How Juries Work

OXFORD MONOGRAPHS ON CRIMINAL LAW AND JUSTICE

This series aims to cover all aspects of criminal law and procedure including criminal evidence. The scope of this series is wide, encompassing both practical and theoretical works.

OTHER TITLES IN THIS SERIES

Civil Recovery of Criminal Property
Colin King, Jennifer Hendry

The Insanity Defence
International and Comparative Perspectives
Ronnie Mackay, Warren Brookbanks

Justice In-Between
A Study of Intermediate Criminal Verdicts
Federico Picinali

Criminal Fraud and Election Disinformation
Law and Politics
Jeremy Horder

Policing the Borders Within
Ana Aliverti

Criminalizing Sex
A Unified Liberal Theory
Stuart P. Green

Reasons to Doubt
Wrongful Convictions and the Criminal Cases Review Commission
Carolyn Hoyle and Mai Sato

Fitness to Plead
International and Comparative Perspectives
Ronnie Mackay and Warren Brookbanks

Criminal Misconducts in Office
Law and Politics
Jeremy Horder

The Preventive Turn in Criminal Law
Henrique Carvalho

Criminal Justice and Taxation
Peter Alldridge

In Search of Criminal Responsibility
Ideas, Interests, and Institutions
Nicola Lacey

Preventive Justice
Andrew Ashworth and Lucia Zedner

Character in the Criminal Trial
Mike Redmayne

Homicide and the Politics of Law Reform
Jeremy Horder

The Insecurity State
Vulnerable Autonomy and the Right to Security in the Criminal Law
Peter Ramsay

Manifest Madness
Mental Incapacity in the Criminal Law
Arlie Loughnan

The Ethics of Plea Bargaining
Richard L. Lippke

Prosecuting Domestic Violence
A Philosophical Analysis
Michelle Madden Dempsey

Abuse of Process and Judicial Stays of Criminal Proceedings
Second Edition
Andrew L.-T. Choo

How Juries Work

And How They Could Work Better

REBECCA K. HELM
Associate Professor of Law and Evidence-Based Justice Lab Director, Law School, University of Exeter, UK

OXFORD
UNIVERSITY PRESS

OXFORD
UNIVERSITY PRESS

Great Clarendon Street, Oxford, OX2 6DP,
United Kingdom

Oxford University Press is a department of the University of Oxford.
It furthers the University's objective of excellence in research, scholarship,
and education by publishing worldwide. Oxford is a registered trade mark of
Oxford University Press in the UK and in certain other countries

Published in the United States of America by Oxford University Press
198 Madison Avenue, New York, NY 10016, United States of America

British Library Cataloguing in Publication Data

Data available

Library of Congress Control Number: 2024934055

ISBN 9780192857293

DOI: 10.1093/9780191948107.001.0001

For my family - Tom, Emilia, and Lily (and Charley, Tiana, and Elmer), and also for Lillian Coggon who always enjoyed discussing my work and who I know would have been thrilled to see this book.

Acknowledgements

I would like to express my thanks to all of the people who took the time to offer comments on or advice in relation to draft chapters in this book, including Valerie Reyna, Valerie Hans, Richard Nobles, Rebecca Probert, Stephen Skinner and Rachel Gimson, and to Rachel Fleetwood who provided formatting assistance. Their helpful suggestions improved this book enormously and I really appreciate it. I would also like to thank UK Research and Innovation who have supported me for the last three years and made it possible to write this book, Anne Barlow and Richard Moorhead who have provided a significant amount of advice relating to my research and writing, and my collaborators and research group members who have inspired me more generally with their great ideas. Finally, I would like to thank Tom, Mum, Dad, and Ali, for their support and feedback, and Emilia and Lily, for being my biggest distractions, who I hope will enjoy this book one day.

Contents

Introduction

Introducing the Jury

The majority of common law jurisdictions, and some civil law jurisdictions, use juries composed of citizens drawn from the general population to deliberate and reach collective verdicts in criminal cases. Juries are often relied on to use their collective judgment to reach verdicts that accord with normative legal goals, for example by being accurate and fair. In many ways, this judgment is key to criminal justice systems since it brings the democratic voice into the criminal justice process. However, despite the important role of the jury in delivering justice across the world, much of the procedure surrounding trial by jury remains predicated on outdated traditions. The legitimacy of the jury system relies heavily on the unverified assumption that twelve people considering evidence are able to reach appropriate judgments in a range of areas purely by virtue of being human and using 'common sense and good judgment'. However, empirical evidence increasingly demonstrates that while common sense and good judgment may lead to verdicts that are democratic, they may be deficient in facilitating the attainment of other goals. For example, they do not necessarily lead to verdicts that are accurate or fair. As Professor Duncan Watts explains in his book on 'how common sense fails us', in situations involving a different complexity from our everyday experience 'common sense turns out to suffer from a number of errors that systematically mislead us'.[1] Ultimately, there is likely to be a disconnect between how legal systems anticipate juries operate and how juries operate in practice. In order to maximize the extent to which juries operate as an effective tool in achieving normative legal goals, and to design effective procedures to help them, jury decision-making must be examined much more critically. We must understand *how juries work*.

The modern criminal law jury dates back to thirteenth-century England, where land-owning white men would draw on their personal knowledge of disputes in order to resolve them. The role of the jury evolved over the next few centuries. Increasingly trial proceedings included witnesses called by the parties, and the role of the jury became to evaluate facts presented to them by others and to make determinations based on those facts. As the jury evolved, it became increasingly powerful and independent and it was exported across the world, partly as a result of the expanding British Empire.[2] Today, the jury is used to make determinations

[1] D Watts, *Everything is Obvious* (Atlantic Books 2011) xiv.

[2] VP Hans, 'Trial by Jury: Story of a Legal Transplant' (2017) 51(3) Law & Society Review 471.

How Juries Work. Rebecca K. Helm, Oxford University Press. © Rebecca K. Helm 2024.
DOI: 10.1093/9780191948107.001.0001

in criminal cases in many countries including England and Wales, Australia, Ghana, Hong Kong, Ireland, Malawi, New Zealand, Northern Ireland, Scotland, the United States of America (USA), and more than forty other nations.[3] While the precise role of the jury varies by jurisdiction, juries are typically required to make 'determinations of fact' in criminal cases. Ultimately this means deciding whether a defendant is 'guilty' or 'not guilty' of an offence, given relevant legal rules. Making this determination can involve a wide variety of judgments including determinations of confidence that a defendant was the person who committed a physical act, that a defendant had certain knowledge (eg knowledge that a victim did not consent),[4] as to whether a defendant's actions were reasonable (either in general or given some characteristics of the defendant),[5] and as to whether a defendant acted 'dishonestly' given community standards.[6] These determinations inevitably involve complex considerations, for example about which actions did or did not take place and about the mindset of the defendant and witnesses. When a jury finds a defendant to be 'guilty' it is read as an authoritative statement that the accused has fulfilled the requirements that make out the relevant criminal offence.

Thus, the jury are making important determinations of truth (or at least assessing their confidence in them)—what did a defendant do? And what was a defendant thinking? However, as Professors Richard Nobles and David Schiff have stated:

> The increasing dominance of ideas associated with truth, as the basis for justifying practices within the legal system, creates pressures on that system, for what can objectively count as truth lies not in law, but in science. The conditioning programmes which, within science, lead to the application of its binary code truth/untruth . . . bear very little resemblance to the conditioning programmes whereby law achieves its operations.[7]

There is nothing particularly scientific about the current jury system. There is no scientific basis to suggest that asking laypeople to discuss evidence and reach a verdict is the most effective—or the fairest—way to make judgments relating to what happened in the past and, relatedly, to judge whether a defendant committed a criminal offence. Current procedure surrounding jury trial has not been designed and validated based on scientific evidence, despite normative legal goals providing usable benchmarks. Although different jurisdictions have introduced a variety of interventions designed to reduce juror mistakes, for example Turnbull

[3] N Vidmar (ed), *World Jury Systems* (OUP 2000).

[4] See eg Sexual Offences Act 2003.

[5] See eg *R v Duffy* [1967] 1 QB 63 (CA); *R v Bowen* [1996] 4 All ER 837 (CA).

[6] *Booth v The Queen* [2020] EWCA Crim 575; [2021] QB 685.

[7] R Nobles and D Schiff, 'Miscarriages of Justice: A Systems Approach' (1995) 58 Modern Law Review 299, 304.

instructions in England and Wales[8] and Henderson instructions in New Jersey, USA,[9] introduced to help jurors effectively assess eyewitness testimony, there is little evidence to suggest that these interventions reduce mistakes in practice. In fact, the legal system may not claim to conclusively determine factual guilt or innocence at all, preferring to view guilt as a legal concept, justified by reference to non-scientific concepts such as fairness and reasonableness.[10] However, factual accuracy remains important to many legitimations and rationales underlying the criminal justice system, and accumulating research makes the goal of achieving accurate convictions far more attainable than it was when the jury system was first developed. In any case, there is also a lack of evidence that juries convict defendants fairly, and decades of empirical research demonstrate that jurors and juries are not immune to the influence of stereotypes, biases, and misconceptions.

In fact, accumulating evidence suggests that as a tool to achieve important normative goals, juries are malfunctioning. In other words, juries are not consistently performing in a way that achieves relevant goals of criminal justice systems. For example, evidence suggests that juries convict defendants who are factually innocent, and overturned verdicts suggest that this happens across jurisdictions and with some frequency.[11] The case studies below provide some illustrative examples.

Stefan Kiszko—England and Wales

Acquitted in 1992 after sixteen years in prison

Stefan Kiszko was convicted of the rape and murder of eleven-year-old Lesley Molseed. Shortly after Lesley was killed, four teenage girls came forward and accused Kiszko of exposing himself to them the day before the murder. The police arrested Kiszko. After three days of intensive questioning, he confessed to the crime. He did not have a lawyer present, was not asked if he wanted one, and his requests for his mother to be present were denied. Kiszko had the mental age of a seven-year-old. Kiszko was convicted by a jury, meaning that they were sure 'beyond reasonable doubt' that he committed the murder.

[8] *R v Turnbull* [1977] QB 224.

[9] *New Jersey v Henderson* 27 A 3d 872 (2011).

[10] See eg Nobles and Schiff (n 7).

[11] For databases logging recognized wrongful convictions (and containing further detail on the examples provided below), see The National Registry of Exonerations <www.law.umich.edu/special/exoneration/Pages/about.aspx> accessed 14 September 2020 (USA); Evidence-Based Justice Lab, 'Miscarriages of Justice Registry' <https://evidencebasedjustice.exeter.ac.uk/miscarriages-of-justice-registry/> accessed 10 May 2022 (England and Wales); The Canadian Registry of Wrongful Convictions, <www.wrongfulconvictions.ca/> accessed 10 May 2022 (Canada). For a related database in the European context, see the European Registry of Exonerations < https://www.registryofexonerations.eu/about-eurex/> accessed 8 April 2024.

On appeal, evidence showed that material left on the victim's body could not be from Kiszko (due to an illness which rendered him impotent) and the four girls who said Kiszko had exposed himself admitted they had made it up 'for a laugh'. He was psychologically damaged by his time in prison, and died of a heart attack the year after he was released.

Joseph Abbitt—North Carolina, USA

Exonerated in 2009 after fourteen years in prison

Joseph Abbitt was convicted of rape, burglary, and kidnapping, after an intruder raped two sisters in their home. The victims told investigators that their attacker looked like Joseph Abbitt, a man who had previously lived in their neighbourhood, and both separately identified Abbitt in a photo line-up. DNA tests were inconclusive. Despite having an alibi, he was convicted by a jury, meaning that they were sure 'beyond reasonable doubt' that he committed the offences.

On appeal, DNA evidence from the case rape kits excluded Abbitt as the perpetrator. He was released and officially exonerated in 2009. He died in a traffic accident in 2015.

Tammy Marquardt—Ontario, Canada

Acquitted in 2011 after thirteen years in prison

Tammy Marquardt was convicted of murdering her son, Kenneth, who she said she found tangled in bed sheets and gasping for breath. A leading expert testified that in his opinion Kenneth's death was non-accidental. Marquardt maintained that her son had died as a result of complications from an epileptic seizure. She was convicted by a jury, meaning that they were sure 'beyond reasonable doubt' that she had killed her son.

Marquardt was acquitted in 2011 after a forensic pathologist assigned to the case as part of a case review found that the original expert's findings were 'illogical and completely against scientific evidence-based reasoning', and experts agreed that a natural cause of death could not be ruled out.

In these cases, juries were *sure beyond reasonable doubt* that the defendant was guilty, when they were, in all likelihood, not in fact guilty. In other words, juries are making mistakes, whether as a result of their own intuitions or as a result of misleading information being provided to them that they are ill-equipped to effectively evaluate. Importantly, in these cases errors may be due to misconceptions, for example as to the reliability of eyewitness testimony or the likely behaviours of those with mental health conditions, which may be entirely predictable. The number of factually innocent defendants who are convicted at jury trial is very difficult to estimate, particularly since legal exoneration is typically not equivalent to a finding of innocence. However, evidence does show that an alarming number of defendants are wrongfully convicted from a legal perspective. For example, the United States National Registry of Exonerations records approximately 2,000 defendants who have been exonerated after being convicted by a jury since 1989.[12] A similar database detailing miscarriages of justice in England and Wales records more than 300 miscarriages of justice that have resulted from trial by jury since 1970.[13] Empirical work has also used different approaches to examine the scale of wrongful convictions. One study using statistical modelling known as survival analysis estimated that if all death-sentenced defendants in the USA remained under sentence of death indefinitely, at least 4.1 per cent would be exonerated.[14]

In addition, juries have been implicated in systematic failures to prosecute defendants in certain types of case, most notably in what is known as the 'rape conviction crisis' where failures to successfully prosecute rape have been said to have led to an effective 'decriminalization' of many types of rape.[15] This failure has been attributed, in part, to juror endorsement of 'rape myths', that can lead to blaming victims in place of defendants.[16]

Thus, the real effectiveness of the jury as a legal tool is unclear. Jury error is far from being the sole cause of miscarriages of justice, particularly since juries are reliant on the information presented to them. However, there are weaknesses in the way that juries function and make decisions in the current system that mean that they are not operating as effectively as they could be. We need to understand better how juries function in order to assess these potential weaknesses and to make improvements. For example, we need to understand what causes juries to be sure of guilt beyond reasonable doubt, what conscious and unconscious influences affect their decisions, what information they rely on, and how effective their ability to critique evidence presented to them is. Scientific evidence and research

[12] The National Registry of Exonerations (n 11).

[13] Evidence-Based Justice Lab (n 11).

[14] S Gross and others, 'Rate of False Conviction of Criminal Defendants Who Are Sentenced to Death' (2014) 111(20) PNAS 7230.

[15] See eg L Kelly, J , and L Regan, *A Gap or a Chasm? Attrition in Reported Rape Cases* Home Office Research Study 293 (Home Office Research, Development and Statistics Directorate 2005); End Violence Against Women, 'CPS Data Shows Survivors Still Being Failed as Record Numbers of Sexual Offences Are Recorded' (*End Violence Against Women*, 21 July 2022) <www.endviolenceagainstwomen.org.uk/cps-data-survivors-failed-record-number-sexual-offences/> accessed 10 May 2022. Although see also C Thomas, 'Juries, Rape and Sexual Offences in the Crown Court 2007–21' (2023) 3 Criminal Law Review 200.

[16] F Leverick, 'What Do We Know About Rape Myths and Juror Decision Making?' (2020) 24(3) The International Journal of Evidence and Proof 255.

in behavioural science generally and jury decision-making specifically now have the potential to provide such insight. Just as the functioning of scientific instruments can be improved based on evidence, the jury can alter and improve as a legal tool, based on robust evidence.

Empirical Analysis of the Jury

Examining how juries function is hard for at least three reasons. First, juries are generally not required to give reasons for their decisions. Secondly, research in cognitive science suggests that jurors themselves may not have complete insight into factors affecting their decision processes. Thirdly, real cases vary in so many ways that it is difficult to tell what is driving decisions and which factors might be influencing outcomes. While study of human behaviour can be made easier through being human and therefore having insight into how humans think, it is also clear that human behaviour and decision-making are incredibly complex. It is therefore necessary to use scientific research techniques (rather than common sense or 'folk psychology') to understand how juries work generally, and how they are likely to respond to changes in law and legal procedure.

First, qualitative and quantitative analyses of case data from real cases can help us understand how juries are functioning in practice. This can include examining statistically variables associated with a greater number of guilty verdicts from juries (eg there may be more guilty verdicts in cases involving defendants of a particular gender or ethnicity). These studies are most informative when the influence of one variable is examined, while controlling for other important variables (this means examining the influence of one variable, while holding others constant). For example, in a study in England and Wales, Professor Cheryl Thomas examined a possible influence of defendant ethnicity on jury verdicts, controlling for the offence-type which defendants were accused of.[17] When conducting this type of work, it is important to have sufficient data to draw reliable conclusions (the specific amount of data required will vary depending on the analysis conducted), to ensure that the data analysed is representative of the population of interest (eg all juries in a jurisdiction), and to ensure that as many potentially important variables as possible are controlled for. This is most easily achieved where data is available for all jury decisions of interest. For example, in the study mentioned above, Professor Thomas analysed data from CREST, the HM Court and Tribunal Service case management and reporting system, which covers all Crown Court cases in England and Wales in a set time period, including almost 400,000 jury verdicts at the time of Professor Thomas's analysis. This type of work has the obvious advantage of using data taken

[17] C Thomas, 'Ethnicity and the Fairness of Jury Trials in England and Wales 2006–2014' (2017) 11 Criminal Law Review 860.

from real cases, and therefore accurately representing what is happening in practice. However, the work is limited in the extent to which it can be used to draw causal inferences, largely because it is impossible to control for all potentially relevant variables. For example, if it is shown that juries tend to convict male defendants more often than female defendants, this could be because of a bias in favour of female defendants or it could be because evidence tends to be stronger in cases involving male defendants, either because male defendants tend to commit crimes that are easier to evidence or because prosecutions against woman are brought on the basis of less evidence than prosecutions against men are. Since no two cases are the same and the evidence in cases is often open to subjective interpretation, it is difficult to directly measure and control for evidence strength and to test these hypotheses. It is also not possible to control for or to examine the influence of cognitive mechanisms in this type of work. In the example above relating to gender, it is possible that such an association could be caused by a tendency in jurors to view men as more 'dangerous', but this hypothesis could not be tested without additional information on juror viewpoints that is typically not available.

Secondly, in jurisdictions where it is permitted, people who have acted as jurors in real cases can be interviewed about their experiences and decision-making. This approach can provide insight into what jurors themselves thought about case facts, evidence presented to them, and their ultimate decision. For example, in a study using data from South Carolina, USA, Professors Theodore Eisenberg and Martin Wells presented data from detailed interviews with 114 jurors who had made judgments in death-penalty cases.[18] The fifty-page interview instrument that they used included questions about the crime, characteristics of the defendant and victim, the process of juror deliberation, the conduct of the case by legal professionals, and the background of the juror themselves. As with quantitative analysis of case data, analysis of interview data has the advantage of providing insight into what is happening in practice. Interviews also have the advantage of providing very rich and descriptive data covering a large variety of variables that can be analysed both qualitatively and quantitatively. In addition, interviews (particularly semi-structured interviews) are valuable in that they can provide insight into factors that may be important but that researchers were not specifically looking for. However, there are also limitations of this approach. Perhaps most importantly, psychological research has shown that people are not necessarily good at understanding or assessing the influence that factors have on their own thinking and decision-making.[19] The data will also be influenced by jurors' own biases and by the impressions that they want to present to the interviewer (which may not always accurately capture reality).

[18] T Eisenberg and M Wells, 'Deadly Confusion: Juror Instructions In Capital Cases' (1993) 79(1) Cornell Law Review 1.

[19] See eg J Haidt, *The Righteous Mind* (Penguin 2012).

Because of the limitations in observing and understanding juries in the real world, experimental work grounded in behavioural sciences has the potential to be vitally important in complementing work with real juries to advance our understanding of how jurors and juries are likely to make decisions in practice, and what factors influence those decisions. Specifically, experimental and quasi-experimental work can be used to examine influences on decision-makers and to test predictions about individual and group decision-making. This work typically involves using mock jurors or mock juries, who are asked to participate in a mock trial or review evidence from a mock trial and deliver a verdict. Other variables will also be recorded. For example, mock jurors might be asked to give information about their own attitudes, values, or emotions when learning about a case, or the dominance of particular jurors during deliberations may be recorded by research assistants. Interventions can also be tested to explore their impact on juror decisions. In one study, Professors Susan Bandes and Jessica Salerno examined the influence of gruesome photographs on juror verdicts by asking half of a sample of mock jurors to make a decision in a case involving a gruesome photograph and half of a sample of mock jurors to make a decision in the same case but without the gruesome photograph.[20] Through asking mock jurors to report their emotional reactions, the authors were able not only to examine a potential influence of gruesome photographs, but also to test predictions regarding the psychological mechanisms through which the photographs impacted verdicts. This approach has the advantage of allowing researchers to examine causal influence more effectively and to control for and explore the influence of a wide variety of variables, through what is known as randomized control trial methodology (where participants are randomly assigned to groups which only differ from each other in terms of a particular variable of interest, and differences in outcomes between groups can therefore be attributed to that variable). However, experimental work also has weaknesses. Most importantly, the experiments can be somewhat artificial and may not reflect reality in important ways. For example, jurors are unlikely to feel as emotional in a mock case as they would in a real case, jurors may not care as much about reaching the correct verdict in a mock case as they would in a real case, materials in a mock case may be less detailed and realistic than in a real case, and jurors may behave differently knowing that their decision will not have consequences for a real defendant. The work is also dependent on having sufficiently large sample sizes, using sufficiently robust statistical techniques and experimental design, and recruiting appropriate and representative samples, to be able to draw reliable conclusions (something that is particularly important given the current 'replication crisis' in the social sciences).

[20] S Bandes and J Salerno, 'Emotion, Proof and Prejudice: The Cognitive Science of Gruesome Photos and Victim Impact Statements' (2014) 46 Arizona State Law Journal 1003.

Theory and research in social science generally is therefore important in informing any research in this area and in understanding how juries are likely to function. Utilizing underlying theory to inform research is important since empirically there is a big difference between, on the one hand, predicting an effect for good reasons and then finding that this effect exists, and, on the other hand, gathering data and interpreting trends or patterns *post hoc*. Put simply, findings supporting *ex ante* theoretical predictions are far more likely to be reliable in terms of the presence of effects and of conclusions as to causes of those effects and the situations to which they can be expected to generalize. The theory and research underlying jury work can include work in both social and cognitive psychology examining group and individual-level evidence evaluation and decision-making. For example, Professors Dan Kahan and Donald Braman have applied work from social psychology (specifically work showing that individuals have a tendency to resolve factual ambiguities in a manner supportive of their defining values) in order to formulate and test predictions relating to mock juror judgments in ambiguous cases involving self-defence.[21] As noted above, using psychological research and theory in this way is incredibly important as it has the potential to provide more reliable insight not only into what influences jury decisions, but also into why particular factors influence jury decisions. Knowing why a variable influences jury decisions can be key to analysing jury performance. For example, an influence of emotion on juries may be seen as beneficial if it leads jurors to pay greater attention to facts and really gain insight into the experience of the defendant or the victim. On the other hand, an influence of emotion in juries may be seen as harmful if it leads jurors to lack rationality and thus be influenced by misperceptions despite judicial instructions, or to systematically show bias against an 'out-group' defendant. Knowing when and why emotion has an impact should therefore be key in informing legal procedure to allow or limit emotionally evocative evidence such as gruesome photographs. Underlying theory also has the potential to be helpful in drawing together disparate strands of research in a coherent form that is useful in enhancing cohesive understanding and in ensuring that findings of individual studies are not based on idiosyncrasies.

This book draws on psychological theory and accompanying research in order to develop conceptual models of juror and jury decision-making that are used to structure and examine data relating to juries drawn primarily from controlled experimental studies, but also from field experiments. The book therefore adopts an approach to understanding jurors and juries that is grounded in science, asking how human decision-makers function individually and in groups when considering evidence and applying legal standards to that evidence to reach a verdict. Essentially, it views jurors' and juries' behaviour as predictable, given sufficient

[21] D Kahan and D Braman, 'The Self-Defensive Cognition of Self-Defense' (2008) 45(1) American Criminal Law Review 1.

information (although note that much more information is needed to predict human behaviour than to predict the behaviour of simpler organisms). Because the book is grounded in science, it draws on evidence from outside the jury context and from a range of jurisdictions that examines or provides insight into relevant psychological mechanisms. These general psychological mechanisms would, scientifically, be expected to replicate in more ecologically valid jury contexts and across jurisdictions (although how general processes might be altered by law and legal procedure is discussed). However, it is important to note that in real cases involving trial by jury, decision-making may be complicated by additional factors not discussed in this book, and the research presented here is intended to complement rather than replace observations of real jury decisions.

The aim of this book is not to summarize the entire body of jury and mock jury research, which is now incredibly voluminous and considers different issues using different stimuli and different methods with varying degrees of reliability. Instead, the book has two underlying aims. One aim is to improve our understanding of how juries work (and how they can work better) through the creation of conceptual models that have a robust basis in empirically supported research in cognitive science. These models are complemented and extended through reviews of empirical research and used to critique jury performance. The second aim is to provide a theory-based structure to facilitate the interpretation of the huge body of research on juror and jury decision-making in a way that has the potential to be useful to lawyers and policymakers and to inform research moving forwards.

Organization of This Book

This book is split into three primary parts. The first part of the book considers normatively the role of juries and the regulation introduced by different jurisdictions to achieve relevant normative aims (*how do juries work in theory?*). Historical context (Chapter 1), comparative legal procedures (Chapter 2), and modern developments and jurisprudence (Chapter 3) are considered in order to identify how the jury has evolved to meet requirements of society, the broad principles underlying modern jury systems, and the specific requirements of the jury today. Uncertainty surrounding clear normative benchmarks against which jury performance can be evaluated is discussed. It is suggested that the jury really has two roles—a fact-finding role and a democratic role—and that success in each of these roles should be measured against different benchmarks. This part provides benchmarks that can be used to measure the success of the modern jury in each of these roles, and also begins to examine the empirical presumptions underlying existing infrastructure surrounding trial by jury.

The second part of the book assesses how juries work from an empirical perspective (*how do juries work in practice?*). Juries are conceptualized like complex machines that function in predictable ways when sufficient predictor variables are considered. This conceptualization is not the same as seeking to predict jury decisions, since judgments are highly contextual. It is about identifying the influences likely to be driving juries, which can then be compared to the influences that should be driving juries from a normative perspective. This part of the book develops a new 'Representation-Based' Model of juror decision-making based on psychological theory (specifically Fuzzy-Trace Theory) and Fuzzy Logic. This model emphasizes the importance of meaningful as opposed to precise representations of information and suggests that understanding how jurors assign meaning to evidence, trial participants, the body of evidence, and legal standards is central to understanding juror decision-making. This part then collates and examines literature from empirical law and psychology identifying associations between juror characteristics (Chapter 5), case characteristics (Chapter 6), and legal standards and procedures (Chapter 7) and juror decisions to demonstrate how these associations can be explained by juror assignment of meaning. Through this collation and examination, the potential for the Representation-Based Model to tie together disparate strands of literature is demonstrated, and normatively desirable and problematic influences on the jury (categorized based on the criteria outlined in Part I) are identified. Finally, the role of group deliberation in impacting how individual determinations are translated into ultimate group verdicts is examined (Chapter 8). A Representation-Based model of the translation of individual preferences into juror verdicts is developed and drawn on in order to demonstrate how deliberation can change the influences on legal decisions in both positive and negative ways, depending on a range of contexts.

The final part of the book (Chapters 9 and 10) considers the general coherence between the normative requirements of juries identified in the first part of the book and the operation of juries in practice examined in the second part of the book, and considers the question '*how can juries work better?*' What might the jury and related procedure look like if designed today, based on scientific evidence and with the goals of the jury today in mind, rather than being at least in part a product of history? This analysis draws on the Representation-Based models developed earlier in the book to identify evidence-based paths for reform to improve coherence between normative goals and performance in practice. Suggestions for reform show how changes in legal regulation can maximize the extent to which the jury functions effectively as a legal tool from a normative perspective. These suggestions for reform are the culmination of the analyses and arguments made throughout the book and provide evidence-based ideas that can be drawn on to improve the administration of justice in jury systems around the world.

1
The Development of the Jury: Changing Regulation and Function

Introduction

In the 1920s, Roscoe Pound wrote that 'law must be stable, and yet it cannot stand still'.[1] A similar idea is of central importance when seeking to understand the criminal law jury. Over hundreds of years the jury system has endured both in England and Wales, where the modern criminal law jury originates, and across the world. In many of these systems the jury is seen as central to liberty and freedom. In England and Wales, the jury has been described as a 'lamp that shows that freedom lives'[2] and the 'grand bulwark' of liberties.[3] In Scotland, calls to hold criminal trials without juries during the recent Covid-19 pandemic were widely condemned and then dropped.[4] However, while the jury has acted as a relatively stable symbol in the criminal justice process, which may be key to its enduring popularity, the jury has not worked in a consistent way over time. The jury has not stood still, and in many ways the jury today is not the same institution that it was when it was introduced in England in the thirteenth century. The system has had to continually and pragmatically change and adapt to meet the needs of society and to reflect changing societal aspirations for justice and security. This organic evolution of the jury makes it a powerful symbolic representation in society, but also means that the goals of the jury are not well defined, and that the jury is not necessarily well designed for achieving specific goals.

In this chapter I examine the changing role of the jury, specifically in England and Wales, in order to demonstrate the different ways that the jury has functioned and the different roles that it has assumed over time, and the priorities that have shaped its evolution. I review the history of the modern jury based on contemporary commentaries,[5] categorizing jury development into four suggested key

[1] R Pound, *Interpretations of Legal History* (CUP 1923) 1.

[2] P Devlin, *Trial by Jury* (Stevens & Sons Ltd 1956) 164.

[3] W Blackstone, *Commentaries Book 4* (1769) 342.

[4] S Carrell, 'Scotland Drops Plans to Suspend Jury Trials During Coronavirus Crisis' *The Guardian* (1 April 2020) <www.theguardian.com/uk-news/2020/apr/01/scotland-drops-plans-to-suspend-jury-trials-during-coronavirus-crisis> accessed 30 May 2022.

[5] Note that this is not intended to be a comprehensive history of trial by jury, but rather to highlight and explain important phases in its development. For more comprehensive information on jury history, see TA Green, *Verdict According to Conscience: Perspectives on the English Criminal Trial Jury, 1200–1800* (University of Chicago Press 1985); L Levy, *The Palladium of Justice: Origins of Trial by Jury*

How Juries Work. Rebecca K. Helm, Oxford University Press. © Rebecca K. Helm 2024.
DOI: 10.1093/9780191948107.003.0001

phases in which the role of the jury evolved. I then draw on the history of the jury to show that there is nothing about the jury system that makes it inherently appropriate as the best tool to fulfil a particular role, and that the way in which the jury functions must be shaped by policy surrounding trial by jury. I conclude by suggesting that the variety of ways that the jury can function demonstrates the importance of articulating what we want the jury to do in society and designing evidence-based policy to ensure the jury is functioning to do that.

Phase I: Self-Informing Community Experts (1166–1300s)

Medial judgments

The precise roots of the modern criminal law jury system are unclear, but it is likely that the system was formed as an amalgamation of ancient customs, including influences from the Anglo-Saxons and Normans.[6] The jury was established in its modern form, as a decision-making body making determinations of factual guilt or innocence, when trial by 'ordeal' was abolished by an edict of the Roman church in 1215. However even before this time, probably from around 1166 when King Henry II reformed the public prosecution system in England, two jury systems making judgments relevant to determinations of guilt were operating.[7]

Prior to the abolition of trial by ordeal, there were two major forms of 'juries' in use—the *presenting jury* (a jury which reported those alleged to have committed crimes) and the *de odio jury* (a jury which determined whether private prosecutions had a just cause or were brought out of hate or spite). These juries made decisions that have been described as medial, since although they influenced the criminal justice process, they did not, at least officially, convict defendants.[8]

Presenting juries are conventionally dated from an ordainment of the Assize of Clarendon in 1166 (although note that communal accusations likely predate this ordainment).[9] These juries consisted of 'twelve lawful men' representing their 'hundred' (a political subdivision of a county).[10] These hundred jurors, alongside representatives of local 'vills' (smaller administrative units), had the job of

(Ivan R Dee, Inc 1999); JS Cockburn and TA Green (eds), *Twelve Good Men and True: The Criminal Trial Jury in England, 1200-1800* (Princeton UP 2014).

[6] R Moschzisker, 'The Historic Origin of Trial by Jury' (1921) 70(1) University of Pennsylvania Law Review 1.

[7] RD Groot, 'The Early Thirteenth Century Criminal Jury' (n 5) 5–9.

[8] ibid.

[9] ND Hurnard, 'The Jury of Presentment and the Assize of Clarendon' (1941) 56(223) English Historical Review 374, 374; Groot, 'The Early Thirteenth Century Criminal Jury' (n 7) 3.

[10] The use of twelve men specifically had historical precedent. For example, in the tenth century twelve men, six English and six Welsh, would be gathered together to reach compromises where disputes occurred between their two countries, see D Stenton, *English Justice between the Norman Conquest and the Great Charter 1066–1215* (George Allen & Unwin 1965) 7.

reporting to royal justices during periodic visits (*eyres*) 'any man accused or notoriously suspect' of being a robber, murderer or thief in their hundred.[11] These reports were made through what was known as a *veredicta*.[12]

Where a person was clearly guilty or made a confession in front of local officials a case would proceed to punishment.[13] In other cases, presenting juries also had a screening role in deciding whether they *suspected* the person. If the hundred jurors suspected a defendant was guilty and either produced supporting evidence or were joined in their suspicion by four vill representatives, the accused would be tried by ordeal.[14] If not, the defendant would not be tried. Jurors never officially convicted defendants themselves, although they were sometimes so certain of the guilt of an accused, based on their own knowledge, that they would say that the accused committed the crime rather than just that they were suspected.[15] The ordeal would be what officially determined guilt, and was seen as representative of the voice of God.[16] For example, an accused could be subjected to the ordeal of water, where they would have their hands and feet bound and be thrown into a body of water. If the accused sank, then they were considered not guilty and saved. If the accused floated then they were judged to be guilty.[17] Essentially, presenting juries could acquit a defendant (by determining that they did not suspect the defendant) but could not officially convict them.

Another type of jury— the *de odio* jury—had a role in private criminal prosecutions (known as appeals) where a victim would make an accusation directly against a defendant. The role of the jury in these cases was to decide, generally when asked to by the accused, whether an appeal was motivated by hate or spite (*de odio et atia*) or whether the appeal had just cause. Although this judgment was framed as a judgment about hate and spite, it was essentially a judgment as to whether the jury believed that the crime had occurred, and the accused was responsible. If the jury determined that the appeal was not motivated by hate or spite, then the case could be sent for resolution by combat or by ordeal. If they determined that the appeal was motivated by hate or spite then it could not.[18] Similarly to presenting juries,

[11] Assize of Clarendon (1166), cited in DC Douglas and GW Greenaway (eds), *English Historical Documents, Volume 2: 1042–1189* (Eyre & Spottiswoode 1968) 408.

[12] RD Groot, 'The Jury of Presentment Before 1215' (1982) 26(1) American Journal of Legal History 1, 6. See also W Stubbs and HWC Davis, *Select Charters and Other Illustrations of English Constitutional History from the Earliest Times to the Reign of Edward the First* (9th edn, Clarendon Press 1921).

[13] Groot, 'The Early Thirteenth Century Criminal Jury' (n 7) 6–7.

[14] ibid. Note that the jury had a duty to report people accused of crimes but could spare them being tried by ordeal by not 'suspecting' them of the crime.

[15] M Kerr, D Forsyth, and M Plyley, 'Cold Water and Hot Iron: Trial by Ordeal in England' (1992) 22(4) The Journal of Interdisciplinary History 573, 577.

[16] C Radding, 'Superstition to Science: Nature, Fortune, and the Passing of the Medieval Ordeal' (1979) 84(4) The American Historical Review 945, 945–46. Although, another possibility is that the jurors' decision to suspect the accused was essentially the real determination of guilt, and the ordeal was a method through which the lives of some of the guilty were spared. See Kerr, Forsyth, and Plyley (n 15).

[17] Kerr, Forsyth, and Plyley (n 15) 582–83.

[18] Groot, 'The Early Thirteenth Century Criminal Jury' (n 7) 8–9.

de odio juries could essentially acquit a defendant, but could not officially convict them.[19]

This jury system, and the early formulation of trial by peers, reflected society at the time—small, close-knit communities where people typically knew each other and about each other (eg as a result of shared agricultural and policing responsibilities), and often knew or at least had significant knowledge relating to who committed crimes (eg who had inflicted wounds or who had been found with stolen property).[20] Juries were self-informing, meaning that they investigated allegations of wrongdoing themselves, rather than relying on evidence presented to them by others. They made judgments akin to declarations of factual guilt or innocence based on their knowledge of events in the community (eg when presenting juries sent a defendant to an ordeal by determining that they suspected them and providing accompanying evidence) but also judgments that were more like statements about a defendant's character and propensity to commit the crime they were accused of than substantiated judgments about factual guilt (eg when presenting hundred jurors sent a defendant to an ordeal due to suspicion in the absence of proof but supported in their suspicion by four vill representatives).[21]

This system, utilizing juries combined with the ordeal, can be seen as reinforcing stability and cohesiveness that was needed in society at that time. Research has suggested that a need for community involvement in the justice process may have been inherited from the Anglo-Normans, who recognized that community settlements under the authority of a court were preferrable to judicial decisions, which had the potential to leave one party dissatisfied and motivated to retaliate.[22] Involving the community in dispute resolution had the potential to increase the effectiveness of the legal system in restoring harmony in a community and preventing retaliation.[23] In addition, utilizing jurors from the community potentially provided the best fact-finding mechanism available at the time, through tapping into the knowledge of community members. This expertise arguably made up for deficits in formal investigation.[24] As noted above, community members had significant knowledge of the community and events in the community, and thus the best information on which to base decisions. Ultimate fairness and accuracy were then ensured by God, through the ordeal, potentially reducing the pressure on the jury system to ultimately guarantee these outcomes. Therefore, even prior

[19] For more information on the *de odio* jury, see RD Groot, 'The Jury in Private Criminal Prosecutions Before 1215' (1983) 27(2) American Journal of Legal History 113.

[20] Kerr, Forsyth and Plyley (n 15) 576–77.

[21] Groot, 'The Early Thirteenth Century Criminal Jury' (n 7) 7–8.

[22] See R Gimson, 'The Mutable Defendant: From Penitent to Rights-bearing and Beyond' (2020) 40(1) Legal Studies 113, 116.

[23] Groot, 'The Early Thirteenth Century Criminal Jury' (n 7) 10

[24] J Langbein, 'The Four Epochs of Jury Trial in England' (Talk at The British Academy, London, 17 March 2015) <www.thebritishacademy.ac.uk/events/four-epochs-jury-trial-england/> accessed 30 May 2023.

to 1215 we see early roots of the jury as a mechanism with the potential to promote community involvement, fairness, and accuracy in legal decisions.

Abolishment of the ordeal and judgments of guilt

In 1215, an edict of the Roman church (the Fourth Lateran Council) abolished trial by ordeal.[25] Historians have suggested that theologians had increasingly viewed the ordeal as wrong since it involved clerics in a process that ended in bloodshed, lacked canonical authority, and tempted God (through using a constructed human procedure to 'force' a judgment from God).[26] For a short time after the abolition of trial by ordeal, those suspected of serious crimes were detained pending an alternative way to make formal determinations of guilt. But the role that juries had begun to play in making determinations akin to those of guilt prior to 1215 made them a natural alternative to replace the ordeal, and prevented the need for utilizing other approaches, such as pressured confessions.[27] In 1220, after a period of apparent experimentation, four men became the first people to be convicted by an English trial jury.[28]

Presenting juries continued in their role in reporting those alleged to have committed criminal offences, but no longer engaged in significant screening, and instead named *all* of those who had a soundly-based accusation against them.[29] Guilt would then be determined by the trial jury. Initially, the accused had to consent to trial by jury (since judgments were known to be made by man rather than God);[30] however, increasingly coercive measures were adopted to pressure people to have their case heard by a jury, essentially culminating in torture for those unwilling to stand trial by jury by the 1300s.[31]

The development of rudimentary procedure and procedural protection, and early 'democratization'

Shortly after 1222, after a short period in which larger juries were utilized, the trial jury became composed of twelve men from the hundred in which an alleged crime

[25] The Magna Carta also issued in 1215 but is not thought to have had any significant impact on the development of the jury at that time. See Groot, 'The Early Thirteenth Century Criminal Jury' (n 7) 10.
[26] RC Palmer, 'Trial by Ordeal' (1989) 87(6) Michigan Law Review 1547, 1553.
[27] Groot, 'The Jury of Presentment Before 1215' (n 12) 24.
[28] These cases were heard by the jury because the accuser, Alice, was a woman and therefore could not offer combat as proof. See Groot, 'The Early Thirteenth Century Criminal Jury' (n 7) 18.
[29] Green (n 5) 14.
[30] S Anand, 'The Origins, Early History and Evolution of the English Criminal Trial Jury' (2005) 43(2) Alberta Law Review 407, 415.
[31] ibid 416.

occurred.[32] Initially these juries were often at least partly made up of men from the presenting jury that reported the alleged crime (evidence suggests that the majority of trial juries included at least a third of the original presenting jury).[33] However, as hearings came to be held more frequently, partly due to a transition from trials taking place during eyres to trials taking place during gaol deliveries, men of lower status increasingly sat on trial juries. This may have been due to those men being less able to avoid what was seen as the burden of serving on a jury than men of higher status were.[34] This has been referred to as apparent 'democratizing' of the trial jury; however, at the time this was not seen as a desirable change since such men were more often susceptible to pressure from more powerful members of society.[35]

By the 1340s, there was a general trend towards questioning previous practices and calling for more formal court procedure,[36] and, relatedly, an increasing belief that defendants ought to be tried primarily by people who had not 'presented' them.[37] In 1352, legislation was passed allowing an accused to challenge (for cause) members of their presenting jury sitting on their trial jury.[38] This established the general principle that a person should not be tried by the people bringing the case against them, and marked the formal separation of the presenting jury (which would become the grand jury) and trial jury (hereafter the jury).[39] However, trial jurors continued to be drawn from the community in which a crime was alleged to have occurred. Although the accused were able to prevent potential jurors sitting on a jury by exercising a right to 'challenge' a juror, it seems that knowledge of the facts or the parties was not a ground for exclusion (which could be, for example, due to a juror having a 'greedy desire' to get land).[40]

Jurors continued to have extensive knowledge of communities and events that occurred within them.[41] They also continued to be self-informing, meaning that they investigated allegations of wrongdoing themselves and reported what they had found at trial.[42] Jurors conducted investigations and, in some cases, made conclusions

[32] Levy (n 5) 19.

[33] A Musson, 'Twelve Good Men and True? The Character of Early Fourteenth-Century Juries' (1997) 15(1) Law and History Review 115, 135–37.

[34] See BW McLane, 'Juror Attitudes Toward Local Disorder: The Evidence of the 1328 Lincolnshire Trailbaston Proceedings' in Cockburn and Green (n 5) 36, 42 for a comparison of the composition of trial juries and presenting jurors in Lincolnshire proceedings in 1328, suggesting men on presenting juries were generally of higher social status than men on trial juries.

[35] Green (n 5) 22.

[36] Musson (n 33) 141.

[37] Green (n 5) 22.

[38] Musson (n 33) 141.

[39] ibid 141.

[40] D Klerman, 'Was the Jury Ever Self-Informing?' (2003) 77(1) Southern California Law Review 123, 134.

[41] Anand (n 30) 417.

[42] Note that some commentators believe that jurors did hear from the defendant, victim, and occasionally other witnesses at trial, but it is generally agreed that jurors were sufficiently well informed that testimony was not seen as important, and judges knew significantly less about the facts than jurors did, see Klerman (n 40).

about the guilt of the defendant prior to trial. These conclusions were often well known enough to influence the willingness of a defendant to be tried by a jury.[43] However, these juries (unlike presenting juries) did give verdicts in open court and began to base them not only on their prior knowledge, but also on witnessing the accused and even other witnesses being questioned by a justice in court.[44]

Technically, jurors could be held liable for perjury—giving false verdicts under oath—if they deliberately reached an incorrect verdict.[45] However, the local knowledge of jurors and the importance of that knowledge at trial left the jury in almost total control of cases. The judge was not in a position to challenge jury decisions, as they did not have independent information on which to base challenges to them (although they may have been suspicious of frequent acquittals).[46] This lack of meaningful oversight contributed to an inscrutability of jury judgments, which were treated as final in the same way as outcomes of the ordeal had been.[47] This inscrutability has also been linked to other characteristics of the jury system. First, inscrutability may have been related to the fact that the accused had, at least technically, consented to accepting the judgment of the jury as proof.[48] Second, inscrutability may have reflected early forms of jury discretion and particularly the ability of the jury to reflect social understanding about when a person's life should be taken rather than simply applying formal law (this discretion would only be considered abused if a decision was made in bad faith).[49] A verdict rendered by the jury 'according to conscience' may have been seen as beyond judicial 'reproach'.[50] However, there are also indications that the inscrutability of jury judgments may have been problematic, particularly in the context of the period, in which crime was high (evidence suggests that there was an 'epidemic' of crime throughout England particularly in the late thirteenth and early fourteenth centuries) and conviction rates were low.[51]

Phase II: Evidential Trials, Judicial Control, and the Regulation of Behaviour (Approximately 1400s–1600s)

From the self-informing jury to evidential trials

From the late fourteenth to the sixteenth century, the self-informing nature of juries was slowly eroded as changes in society made use of self-informing juries less

[43] Green (n 5) 17.
[44] ibid 14. Note that such exchanges are likely to have been brief but would have given justices some leeway to test a defendant's story.
[45] ibid 19.
[46] ibid 18; See also McLane (n 34) 36, 36–37.
[47] Anand (n 30) 416.
[48] ibid.
[49] Green (n 5) 20.
[50] ibid 20.
[51] McLane (n 34) 36, 36.

appropriate (note that there is some uncertainty about the relative importance of these factors). First, as a result of the Black Death, a bubonic plague pandemic that reached England in 1348, the social and demographic conditions that underlay the self-informing jury declined. Population loss and social change caused by the pandemic left many villages abandoned and created new patterns of labour movement.[52] Increasingly, jurors had less knowledge about their neighbours and needed to rely on information presented in court. In addition, the ability of the defendant to challenge members of their presenting jury from sitting on their trial jury and exemptions from jury service reduced the available pool of jurors and led to the exclusion of many people who knew something about a case.[53] Finally, the number of cases that needed to be heard made it unrealistic to have a different specialist local jury to hear each case, and juries came to try several cases at a time.[54] Evidence suggests that while there were attempts to ensure juries were drawn from the neighbourhood in which an offence occurred, these were often unsuccessful and the geographical link between jurors and the offences that they were hearing was eroded.[55] Instead, jurors may have been selected based on experience and reputation and some jurors served regularly.[56] In this context, it was impossible for jurors to come to court knowing about all of the cases that they were going to hear. Although some jurors may still have had knowledge of the people involved in a case and basic case facts, the idea of jurors being best placed to know or to find out who committed an offence due to their involvement in a community was gone. They needed to receive information at trial. From 1555, public officers known as Justices of the Peace were charged with assisting the accuser (usually the victim or the victim's kin) in investigating the crime.[57] Justices of the Peace were required to compel the victim and witnesses whose testimony would be material to testify against the accused (although note that defence witnesses could not be compelled to testify).[58] Research suggests that by the sixteenth century at the latest, juries were more dependent on evidence presented to them than evidence they had gathered themselves,[59] although it was not until the second half of the eighteenth century that jurors were precluded from relying on evidence given to them outside of court.[60]

[52] See Langbein, 'The Four Epochs of Jury Trial in England' (n 24) outlining estimates that in Warwickshire sixty villages, thought to be half of the total number of villages in the county, were abandoned; 40 per cent of the population were lost.

[53] Green (n 5) 22.

[54] E Powell, 'Jury Trial at Gaol Delivery in the Late Middle Ages: The Midland Circuit, 1400–1429' in Cockburn and Green (n 5) 78, 83–84.

[55] ibid 78, 88.

[56] ibid 78, 88–89.

[57] Anand (n 30) 422.

[58] ibid.

[59] JH Langbein, 'The Criminal Trial Before the Lawyers' (1978) 45(2) University of Chicago Law Review 263, 299. Note that some commentators believe the shift to an 'active' rather than self-informing jury was much earlier, see Powell (n 54) 78.

[60] JH Langbein, *The Origins of Adversary Criminal Trial* (OUP 2003) 320.

Prosecutorial advantage and the absence of lawyers

At this time, lawyers were still not used in trials, at least in cases involving felonies (more serious criminal offences). Defence lawyers were specifically prohibited (perhaps because the defendant was thought to know more about the facts than a lawyer would[61]) and victim prosecutors rarely retained lawyers.[62] The victim prosecutor could call witnesses in these trials and, as noted above, Justices of the Peace could compel witnesses to testify against the accused. However, initially the defendant could not call witnesses.[63] In addition, while the victim's testimony and the testimony of witnesses for the victim were sworn under oath, the defendant's testimony could not be sworn under oath.[64] Similarly, when the defence started being able to call witnesses around the late sixteenth century, these witnesses could not be sworn under oath either.[65] This rule was in place in order to avoid contradictions in sworn testimony, which would force one party to commit perjury.[66] However, it likely created an imbalance since statements were seen as more credible when they were made under oath.[67]

The trial process at this time has been described as a 'altercation', in which the victim and accusing witnesses engaged in a confrontational dialogue with the defendant about the alleged offence.[68] As juries gradually gave up their investigatory role, they became more passive participants in the trial process, but were still able to call for witnesses to be summoned, and to ask direct questions of witnesses.[69] This shift to reliance on evidence presented in court would certainly have protected the accused from community prejudice, although the change may have come at the cost of accuracy. Trials had always been conducted at breakneck speed, which may have worked when the jury was self-informing but was likely more problematic when it continued into the period where jurors were learning about the case at trial. In the provincial assize courts (hearing felony cases) between 1558 and 1625, commentators have estimated that trials, including jury deliberations, lasted on average between fifteen and twenty minutes.[70] In one case, reports suggest that a trial that was concluded before anyone realized that the court had tried the wrong person.[71]

[61] JH Langbein, 'The Lawyer-Free Criminal Trial' in ibid 10, 34.
[62] ibid 13.
[63] G Fisher, 'The Jury's Rise as Lie Detector' (1997) 107 Yale Law Journal 575, 603.
[64] ibid 604.
[65] ibid.
[66] ibid.
[67] ibid 604.
[68] Langbein, 'The Lawyer Free Criminal Trial' (n 61) 13.
[69] Anand (n 30) 432.
[70] Langbein, 'The Lawyer Free Criminal Trial' (n 61) 16.
[71] ibid 18.

A shift to more powerful judges

This shift from a self-informing jury to a jury considering evidence presented in court was accompanied by a shift of power from jurors to judges. Since trial judges heard the same evidence as jurors, they could comment on evidence and advise the jury.[72] By the sixteenth century, evidence suggests that judges dominated proceedings, and frequently intervened in criminal trials.[73] Jury discretion (and in particular the ability to reach decisions that reflected social understanding rather than formal law) was likely to have been more limited since judges heard and knew evidence. Some commentary has suggested that in the 1500s and 1600s, the role of the jury was 'subordinate to and conditioned by' the will of judges.[74] As central government became more powerful and built up more significant criminal justice infrastructure, jurors were less needed by the government, and may even have become seen as problematic.[75] As Crown officials took increasing responsibility for the initiation and prosecution of criminal cases, great skill was used in persuading jurors of a defendant's guilt, and, since the jury relied on evidence presented to them, they were less able to manipulate evidence. Judges had the power to question juries about their verdicts and jurors would therefore be required to disclose their reasoning, which judges could refuse to accept.[76] Judges could also put pressure on the jury through commenting on the evidence.[77] Juries who acquitted despite inculpatory evidence could be pressured, fined, and even imprisoned. However, this would have been most likely to occur in cases in which the state had an interest, rather than routine cases.[78] In more routine cases, judges would have been more likely to depend on the jury due to large case volumes, which may have aligned efficiency with judicial discretion.[79]

The control of judges over juries, and the acceptability of the exercise of some form of jury discretion, discussed below, were potentially enhanced by the fact that jurors were still not drawn from the lowest social groups (despite the lack of availability of jurors having led to men of lower status becoming jurors, as discussed above). Some work examining juries in the early fifteenth century has identified a significant minority of jurors from the fringes of the gentry and just below, who regularly served as jurors, and likely exercised a decisive influence in many deliberations.[80] Other work examining Hertfordshire juries, specifically in the late

[72] JH Langbein, 'History of Evidence' (1996) 96 Columbia Law Review 1168, 1171.
[73] Powell (n 54) 114.
[74] PG Lawson, 'Five Lawless Juries? The Composition and Behavior of Hertfordshire Juries, 1573–1624' in Cockburn and Green (n 5) 117.
[75] Green (n 5) 105.
[76] Langbein, 'The Four Epochs of Jury Trial in England' (n 24).
[77] ibid.
[78] Green (n 5) 106.
[79] ibid 130.
[80] Powell (n 54) 96–97.

1500s and early 1600s, has highlighted the fact that jurors were generally still men of property, and more socially and economically aligned with the gentry than labourers and small property owners.[81] There is evidence that juries maintained discretion during this period. However, it has been persuasively argued that this discretion was not utilized to reflect social understanding or to provide a check on authorities. Rather, jurors who were aligned with the ruling class enforced the spirit of the law as opposed to the letter of the law, in a system focused on the logic of exemplary punishment (harsh punishment aimed at preventing others from committing crimes), which can require selective enforcement of crimes.[82] Jurors are said to have adopted a strategic approach to their task, with evidence being adapted or even ignored to achieve the desired end of regulating behaviour to prevent offending.[83] Jurors were influenced in their judgments by the character of defendants, for example, being less likely to convict the 'respectable poor'—people driven to crime as the result of economic need.[84] It has thus been argued that jurors' principal task was the selection of defendants whose execution would provide an 'appropriate, and therefore deterrent' example.[85] This argument has been supported with empirical data from Hertfordshire juries between 1573 and 1624, showing variation reflecting potentially selective enforcement.[86] Judgments during this period therefore suggest that jurors were not just deciding who had committed certain actions but also whether they should be punished for them.[87]

Phase III: Democratic Voice but Continued Deference (Approximately 1600s–1700s)

Political trials and jury equity

In the mid-1600s, at a time of political crisis relating to the struggle against the Stuart monarchy, reformists campaigned for reform of the law, truly local trials, and increased independence of the jury.[88] Legal writers and reformists tended to misinterpret the history of the jury and presented idealistic, but inaccurate, views of the early jury system. For example, in 1623, Ferdinando Pulton incorrectly claimed in an influential text that that the jury system was founded on the Magna

[81] Lawson (n 74) 117, 133.

[82] ibid 117. Prominent jurist of the time Sir Edward Coke noted that while one hanging might induce terror and thus prevent crime, people might grow to have compassion for offenders if too many people were hung (ibid 149).

[83] ibid 117, 150.

[84] ibid 117, 156.

[85] ibid 117, 157.

[86] ibid 117.

[87] For a slightly differing account, suggesting that juror decisions against the law reflected age-old social attitudes that authorities were 'either unable or unwilling' to resist, see Green (n 5) 107.

[88] Green (n 5) 154.

Carta.[89] In 1649 and 1653, democrat and Leveller[90] leader John Lilburne looked to the jury for protection in his high-profile trials for treason. He argued (in the absence of real historical precedent) that the jury was entitled to make determinations of law as well as fact. Essentially, Lilburne argued that he did not deserve to die because he had not broken a 'true law' of England. Although legal commentators recognized at the time that these claims were weak from a legal perspective,[91] the jury agreed and found him not guilty in his trials.[92] In a series of important works analysing trial by jury, John Jones suggested that trial by jury was an ancient right rooted in God's grant of divine power to the people, whose true purpose had been undermined by the development of the judiciary.[93] Jones's texts supported the ability of jurors to decide the law, based on use of historical evidence that has been described as 'amateurish and manipulative'.[94] But the arguments were consistent with Leveller ideas of the time, which suggested that the law was simply a matter of right and wrong that came to the mind and conscience of all men.[95] These ideas called for a decentralized system of law in which neighbours would judge neighbours, and shared experiences and context would guarantee fairness—all men were equal in the eyes of God and could pass judgment on peers gone astray primarily as a process of community affirmation.[96]

The Quakers continued this movement of jury activism through the 1660s (Quakers, although typically less radical than the Levellers, continued to argue for a jury law-finding power).[97] The movement occurred alongside increasing attempts to control juries by the courts (specifically the King's Bench), which began frequently imposing fines and imprisonment on jurors who refused to return verdicts consistent with the judge's view of a case.[98] In 1671, the independence of the jury was formally recognized in *Bushel's case,* which established the principle that a judge may not punish or threaten to punish jurors for their verdict.[99] Specifically, the court in *Bushel* ruled that jurors could not be fined or imprisoned for returning a verdict that conflicted with the judge's assessment of evidence.[100] The opinion in that case, written by Sir John Vaughan, made no mention of jurors being able to

[89] Levy (n 5) 55.

[90] The Levellers were a movement that campaigned for religious toleration and a radical remaking of politics; see R Foxley, *Levellers: Radical Political Thought in the English Revolution* (Manchester University Press, 2016).

[91] See discussion in Green (n 5) 176.

[92] PB Scott, 'Jury Nullification: An Historical Perspective on a Modern Debate' (1989) 91(2) West Virginia Law Review 389, 402.

[93] Green (n 5) 153–69.

[94] ibid 180.

[95] ibid 185–86.

[96] ibid 185–86.

[97] ibid 200.

[98] Scott (n 92) 403–04.

[99] (1670) 124 ER 1006.

[100] S Stern, 'Between Local Knowledge and National Politics: Debating Rationales for Jury Nullification After Bushell's Case' (2002) 111(7) The Yale Law Journal 1815.

disregard the law.[101] In the early 1680s, this statement of jury independence was translated into what is now known as jury equity, or jury nullification—a jury's power to knowingly and deliberately refuse to apply the law by returning a not guilty verdict even though they believe the defendant is legally guilty—following a political battle over its meaning.[102] Specifically, Whig-dominated juries indicated in some cases involving government-sponsored prosecutions of dissidents from the Whig party for libel and treason that they saw no basis for pursuing the charges, and judges were unable to circumvent them.[103] The judgment in *Bushel's case* was capitalized on in the press to justify those decisions, leading to jury equity (ie jury nullification) being recognized as a right of the jury.[104]

Continued judicial power alongside jury discretion in most trials

This period is important politically due to the recognition of jury equity; however, in the majority of cases trials continued as they had previously. It seems that generally the judge continued to exert authority and influence in the courtroom and that the judge and jury seldom came into conflict.[105] Commentary suggests that the judge was largely dominant because the absence of lawyers gave him an important role in commenting on evidence and shaping the testimony of witnesses,[106] although note that evidence suggests that judges did not exert much control over the evidence that juries saw.[107] Juries seem to have been willing to accept advice from judges, resulting in a system that has been described as largely harmonious.[108]

Jurors did continue to exercise discretion in everyday cases, but in ways that were largely expected and accepted.[109] Jurors would find defendants guilty of lesser offences than those they were charged with, for example by reducing the value of items stolen in verdicts relating to theft, in order to avoid defendants being given capital sentences.[110] For example, Professor John Beattie describes a woman charged with larceny of £1 16s (£1.80) in 1663 who was convicted of theft of goods worth nine shillings to ensure a lenient sentence.[111] However, research suggests that when jurors exercised their discretion in this way, they were not

[101] ibid 1815.
[102] ibid 1817.
[103] ibid 1819.
[104] ibid.
[105] Langbein, 'The Criminal Trial Before the Lawyers' (n 59) 291; JM Beattie, *Crime and the Courts in England 1660–1800* (OUP 1986) 408.
[106] Beattie (n 105) 408.
[107] Langbein, 'The Criminal Trial Before the Lawyers' (n 59) 301.
[108] Beattie (n 105) 408.
[109] ibid 420–21.
[110] ibid 419–24.
[111] ibid 424.

doing so against the wishes of Parliament, who expected the law to be enforced with discretion.[112]

However, even after *Bushel's case* (which, as described above, established that judges could not punish or threaten to punish jurors for their verdicts), judges continued to have the power to question juries about the reasoning behind their verdicts, to argue with the jury, to give the jury further instructions, to ask the jury to engage in further deliberation, and to pardon a defendant following a guilty verdict from a jury.[113] Professor John Langbein has demonstrated how the use of some of these powers could influence jury decisions through an exploration of the case of Stephen Arrowsmith in 1687.[114] In that case, the jury initially found the defendant not guilty of what is now known as statutory rape. The judge used his power of comment to suggest the defendant was guilty, rejected the jury verdict as not being 'according to the evidence', and essentially persuaded the jury to change their verdict to guilty through identifying and 'correcting' mistakes. This case has been described as illustrating the 'outer extreme of judicial dominance' in a system where heavy caseloads required harmony between juries and judges.[115] However, it has been suggested that the real reason for the verdict given in *Bushel's case*, which was against the weight of precedent, was that judges were willing to give up the power to fine disobedient jurors in the 1770s due to the many other ways in which they were able to exert dominance over juries.[116]

Phase IV: Advancing Fairness and the Adversarial Trial (1700s–1900s)

The eighteenth and early nineteenth centuries saw significant change in trial procedure. Between 1730 and 1770—and inspired by Enlightenment ideals focused on rationality and individual liberty—the adversarial trial developed.[117] This development was influenced by recognition of the significant power of the state over individuals, and thus the need to safeguard individuals through use of structural restrictions.[118]

In the 1730s, judges started to allow the defendant to have a lawyer, specifically to examine and cross-examine witnesses in felony cases.[119] Although the reasons

[112] ibid 420–21.
[113] Langbein, 'The Criminal Trial Before the Lawyers' (n 59) 291.
[114] ibid 291–95.
[115] ibid 295.
[116] ibid 298–300.
[117] R Vogler, *A World View of Criminal Justice* (Routledge 2017) 129–30.
[118] ibid.
[119] JH Langbein, 'The Prosecutorial Origins of Defence Counsel' in *The Origins of Adversary Criminal Trial* (n 60) 106. Note that defence lawyers had been allowed in high treason trials only

for this change are not well understood, it has been suggested that changes in prosecution practice, particularly the use of lawyers to prepare and conduct prosecutions and the development of new incentives for prosecution moved the trial process away from the previous conception as a 'contest of citizen equals' and made prosecutorial advantages and defendant vulnerability clearer.[120]

The increased involvement of defence lawyers in the trial process had a significant impact on the development of the criminal trial and thus the role of the jury. One important influence of this involvement was the development of rules of evidence (discussed further below), which were likely at least partly a result of objections raised by lawyers.[121] The rise of the law of evidence has also been linked to the need for judges to have continued power in jury trials, in which the rise of lawyers meant that they had lost their command over the jury.[122] While in 1700 rules of evidence had been almost non-existent, at the end of the eighteenth century they had been developed and refined into a substantial jurisprudence.[123] For example, by the middle of the eighteenth century judges were preventing hearsay evidence from being given at trial.[124] The most influential eighteenth-century book on evidence was written by Judge Geoffrey Gilbert and published in 1754.[125] This book summarizes jurisprudence that had developed on, for example, the disqualification of witnesses with an interest in a case outcome, and the exclusion of hearsay evidence (primarily due to the witness not having taken an oath).[126] Crucially, focus in trial proceedings shifted from asking what really happened, to asking whether the defence had raised sufficient doubt about the prosecution case.[127]

In the nineteenth century, 'adversarial procedure', where opposing sides each present evidence in support of their case, was formally established. The Prisoners' Counsel Act of 1836 gave those accused of crimes the right to be represented by a defence lawyer, who could directly address the jury.[128] This change enforced jury independence, since lawyers rather than judges took responsibility for the production and presentation of evidence.[129] The role of juries in the trial process became

since the Treason Trials Act of 1969; see JH Langbein, 'The Treason Trials Act of 1969: The Advent of Defense Counsel' in *The Origins of Adversary Criminal Trial* (n 60) 67–68.

120 Langbein, 'The Prosecutorial Origins of Defence Counsel' (n 119) 108–09.
121 Beattie (n 105) 363.
122 Langbein, 'The Criminal Trial Before the Lawyers' (n 59) 306.
123 Vogler (n 117) 142.
124 Beattie (n 105) 364.
125 G Gilbert, *The Law of Evidence* (1754).
126 JH Langbein, 'Historical Foundations of the Law of Evidence' (1996) 96 Columbia Law Review 1168, 1174.
127 See TP Gallanis, 'Reasonable Doubt and the History of the Criminal Trial' (2009) 76(2) University of Chicago Law Review 941.
128 Gimson (n 22) 120.
129 Anand (n 30) 430.

more passive, since their ability to question witnesses, to ask for witnesses to be called, and to comment on evidence was restricted or eliminated.[130] Essentially, the jury became bystanders to a trial process controlled by lawyers.[131] The increased independence of jurors during this period enhanced the possibility for jury error or jury equity (nullification). Lawyers argued against the practice of allowing judges to ask juries for reasons for their findings and the practice of judges returning a case for further discussion where reasons did not appear grounded on evidence, and began to successfully insist that judges stop inquiring into the basis for jury verdicts.[132]

As judges lost their control over the jury, rules of evidence continued to build up that constrained jury decisions by limiting which evidence jurors would be able to see. Rules also demanded that certain types of evidence (eg unsworn evidence from child witnesses) be corroborated to be admissible, and in other cases required the judge to warn the jury to view evidence of certain witnesses (complainants in sexual assault cases, accomplices, and children giving sworn testimony) with caution.[133] These rules of evidence were designed to protect the defendant from evidence that could be prejudicial. These rules also represented, at least to some extent, a distrust in the jury. The rules have been said to be 'rooted . . . in the system of trial by jury', since jurors may be susceptible to giving such evidence a 'force it does not deserve'.[134] Professor James Thayer (a late nineteenth-century legal commentator) argued that the rules of evidence developed because the jury system needed 'so much watching and so many safeguards' due to the potential for jurors to misunderstand or be misled by evidence.[135] Thus, as judges relinquished their power over the jury, rules of evidence were used to curtail the discretion of the jury.

During this period, other important changes also occurred. In 1898, the rule that defendants could not testify under oath ended as part of a general trend away from reliance on the oath as a method of determining truthfulness in uncertain cases.[136] As a result, jurors were required to resolve conflicting testimonies under oath, and in order to convict a defendant who maintained their innocence they had to determine that a story told under oath was a lie beyond reasonable doubt. Arguably, this change gave the jury a more significant role in lie detection than they had had previously. The composition of juries also continued to become more representative during this period. In 1919, the Sex Disqualification (Removal) Act abolished the ban on female jurors (although note they were often still excluded

[130] ibid 428.

[131] ibid 432.

[132] ibid 431. See also Langbein, 'Historical Foundations of the Law of Evidence' (n 126).

[133] R Munday, *Evidence* (10th edn, OUP 2019) 48.

[134] *R v Blastland* [1986] AC 41, 54.

[135] JB Thayer, *A Preliminary Treatise on Evidence at the Common Law (1898)* (Little, Brown, and Company 1898) 2.

[136] Fisher (n 63) 662.

in other ways, eg by property qualifications).[137] This reform was the start of a process of broadening the membership of juries; however, even in the 1960s, juries remained overwhelmingly male.[138] The Juries Act 1974 finally abolished property qualifications for jurors, and gender equality in juries was achieved around that time.[139] Thus, it is only relatively recently that the jury in England and Wales has become a truly representative institution.

The development of the adversarial trial in some ways increased the independence of the jury since evidence was presented from lawyers rather than from judges. However, in some ways it limited the role of the jury, since the evidence that they could see became increasingly policed by judges. In some ways this development limited the extent to which jurors could exercise their discretion and community judgment, since factors that may have been relevant to this discretion were susceptible to being withheld in the interests of fairness. The resulting jury considers evidence according to strict rules to make determinations of whether guilt has been proven, in cases involving defendants about whom they have no background knowledge. This jury differs significantly from the first trial jury of the thirteenth century.

Lessons from History and Jury Malleability

The jury is a legal instrument used to determine who should be held legally liable for alleged wrongdoing. The development of instruments is typically informed by a feedback loop—the performance of an instrument is assessed based on how well it works against objective outcomes, and analysis of those outcomes is used to inform changes to enhance future performance. However, the jury has not developed in this way, either artificially or organically, since objective outcomes that the jury should be designed to achieve have evolved subtly over time.

Over time, the jury has had a role in reinforcing cohesiveness in society, effectively investigating community crime, ensuring mercy for deserving defendants, promoting exemplary justice, ensuring that the legal system represents the voices of the people, and neutrally adjudicating crime. The jury itself as an institution of peers is not necessarily carefully designed to fit any particular role. The way in which juries function in society is likely to be dependent on the procedure and regulation surrounding their use. The jury has, at different times, functioned as a tool of those in power to control behaviour in society and as a protective institution

[137] K Crosby, 'Restricting the Juror Franchise in 1920s England and Wales' (2019) 37(1) Law and History Review 163.

[138] A Logan, 'Building a New and Better Order? Women and Jury Service in England and Wales *c.*1920–70' (2013) 22(5) Women's History Review 701.

[139] ibid.

drawing on community voice to protect individuals in society from those in power. It has been a mechanism through which those close to a crime, and arguably most likely to make accurate judgments, have been able to adjudicate upon those in their community, and also a tool where defendants are protected from partiality by having someone who does not know them adjudicate their case. Legal infrastructure and regulation are what determine how the jury functions. One recent article made this point, specifically in the context of information presented to juries, by analogizing the jury trial to Socrates 'cave' where what people see is merely the shadow of objective truth—a reflection of what they are allowed to see.[140] The ability of the jury to make effective decisions is largely dictated by the way in which they are regulated and the information that is presented to them. Through regulating, among other things, the size of juries, who can sit on juries, the evidence that juries hear, and the control of judges over juries, the criminal justice system can change how juries function and the role that they fulfil in society.

Today, control over the jury is less clear than it has been in the past, and jury independence is valued, although it is important to note that rules of procedure and evidence still act as levers that effectively control and constrain jury function. However, rules of procedure and evidence surrounding the jury are not consistently designed with the aims and abilities of the modern jury sufficiently in mind. Consider, for example, the basic composition of the jury as a body comprising of twelve citizens. This number of citizens was chosen, primarily based on tradition, when juries were local men charged with reporting crimes in their communities. These men represented their hundred, which could have consisted of several thousand people, or even fewer.[141] This number remained when juries started doing a different job and representing a different body of people, as they increasingly became drawn from outside communities to hear evidence presented in court. Today, in England and Wales twelve jurors represent a population of tens of millions of people from across a wide range of groups in society rather than the several thousand people they represented when they were first utilized (and although they are still drawn from areas in which crimes occurred, these areas are made up of significantly more than several thousand people).[142] Jury size has stayed the same despite juries performing vastly different roles. It is clear that there is no scientific reason to use twelve jurors in particular.[143] However, juries in England and Wales

[140] CD Hatcher, 'The Whole Truth or Anything But: How Fairness, Reliability, and the Rule of Completeness Affect the Jury's Truth-Seeking Function' (2016) 39 American Journal of Trial Advocacy 683, 685–86.

[141] See eg T John, 'Population Change in Medieval Warwickshire: Domesday Book to the Hundred Rolls of 1279–1280' [1997] Local Population Studies 41.

[142] Office for National Statistics, 'Population Estimates for the UK, England and Wales, Scotland and Northern Ireland: Mid-2020' (*Office for National Statistics*, 25 June 2021) <www.ons.gov.uk/peoplepopulationandcommunity/populationandmigration/populationestimates/bulletins/annualmidyearpopulationestimates/mid2020> accessed 5 June 2023.

[143] Devlin (n 2) 4.

have continued to use twelve members, probably because many people believe that the jury system functions effectively, and do not want to do anything to disrupt that.[144]

Consider also the role of 'lie detectors' that the jury has assumed in a significant number of cases, including cases which typically rely largely on testimony, such as sexual assault cases. Juries were not designed as lie detectors, and likely relied heavily on the oath in cases of uncertainty (since, for a long period, only prosecution evidence would be sworn under oath, this would have led to favouring the prosecution) until the late 1800s when they had to decide between competing sworn testimony for the first time.[145] Importantly, a significant amount of evidence today suggests that jurors may be unlikely to perform effectively in this role.[146] The jury was not designed as a lie detector, and if we want it to now function as a lie detector then more work needs to be done to ensure that the jury is competent at this task and to facilitate maximally effective performance.

It is true that public support for juries seems relatively high: a 2009 international literature review noted that 'polls repeatedly suggest that the public strongly support the concept of the jury' and 'the right to trial by jury is seen as one of the most important rights in a democratic society'.[147] However, there are also clear suggestions that the jury system could be functioning better (although it is unclear which issues are caused by the jury themselves and which are caused by the evidence put to them). Over the last fifty years there have been relatively steady rates of wrongful convictions in trials by jury in England and Wales,[148] which have been broadly tolerated, with some underlying causes being addressed.[149] Recently there has also been growing dissatisfaction with failures to effectively prosecute defendants, and the potential role of juror bias in these failures.[150] Critics of the jury have labelled

[144] See eg Tana Adkin QC, 'How Will Restricting Jury Trial and Reducing Jury Numbers Affect the Delivery of Justice?' (*The Bar Council Guest Blog*, 10 July 2020) <www.barcouncil.org.uk/resource/guest-blog-how-will-restricting-jury-trial-and-reducing-jury-numbers-affect-the-delivery-of-justice.html> accessed 14 October 2021.

[145] Fisher (n 63) 662.

[146] See eg A Vrij and S Mann, 'Telling and Detecting Lies in a High-Stake Situation: The Case of a Convicted Murderer' (2001) 15(2) Applied Cognitive Psychology 187; CF Bond Jr and BM DePaulo, 'Accuracy of Deception Judgments' (2006) 10(3) Personality and Social Psychology Review 214; CF Bond Jr and BM DePaulo, 'Individual Differences in Judging Deception: Accuracy and Bias' (2008) 134(4) Psychological Bulletin 477.

[147] J Roberts and M Hough, *Public Opinion and the Jury: An International Literature Review* (Ministry of Justice Research Series 1/09 2009) i.

[148] See Evidence-Based Justice Lab, 'Miscarriages of Justice Registry' (*Evidence-Based Justice Lab*, 2021) <https://evidencebasedjustice.exeter.ac.uk/miscarriages-of-justice-registry/> accessed 14 October 2021.

[149] R Nobles and D Schiff, *Understanding Miscarriages of Justice: Law, the Media, and the Inevitability of Crisis* (OUP 2000); H Quirk, 'Identifying Miscarriages of Justice: Why Innocence in the UK is Not the Answer' (2007) 70(5) Modern Law Review 759, 760; R Helm, 'The Anatomy of "Factual Error" Miscarriages of Justice in England and Wales: A Fifty-Year Review' (2021) 5 Criminal Law Review 351.

[150] See eg A Topping and C Barr, 'Rape Conviction Crisis: The Systemic Failures that Deny Justice for Victims' *The Guardian* (6 October 2018) <www.theguardian.com/membership/2018/oct/06/conviction-crisis-rape-uk-cps> accessed 5 June 2023.

it as antiquated and absurd,[151] archaic and irrelevant,[152] untrustworthy,[153] the 'apotheosis of the amateur',[154] and as having 'infinite capacity for mischief'.[155]

The jury needs to respond to this criticism in order to continue to meet society's aspirations for security and justice. The jury needs to evolve again, into a more sophisticated legal instrument. However, the organic and often pragmatic evolution of the jury means that the philosophical and political assumptions on which the current jury system is based are relatively opaque, and that procedure can be the result of historical artefact and 'common-sense' principles rather than careful planning. As a result, aspirations for the jury are often based on myth and vague ideology rather than precise science.[156] One way to examine what informs current jury procedure is to compare procedure surrounding jury trial in different jury systems. These systems have been transplanted from the early English or early French juries, and examining how they have evolved in different ways from those early systems and from each other can provide insight into the drivers underlying modern jury procedure. Such an examination will be conducted in the following chapter.

[151] C Becker, *Freedom and Responsibility in the American Way of Life* (Vintage Books 1945) 81–82.

[152] S Jenkins, 'Our Justice System is in Crisis, So Why Not Abolish Jury Trials?' *The Guardian* (22 January 2021) <www.theguardian.com/commentisfree/2021/jan/22/justice-system-crisis-abolish-jury-trials-covid> accessed 5 June 2023.

[153] J Bindel, 'Juries Have No Place in Rape Trials. They Simply Can't Be Trusted' *The Guardian* (21 November 2018) <www.theguardian.com/commentisfree/2018/nov/21/juries-rape-trials-myths-justice> accessed 5 June 2023.

[154] EN Griswold, 'Harvard Law School Dean's Report' (1962–1963) 5–6, as cited in H Kalven and H Zeisel, *The American Jury* (Little, Brown 1966).

[155] Judge Jerome Frank in *Skidmore v Baltimore and Ohio Railroad* (1948) 167 F 2d 54: 'While the jury can contribute nothing of value as far as the law is concerned, it has infinite capacity for mischief, for twelve men can easily misunderstand more law in a minute than the judge can explain in an hour.'

[156] See P Duff and M Findlay, 'Jury Reform: Of Myths and Moral Panics' (1997) 25(4) International Journal of the Sociology of Law 363.

2
Jury Systems Worldwide

Introduction

As Chapter 1 demonstrated, differences in society's need for the jury and related changes in jury procedure have changed the way in which the jury has functioned over its more than 800-year history. Today, the jury system has been 'transplanted' and 'translated' in jurisdictions across the world from both the early English jury and the early French jury.[1] Over time, these systems have evolved in multiple ways to differ from their ancestors and from other jury systems. Differences in prioritizations and differences in presumptions relating to the effects of procedure underlie these different jury systems.

In this chapter, I outline different procedures surrounding jury trial in jurisdictions across the world in order to explore some of the prioritizations and presumptions underlying modern jury systems. I begin by providing some context on how jury systems around the world have developed. I then introduce a range of differing approaches to jury regulation, framed around common debates on how best to regulate juries. Specifically, I focus on the number of people on a jury and unanimity or majority verdict requirements, eligibility and selection of jurors, and juror decision-making freedom. I suggest that many jurisdictional approaches reflect imprecise normative goals and reliance on common-sense-type reasoning or weak empirical foundations, which are not firmly grounded in precise science and so may differ by jurisdiction. Put simply, I suggest regulation is still more opinion-based than science-based. I conclude by highlighting the importance of clearly articulating desired goals of the jury and gathering evidence to facilitate the tailoring of function to those goals.

Section I: The Development of World Jury Systems

The all-citizen jury has been described as a legal transplant—an institution from one country's legal system that is adopted, in whole or in part, by another legal system.[2] Modern jury systems were transplanted from the early English jury (discussed in Chapter 1), and also from the early French jury. The early French

[1] V Hans, 'Trial by Jury: Story of a Legal Transplant' (2017) 51(3) Law and Society Review 471.
[2] ibid.

How Juries Work. Rebecca K. Helm, Oxford University Press. © Rebecca K. Helm 2024.
DOI: 10.1093/9780191948107.003.0002

jury was adopted largely due to its democratic appeal following the French Revolution of 1789.[3] This jury, as an institution in a civil legal system with an inquisitorial (rather than adversarial) tradition, did not reach its own general verdicts but instead answered specific questions asked by a presiding judge.[4] The English and French jury systems were emulated by some jurisdictions independently, but the primary means by which they spread was by being imposed in overseas jurisdictions as the British and French empires expanded.[5] While some countries that had been part of those empires chose to end trial by jury once they achieved independence, others decided to retain the institution, and their own form of trial by jury evolved alongside, but independently of, juries in England and France.[6]

Many common law jury systems transplanted from the English system have had a significant degree of longevity. Juries which descended from the English common law jury remain important parts of legal systems in countries including England and Wales, Australia, Canada, Ghana, Gibraltar, Guyana, Hong Kong, the Republic of Ireland, Jamaica, Malawi, Malta, New Zealand, Northern Ireland, Scotland, Sri Lanka, Tonga, and the United States of America (USA).[7] Despite limitations on their use—most notably the fact that only sufficiently serious offences tend to be tried before a jury,[8] and the fact that incentives to plead guilty mean that relatively few defendants ever reach trial in some jurisdictions[9]—juries remain important in these jurisdictions and are often viewed as significant both symbolically and politically. This significance is particularly obvious in the USA, where historically juries were important in creating a sense of fairness among early colonials, who could be tried by their peers rather than imported English judges.[10]

[3] JM Donovan, *Juries and the Transformation of Criminal Justice in France in the Nineteenth and Twentieth Centuries* (The University of North Carolina Press 2010) 23–48.

[4] Hans (n 1) 481. See also V Hans and C Germain, 'The French Jury at a Crossroads' (2011) 86(2) Chicago-Kent Law Review 737.

[5] Hans (n 1) 481.

[6] ibid 482.

[7] N Vidmar, 'A Historical and Comparative Perspective on the Common Law Jury' in N Vidmar (ed), *World Jury Systems* (OUP 2000) 1, 3.

[8] eg in England and Wales, juries hear cases involving 'indictable only' offences (the most serious offences) or 'either way' offences (intermediate offences) where the lower court's sentencing powers are insufficient (where the crime potentially warrants a custodial sentence of over a year) or where the defendant elects to have their case heard by a jury. The remainder of cases are heard in the lower court, known as the magistrates' court (see S Machura, '"... And My Right" The Magistrates' Courts in England and Wales' in S Ivković and others, *Juries, Lay Judges, and Mixed Courts: A Global Perspective* (CUP 2021). Canada adopts a similar system: summary offences (the least serious) are tried by a judge alone in a lower court, indictable offences (the most serious) are tried in a higher court by a judge and jury, and hybrid offences (intermediate offences) can be tried either as indictable or summary offences based on a determination by the prosecuting Crown Attorney, see C Granger, *The Criminal Trial Jury in Canada* (2nd edn, Carswell 1996) 37–42.

[9] See eg J Blume and RK Helm, 'The Unexonerated: Factually Innocent Defendants Who Plead Guilty' (2014) 100 Cornell Law Review 157; RK Helm, 'Constrained Waiver of Trial Rights? Incentives to Plead Guilty and the Right to a Fair Trial' (2019) 46(3) Journal of Law and Society 423.

[10] Hans (n 1) 481.

The right to a trial by jury in criminal cases is considered so important in the USA that it is enshrined in the US Constitution.[11] Although juries descended from the English system can be seen as transplanted from that system, they have evolved independently and now differ both from each other and from the system in England and Wales in important ways.

All-citizen juries in many civil law countries have not shown this longevity and have largely been abandoned, often in favour of mixed courts, in which jurors (sometimes called lay judges) and professional judges decide cases together.[12] These systems were considered more compatible with the inquisitorial approach adopted in civil law systems, in which the court is actively involved in investigating case facts.[13] Even the French jury itself was replaced by a mixed court of jurors and professional judges, who make determinations of guilt and punishment together, in 1941. This transition was triggered at least in part by citizen unrest about high numbers of acquittals (particularly for certain classes of defendant), and by an increasing move towards government by experts in politics more generally.[14] In 1928, a prominent liberal jurist in France stated that the jury was 'beaten and battered' by 'those who want to replace a justice of "impression" with a truly rational and scientific one'.[15] There are now only a small number of civil law jurisdictions that still utilize all-citizen juries. These include jurisdictions that have traditionally used juries, such as Brazil and Belgium, and jurisdictions that have reintroduced juries more recently, including Spain (which re-introduced trial by jury in 1995)[16] and Russia (which re-introduced trial by jury in 1993).[17]

Examining approaches adopted in different jurisdictions within either the common or civil law tradition and between traditions is informative in illustrating how regulation surrounding the jury has developed and is justified, and the effect that changing regulation might have on function. However, it is important to bear in mind important underlying differences in common and civil law traditions that underlie different choices in terms of jury regulation.

[11] Art 3 and the Bill of Rights. Note that the right to trial by jury is also enshrined in the constitutions of other jurisdictions including Canada (Canadian Charter of Rights and Freedoms, pt I of the Constitution Act 1982) and Australia (Commonwealth of Australia Constitution Act, s 80).

[12] JD Jackson and N Kovalev, 'Lay Adjudication in Europe: The Rise and Fall of the Traditional Jury' (2016) 6(2) Oñati Socio-Legal Series <https://ssrn.com/abstract=2782413> accessed 12 October 2021.

[13] Hans (n 1) 482.

[14] Donovan (n 3) ch 6.

[15] F Lombard, *Les jurés. Justice représentative et représentation de la justice* (L'Harmattan 2000) 272.

[16] S Thaman, 'Spain Returns to Trial by Jury' (1998) 21(2) Hastings International and Comparative Law Review 241.

[17] S Thaman, 'The Resurrection of Trial by Jury in Russia' (1995) 31(1) Stanford Journal of International Law 61.

Section II: Differing Approaches to Jury Regulation

How many people should sit on a jury, and what level of agreement should be required for a guilty verdict?

Jurisdictions differ as to the number of citizens that make up a jury, and how many of those citizens have to agree to reach a verdict. The traditional English jury was composed of twelve citizens who needed to unanimously agree on their verdict.[18] In such systems (systems requiring unanimity), where the jury cannot agree, this is known as a 'hung jury'; the defendant is neither convicted nor acquitted, and the prosecution must retry the case (ie present the case to a new jury) if they want to try to secure a conviction. This composition and unanimity requirement is still used today in a number of jurisdictions, including Canada and the majority of states in the USA.[19] However, many jurisdictions now have different requirements.

First, some jurisdictions maintain the composition of the jury as twelve citizens, but allow majority verdicts, at least under some circumstances. The jury in England and Wales itself is still made up of twelve citizens, but since 1967 jurors can reach a 'supermajority' verdict of ten to two, when they have deliberated for two hours and failed to reach a unanimous decision.[20] The jury in Malawi is also comprised of twelve citizens, but can reach a verdict by a majority of eight to four,[21] as is the jury in New Zealand, which can reach a verdict by a majority of eleven to one.[22] Other jurisdictions adopt different rules altogether. In Scotland, juries are composed of fifteen citizens, and a majority of the jury must agree in order to find a defendant guilty (fewer votes result in an acquittal).[23] In Hong Kong and Ghana, juries are composed of seven members, and a majority of at least five to two must agree on a verdict (other than in death penalty decisions in Ghana where decisions must be unanimous).[24] In Spain's relatively new jury system, the jury is composed of nine citizens—to deliver a not guilty verdict at least five of the jurors must agree on that verdict and to deliver a guilty verdict at least seven of the jurors must agree on that verdict.[25]

[18] Vidmar, 'A Historical and Comparative Perspective on the Common Law Jury' (n 7) 26.

[19] EJ Leib, 'A Comparison of Criminal Jury Decision Rules in Democratic Countries' (2008) 5(2) Ohio State Journal of Criminal Law 629, 635–38.

[20] Juries Act 1974, s 17.

[21] N Vidmar, 'The Jury Elsewhere in the World' in N Vidmar (ed), *World Jury Systems* (OUP 2000) 421, 433.

[22] Juries Amendment Act 2008.

[23] Leib (n 19) 637. Note that as well as traditional verdicts of 'guilty' or 'not guilty', Scottish juries can return an intermediate 'not proven' verdict, see JM Barbato, 'Scotland's Bastard Verdict: Intermediacy and the Unique Three-Verdict System' (2004–2005) 15 Indiana International & Comparative Law Review 15, although this verdict is likely to be abolished as part of a set of reforms of the Scottish jury system which will also include reducing the number of jurors sitting on juries from fifteen to twelve.

[24] Vidmar, 'The Jury Elsewhere in the World' (n 21) 427, 433.

[25] Ley Orgánica del Tribunal del Jurado (BOE) 5/1995, art 59(1). See also M Jimeno-Bulnes, 'A Different Story Line for *12 Angry Men*: Verdicts Reached by Majority Rule—The Spanish Perspective' (2007) 82(2) Chicago Kent Law Review 759.

Differences in jury size and unanimity requirements are presumed to influence how juries function, particularly in more 'borderline' cases.[26] Smaller juries are thought to be more efficient and lead to cost and time savings for a system. This increase in efficiency underlay a cut in jury numbers in England and Wales from twelve to seven during the Second World War, and, more recently, arguments that jury numbers should be cut to ease delays caused by the Covid-19 pandemic.[27] Larger juries are thought to be more likely to protect defendants from bias and wrongful conviction through requiring a greater number to agree as to guilt prior to conviction, and are thus often seen as protective of, or even required to ensure, that defendants' rights are respected. In addition, larger juries are more likely to be representative of the wider population. Regulations relating to jury size are often based on beliefs about the impact of changes in jury size. In 1970, the US Supreme Court concluded that defendant rights would not be compromised if jury size was cut since it made 'no discernible difference' in results.[28] As a result, several states reduced the size of their juries in an attempt to increase efficiency through speeding up deliberation and reducing the number of mistrials (where juries are unable to reach a verdict). However, as a result of the perceived risks of reducing jury size (particularly to defendant rights), other jurisdictions have refused to do so, at least in the absence of clear benefits that would justify the change. The Law Commission of Canada held a consultation on jury size and decided to retain the requirement that juries must consist of twelve people, concluding that those wanting to decrease jury size had 'failed to prove it would increase the effectiveness or efficiency of trials'.[29]

Jury majority requirements are presumed to influence function in similar ways to size requirements. Allowing majority verdicts is thought to increase efficiency through reducing the potential for hung juries and through ensuring that verdicts cannot be held up by those with unusual and potentially unreasonable views. In England and Wales, the primary rationale for starting to allow a majority verdict rather than insisting on a unanimous verdict was to prevent professional criminals from escaping conviction by bribing individual jurors.[30] However, there were also other arguments for majority verdicts at the time, including the increased efficiency

[26] See RO Lempert, 'Uncovering "Non-Discernible" Differences: Empirical Research and the Jury-Size Cases' (1975) 73(4) Michigan Law Review 643.

[27] See eg L Dearden, 'Coronavirus: Juries Could Be Cut from 12 Members to Seven to Restart Court Trials Amid Mounting Backlog' *The Independent* (30 April 2020) <www.independent.co.uk/news/uk/home-news/coronavirus-juries-court-trials-change-case-backlog-remote-video-a9492166.html> accessed 13 October 2021.

[28] *Williams v Florida* 399 US 78 (1970). In that case, the court described the use of twelve citizens on juries as 'a historical accident … in no way essential to the purpose of the jury trial', at 125.

[29] Law Reform Commission of Canada, 'The Jury in Criminal Trials' (1980) (Working Paper 27, Department of Justice Canada).

[30] S Lloyd-Bostock and C Thomas, 'Decline of the "Little Parliament": Juries and Jury Reform in England and Wales' (1999) 62(2) Law and Contemporary Problems 7, 36.

of majority verdicts[31] and the need to reduce the number of guilty people being acquitted by juries more broadly.[32] The move was also linked, at least in part, to widening eligibility to serve on the jury, which seems to have created apprehension about the ability of the jury to function with unanimity requirements while also including a heterogeneous set of citizens.[33] In Spain, the official rationale for allowing a majority verdict is to avoid hung juries.[34] On the other hand, requiring unanimity is thought to protect defendant rights, particularly in the context of the presumption of innocence. Those opposed to allowing majority verdicts note that if some jurors do not agree with the verdict there is clearly reasonable doubt, meaning a conviction would be contrary to the presumption of innocence.[35] In addition, giving minority jurors a voice is potentially important in reducing majority bias and thus protecting defendants.[36] Essentially, allowing non-unanimous verdicts is seen as potentially suppressing the votes of minority jurors. These considerations underlie the continuing importance of unanimity requirements in some jurisdictions. The perceived importance of unanimity requirements for defendant rights in the US context was demonstrated in the recent case of *Ramos v Louisiana*, where the Supreme Court held that the Constitution (and specifically the Sixth Amendment right to trial by an impartial jury) requires unanimous jury verdicts in all state criminal trials.[37] The Supreme Court of Canada has described the necessity of unanimity as one of the 'fundamental' characteristics of criminal jury trials,[38] noting the need for the jury to behave as a body and not a collection of individuals, and the High Court of Australia has described unanimity as a 'hallmark' of trial by jury.[39]

To some extent these differences between jurisdictions may be normal reflections of different prioritization in terms of how efficiency and rights should be balanced. However, the lack of precision in defining the normative balance that is being aimed for creates difficulties in assessing and critiquing procedure. Ostensibly, all jurisdictions want verdicts to be sufficiently certain to protect defendants but also for the jury system to be manageable in terms of efficiency. However, debates in this area do not provide precise guidance as to how protection of defendant rights and efficiency should be measured, and how the balance

[31] See N Waller and N Sakande, 'Majority Verdicts in England and Wales: A Vestige of White Supremacy?' (2024) Race and Class. https://journals.sagepub.com/doi/full/10.1177/03063968231212992.

[32] '[T]here seems no doubt that the large proportion of acquittals, equivalent to about two of every five jury trials include a substantial number of acquittals of guilty men' ibid.

[33] eg Charles Fletcher Cooke, debate held on 26 April 1967 (cited in APPEAL work on majority verdicts, forthcoming).

[34] Ley Orgánica del Tribunal del Jurado (BOE) 5/1995, preamble, pt V.

[35] See eg New South Wales Law Reform Commission, *Majority Verdicts* (Report 111, 2005).

[36] T Adkin QC, 'How Will Restricting Jury Trial and Reducing Jury Numbers Affect the Delivery of Justice?' (*The Bar Council Guest Blog*, 10 July 2020) <www.barcouncil.org.uk/resource/guest-blog-how-will-restricting-jury-trial-and-reducing-jury-numbers-affect-the-delivery-of-justice.html> accessed 13 October 2021.

[37] 140 S Ct 1390 (2020).

[38] *R v Bain* [1992] 1 SCR 91, 145.

[39] *Cheatlet v R* [1993] HCA 44; 177 CLR 571, 7.

between defendant rights and efficiency should be struck. A more precise approach is required in order to facilitate the design of evidence-based procedure to further specified goals. To give a simplified example in the case of jury size, one approach could be to increase size until a point is reached where the proportion of guilty verdicts no longer changes appreciably with increasing size (ie verdicts are broadly reflective of the decision a community at large would have come to), reflecting sufficient certainty and stability to protect defendants without unnecessarily infringing on efficiency. However, it should be noted that the precise size required by this simplified example would be likely to differ based on case characteristics.

Importantly, much of the rationale underlying existing procedures reflects reliance on common-sense-type reasoning and weak empirical foundations, both of which may differ by jurisdiction due to not being firmly grounded in underlying scientific reality. For example, consider the potential impact of changes in jury size. As noted above, the US Supreme Court decided to allow juries with less than twelve members on the basis that if jury size were cut it would make 'no discernible difference' to results.[40] This conclusion was based on some early evidence from experimental work. In contrast, Canada continues to recognize potential risks to defendants when smaller juries are utilized, an approach which is supported by newer experimental research suggesting potentially important effects of changes in jury size on verdicts.[41] In addition, conclusions as to the efficiency benefits of smaller juries are mixed. The approach adopted by some jurisdictions (eg in some US states and Spain) suggests confidence in increased efficiency in smaller juries; however, in other jurisdictions (eg Canada) the presence of these benefits is seen as less clear. In fact, presumptions that reducing jury size will increase efficiency have been called into question by research in the USA, where states that reduced jury size to speed up deliberation and reduce mistrials did not see the expected reduction in mistrial rates.[42] Finally, the maintenance of unanimity requirements is often justified on the basis of protecting defendants, with unanimity granted special status in jury systems (eg in Australia, Canada, and the USA). However, the role of unanimity may, in reality, be more important symbolically (as a result of tradition) than it is practically. Some recent work suggests that unanimity requirements may not be necessary to protect defendants, particularly when large juries are utilized.[43] It is important to also note the continuing role of tradition rather than design in much

[40] *Williams v Florida* (n 28) 125.

[41] See eg R Roper, 'Jury Size and Verdict Consistency: "A Line Has to be Drawn Somewhere"?' (1980) 14 Law and Society Review 977; MJ Saks and MW Marti, 'A Meta-Analysis of the Effects of Jury Size' (1997) 21(5) Law and Human Behavior 451; K Mukhopadhaya, 'Jury Size and the Free Rider Problem' (2003) 19(1) Journal of Law, Economics, and Organization 24.

[42] See B Luppi and F Parisi, 'Jury Size and the Hung Jury Paradox' (2013) 42(2) The Journal of Legal Studies 399.

[43] A Guerra, B Luppi, and F Parisi, 'Accuracy of Verdicts Under Different Jury Sizes and Voting Rules' (2020) 28(1) Supreme Court Economic Review 221.

jury procedure in this area. Many of the rationales used to justify majority verdicts in England and Wales, for example, are unlikely to be applicable today.

How should jurors be selected?

All-citizen juries are invariably made up of citizens drawn at random from the population in a jurisdiction.[44] However, methods for selecting a final panel of jurors differ significantly by jurisdiction. The primary dichotomy in approach is between systems that allow randomly selected citizens to sit on the jury with relatively little scrutiny, only excluding jurors who do not meet eligibility requirements, and jurisdictions that give the parties to a case some control over the jurors that end up hearing the case. Generally, debates surrounding jury selection and informing approaches to jury selection focus on the need to empanel a jury that is representative and impartial. Jurisdictions differ significantly in their conclusions as to the best way to empanel such a jury.

As discussed in Chapter 1, as early as the fourteenth century the accused in England were allowed to challenge potential jurors who they thought would not be neutral (eg due to the juror allegedly having a 'greedy desire' to get land).[45] For a significant period, the defence were able to exercise peremptory challenges to jurors, meaning that they could prevent a number of potential jurors from sitting on the panel hearing their case without giving a reason (this number decreased steadily from thirty-five in the 1300s to twenty in 1520 to seven in 1948 to three in 1977).[46] The prosecution did not have this power (from 1305) but could utilize a procedure known as 'standing aside', through which they could exclude jurors provided that there were a sufficient number of other jurors remaining to make up a full jury.[47] Evidence suggests that generally the use of peremptory challenges and stand aside powers was relatively rare.[48] In 1989, all peremptory challenges were abolished after a series of high-profile trials in which defence counsel's use of the challenges was deemed abusive.[49]

Of particular importance was a trial known as the 'Cyprus Secrets' case, where it was alleged that the multiple defendants had agreed to exercise their peremptory challenges to ensure a young male jury, who ended up acquitting them all.[50]

[44] Although note that there is variation in terms of where random lists from which jurors are selected are drawn from and eligibility requirements for jurors.

[45] D Klerman, 'Was the Jury Ever Self-Informing?' (2003) 77(1) Southern California Law Review 123, 134.

[46] M Hoffman, 'Peremptory Challenges Should Be Abolished: A Trial Judge's Perspective' (1997) 64(3) University of Chicago Law Review 809, 822.

[47] ibid 821–22.

[48] ibid 822.

[49] Criminal Justice Act 1988, ch 33 s 118(1); Hoffman (n 46).

[50] Lloyd-Bostock and Thomas (n 30) 24.

Challenges were criticized as allowing defendants to essentially bias a jury in their favour.[51] Also in 1989, the power to stand aside was abolished for the vast majority of circumstances.[52] In England and Wales today, the right to challenge jurors is limited to challenge for cause. A juror can be challenged on the grounds of bias which would make them unsuitable to hear a case (eg where they have expressed hostility to one of the parties or are connected to one of the parties).[53] Judges try these challenges for cause, and the burden of proof to demonstrate bias is on the challenging party.[54] The right to challenge for cause has been described as 'an empty right' since the challenging party needs evidence to support their challenge, but has very little information about jurors on which to base such a challenge, and no right to ask questions of the jurors.[55]

This restrictive approach to challenges to jurors was adopted largely on the basis of preserving impartiality. Juries should not be 'rigged' in favour of the prosecution or the defence but instead should be randomly selected.[56] However, in some ways the approach may be seen to actually increase partiality through failing to ensure minority representation on juries. The approach has been criticized for 'failing to address real concerns about jury composition' and not being 'likely to satisfy the deep concerns held about the criminal justice system by many people from an ethnic minority'.[57] Unsurprisingly, research suggests that many juries in England and Wales are all-white.[58]

Other jurisdictions have determined that the best way to ensure impartiality of juries is to allow the parties more control over jury selection, primarily through maintaining peremptory challenges. For example, US federal courts allow the defence and prosecution to exercise peremptory challenges in addition to challenges for cause.[59] While not constitutionally mandated, the right to peremptory challenges has, historically, been recognized in the USA as an important part of ensuring that a jury is impartial.[60] The right has also been introduced in newer jury

[51] ibid 24–25.

[52] Hoffman (n 46) 822. Today the prosecution can ask a juror to stand by only if the juror is manifestly unsuitable and the defence agree, or in a terrorist or security case in which the Attorney General has authorized a check of the jury list, but only on the authority of the Attorney General and where the information affords strong reasons for believing that a particular juror might be a security risk, be susceptible to improper approaches, or be influenced in arriving at a verdict. See Crown Prosecution Service, 'Jury Vetting' <www.cps.gov.uk/legal-guidance/jury-vetting> accessed 12 June 2023.

[53] Crown Prosecution Service (n 52). Note that, in theory, there also remains the potential for the defence to challenge the 'array' of jurors, meaning a panel of jurors as a whole, but this power is almost inoperative, and has been described by the Crown Prosecution Service as 'of historical significance only'.

[54] Criminal Justice Act 1988, s 118(2).

[55] Lloyd-Bostock and Thomas (n 30) 24–25.

[56] See eg *R v Ford* 3 All ER 445 (Eng CA 1989).

[57] Lloyd-Bostock and Thomas (n 30) 25.

[58] For more information, see A Lever, 'Democracy, Epistemology, and the Problem of All-White Juries' (2016) 34(4) Journal of Applied Philosophy 541.

[59] Federal Rule of Criminal Procedure 24(b).

[60] See eg *Swain v Alabama* 380 US 202 (1965) 219, where the Supreme Court acknowledged a 'widely held belief that peremptory challenge is a necessary part of trial by jury'.

systems including Spain,[61] Russia,[62] and the majority of provinces in Argentina.[63] Other systems permitting peremptory challenges include (as examples) Hong Kong,[64] Ghana,[65] and Ireland.[66] In these systems, the parties are typically able to question jurors to probe whether their opinions and experiences could lead them to be biased, and thus to inform their exercise of peremptory challenges (this process is referred to as *voir dire* in the USA).

Jurisdictions that do allow peremptory challenges differ significantly in terms of the nature of those challenges. Firstly, they differ in terms of the number of challenges that each party is able to make. Examples of these differences are outlined in Table 2.1. Secondly, they differ in terms of the procedures through which challenges are made. For example, procedure can require lawyers to assess jurors and decide whether to challenge them one at a time (as in the 'strike and replace' method) or can require lawyers to question and assess all jurors and then decide which to challenge (as in the 'struck jury' method).[67] These differences are likely to have important implications for the nature of the jury that ends up hearing a case, and how it functions in considering evidence.[68] Although it is possible that these differences are the result of differences in underlying context (eg the proportion of extreme views in a jurisdiction) there is no clear evidence that this is the case.

Table 2.1 Number of peremptory challenges permitted by jurisdiction

Jurisdiction	Prosecution challenges	Defence challenges	Relevant legislation
USA (Federal)	Capital Case: 20 Other Felony: 6 Misdemeanor:[69] 3	Capital Case: 20 Other Felony: 10 Misdemeanor: 3	Federal Rule of Criminal Procedure 24(b)
Spain	4	4	Ley Orgánica del Tribunal del Jurado 5/1995 art 40

[61] Ley Orgánica del Tribunal del Jurado (BOE) 5/1995, s 40. See also M Jimeno-Bulnes, 'Jury Selection and Jury Trial in Spain: Between Theory and Practice' (2011) 86(2) Chicago-Kent Law Review 585.

[62] SC Thaman, 'The Nullification of the Russian Jury: Lessons for Jury-Inspired Reform in Eurasia and Beyond' (2007) 40(2) Cornell International Law Journal 355, 364.

[63] C Scherr, 'Chasing Democracy: The Development and Acceptance of Jury Trials in Argentina' (2016) 47(2) University of Miami Inter-American Law Review 316, 347.

[64] The Law Reform Commission of Hong Kong, 'Juries Sub-Committee Consultation Paper' (2008).

[65] Justice DD Adjei, 'Ghana's Jury System on Trial' (Master of Judicial Studies Thesis, Duke University School of Law 2014) 18.

[66] JD Jackson, K Quinn, and T O'Malley, 'The Jury System in Contemporary Ireland: In the Shadow of a Troubled Past' (1999) 62(2) Law and Contemporary Problems 203, 210.

[67] FX Flanagan, 'Peremptory Challenges and Jury Selection' (2015) 58(2) The Journal of Law and Economics 385, 386.

[68] See eg GT Munsterman, RG Strand, and JW Hart, 'The Best Method of Selecting Jurors' (1990) 29 Judges Journal 9; A Moro and M Van der Linden, 'Exclusion of Extreme Jurors and Minority Representation: The Effect of Jury Selection Procedures' (2021) *arXiv preprint arXiv:2102.07222*.

[69] Note that, in many instances, the equivalent of misdemeanour cases (cases carrying a sentence of one year of incarceration or less) are not tried by juries.

Table 2.1 Continued

Jurisdiction	Prosecution challenges	Defence challenges	Relevant legislation
Hong Kong	Power to 'stand by' prospective jurors[70]	5	Jury Ordinance s 29 (Cap 3)
Ireland	7	7	Juries Act s 20 (1976) (Ir)
Neuquén and Córdoba, Argentina	1	1	Neuquén Law 2784Córdoba Law 9182
Buenos Aires, Argentina	4	4	Buenos Aires Law 14.542
Ghana	0	3	Criminal and Other Offences (Procedure) Act, 1960 Act 30 s 250

Note, these jurisdictions are used as examples and do not represent a comprehensive list of jurisdictions allowing peremptory challenges.

Despite their purpose in increasing impartiality, observing the use of peremptory challenges over time shows how they can potentially be used to undermine rather than promote impartiality. In the USA, for example, the peremptory challenge system has been described as being, at one time, an 'incredibly efficient final racial filter' preventing African Americans from sitting on juries.[71] Now, US law forbids the use of peremptory challenges to strike jurors for discriminatory reasons (eg on the basis of race or gender).[72] However, both research and reported experiences demonstrate the ineffectiveness of these rules, for example because of difficulties addressing unintentional bias and because of overlap between factors upon which challenges cannot be based (eg ethnicity or national origin) and factors upon which they can be based (eg language ability).[73] Based primarily on concerns over discrimination, the state of Arizona eliminated peremptory challenges in 2021.[74] In Canada, related concerns over use of

[70] As in English law, this is the power to postpone consideration of the juror until the panel of other possible candidates is exhausted. Thus, the juror will only be considered for inclusion of the panel if there are not sufficient other appropriate candidates in the pool, see The Law Reform Commission of Hong Kong (n 64) 12.

[71] Hoffman (n 46) 829.

[72] See *Batson v Kentucky* 476 US 79 (1986) for more detail on challenges potentially motivated by race.

[73] See eg SL Johnson, 'The Language and Culture (Not to Say Race) of Peremptory Challenges' (1993) 35(1) William and Mary Law Review 21; B O'Brien and CM Grosso, 'Jury Selection in the Post-Batson Era' in C Najdowski and M Stevenson (eds), *Criminal Juries in the 21st Century: Psychological Science and the Law* (OUP 2018).

[74] Order Amending Rules 18.4 and 18.5 of the Rules of Criminal Procedure, and r 47(3) of the Rules of Civil Procedure <www.abajournal.com/files/8.30.21_Arizona_Supreme_Court_order_.pdf> accessed 12 June 2023.

peremptory challenges to exclude Indigenous jurors contributed to the abolition of peremptory challenges in 2019.[75] The new jury system in Neuquén, Argentina, has adopted a different approach to ensuring impartiality of the jury, alongside provision for peremptory challenge. The Neuquén jury must include an equal number of men and women and must also reflect the social and cultural background of the defendant.[76]

Procedures governing jury selection are important. They influence the composition of the jury, and the composition of the jury influences its function. While differing approaches utilized in different jurisdictions may to some extent reflect underlying priorities (eg the degree of protection afforded to a defendant), to a large extent differences reflect varying perceptions as to the best way to empanel a jury that will function in an impartial way. However, assessing the extent to which different procedures achieve this aim is again made challenging by the lack of precise definition. For example, some might consider juries to be impartial if they do not hold explicitly biased attitudes, some might consider juries to be impartial if they do not hold explicitly or implicitly biased attitudes, and some might consider juries to be impartial only if they are equally capable of assessing probative value accurately across defendants with various different characteristics. What specifically is required from a normative perspective is important to understand in assessing and improving procedures surrounding jury selection, particularly since (as detailed in the next paragraph) promoting impartiality in some ways may reduce impartiality in others.[77]

As in the case of jury size and unanimity requirements, approaches to jury selection seem frequently to be driven by weak evidence and common-sense-type reasoning rather than by precise design. For example, in some ways procedure has been responsive to high-profile cases and events (eg the Cyprus Secrets case in England and Wales). This type of learning from experience is unlikely to facilitate maximally effective design since what is experienced can depend on chance or surrounding context rather than inherent limitations of procedures themselves, and alternative options are not thoroughly tested and compared. Other approaches are based on common-sense assumptions that may turn out to be unverified in practice. For example, consider the role of peremptory challenges. Many jurisdictions presume, based on common-sense reasoning, that these challenges minimize bias in juries (at least where legal representatives work effectively and are unbiased). However, empirical work challenges this assumption. Removing extreme views (as would be expected to occur through peremptory challenge) may increase impartiality in one way by removing the influence of extreme biases not held by the

[75] See An Act to amend the Criminal Code, the Youth Criminal Justice Act and other Acts and to make consequential amendments to other Acts (SC 2019 c 25) (21 June 2019).

[76] Hans (n 1) 477.

[77] Flanagan (n 67).

community at large. However, it may also decrease impartiality in another way by resulting in the selected jury being likely to include more members with similar characteristics, including similar biases, and the jury thus being more likely to be influenced by those particular biases.[78]

How much decision-making freedom should juries have?

Systems utilizing juries typically distinguish between questions of fact and questions of law and give the jury the power to make determinations of questions of fact. However, the decision-making freedom of juries varies by jurisdiction, largely as a result of balancing the prioritization of freedom and discretion that allow jurors to reflect community values and act as a check on the power of those in authority, and the importance of ensuring informed decision-making and the absence of influence of mistakes, misconceptions, and biases.

At one extreme, in the USA, jury decision-making freedom is considered to be of paramount importance in both federal and state courts. The system puts a significant amount of faith in jurors rather than judges, partly because of the significance of the role of the jury in protecting the community from authority.[79] This importance may be a result of the jury's roots in the US context. As noted above, in the early USA, utilizing juries created a sense of fairness among early colonials, who could be tried by their peers rather than by imported English judges.[80] General verdicts (where juries simply find the defendant guilty or not guilty) as opposed to special verdicts (where juries respond to questions relating to each element of a charged crime) are favoured as a way of preserving the decision-making freedom of the jury.[81] Relatedly, juries are not required to give any reasons for their verdicts, and retain an implicit power to return a not guilty verdict even when they believe the defendant is legally guilty (discussed in the previous chapter, and known in the USA as jury nullification).[82]

In this context, judges are restricted in their ability to influence or guide the jury. Judges are sometimes permitted to give guidance to jurors in the form of instructions, for example to caution jurors about potential inaccuracies in eyewitness evidence.[83] However, they cannot guide jury deliberations—most states prohibit

[78] ibid.

[79] NS Marder and VP Hans, 'Introduction to Juries and Lay Participation: American Perspectives and Global Trends' (2015) 90(3) Chicago-Kent Law Review 789, 798–99.

[80] Hans (n 1) 481.

[81] See eg *United States v Spock* (1st Cir 1969) (quoting George Clementson): 'It is one of the most essential features of the right of trial by jury that no jury should be compelled to find any but a general verdict in criminal cases, and the removal of this safeguard would violate its design and destroy its spirit.'

[82] See eg AW Scheflin and JM Van Dyke, 'Merciful Juries: The Resilience of Jury Nullification' (1991) 48 Washington & Lee Law Review 165.

[83] See eg *United States v Talfaire* 469 R 2d 552 (DC Cir 1972); *State v Henderson* 208 NJ 208 (2011).

judges from commenting or expressing opinions on any evidence in a case.[84] At most, judges might provide jurors with vague guidance such as to listen to each other's arguments and to be respectful of one another.[85]

Relatedly, interventions such as 'decision trees' or 'question trails' designed to guide jurors through their decision-making process in a logical way are not utilized in the USA as these are thought to constrain the structure of jury deliberations and, as a result, limit the freedom of the jury.[86] Systems in the USA are therefore largely reliant on procedures surrounding jury selection (eg the *voir dire* process and peremptory challenges) and deliberation (eg requirements that jurors must deliberate as a group and reach unanimous verdicts) rather than any intervention in, or scrutiny of, jury decisions to ensure the integrity of those decisions.[87]

Many other jurisdictions choose to guide jurors more in their decision-making, while still primarily utilizing general rather than special verdicts. For example, in England and Wales, in addition to giving guidance to jurors in the form of instructions,[88] judges have a role in summarizing the evidence for jurors. Judges are responsible for providing jurors with a correct and concise summary of: (1) the evidence presented by both parties, (2) the arguments presented by both parties, and (3) the inferences which the jurors are entitled to draw from their conclusions about primary facts.[89] As part of this process the judge has the power to comment on the weight of the evidence, which can be used to counterbalance persuasive but weak arguments of advocates.[90] This power has the potential to influence decisions of juries, particularly given the relative experience of the judge, and has in the past been referred to as an informal power of control over the jury.[91] Similarly, throughout Australia and in Canada and New Zealand, judges are generally required to sum up evidence for the jury and are entitled to give their opinions on the weight of evidence in the case provided that it is done with moderation and making clear that the jury can disregard the opinions should they wish to.[92] These jurisdictions (including England and Wales) have also embraced tools such as 'decision trees', 'question trails', and 'routes to verdict' to guide juror decisions and to help ensure that these decisions are made in a logical manner.[93] However, they

[84] Y Ma, 'Lay Participation in Criminal Trials: A Comparative Perspective' (1998) 8 International Criminal Justice Review 74, 80. However, some state judges do guide fact-finding by commenting on evidence.

[85] Marder and Hans (n 79) 797.

[86] ibid 796–98.

[87] ibid 796.

[88] See eg *R v Turnbull* [1977] QB 224.

[89] *R v Lawrence* [1981] 2 WLR 524.

[90] Ma (n 84) 81.

[91] P Devlin, *Trial by Jury* (Stevens & Sons Ltd 1956) 111, 116.

[92] P Marcus, 'Judges Talking to Jurors in Criminal Cases: Why US Judges Do it so Differently from Just About Everyone Else' (2013) 30(1) Arizona Journal of International & Comparative Law 1, 5–9.

[93] Marder and Hans (n 79) 796–97; D Ormerod and C Thomas, 'Routes to Verdict—What We Know and What We Need to Know' (2021) 8 Criminal Law Review 615.

generally maintain the right of jurors to disregard guidance they are provided with (particularly in acquitting a defendant) and do not ask jurors to give reasons for their verdicts. As a result, jurors are still free to acquit a defendant against the evidence, should they wish to, as in the USA.

Some other jurisdictions, particularly those in civil law traditions, have taken different steps to guide juries and ensure that their decisions are made in a logical way. The clearest example of this is in Spain. Spain removed their requirement that judges summarize evidence from a case on the basis that it was inappropriate for a neutral judge to be giving an opinion without the defence being able to respond.[94] However, jury decisions are more directly monitored. In Spain, juries give special verdicts, providing answers to a series of propositions presented to them by the judge. Juries must also provide reasons for each of their answers.[95] Contradictions in reasoning can be viewed as defects in a verdict that need to be corrected, and although juries are asked whether the defendant committed a criminal act, they do not make the final determination of legal guilt.[96] This approach has been described as 'anti-nullification' but does not prevent jurors from acquitting a defendant against the evidence in all circumstances, for example where jury findings on the subject of *mens rea* necessitate a verdict of not guilty.[97]

The Spanish approach has been criticized as compromising the independence and impartiality of the jury; however, it has the advantage of identifying possible mistakes and misconceptions in jury reasoning, enhancing the extent to which the process the jury follow is likely to be logical, and allowing litigants to understand verdicts. In fact, case law of the European Court of Human Rights has established that a failure by the jury to give reasons can undermine the defendant's right to a fair trial under the European Convention on Human Rights where the defendant is not able to understand a jury's basis for a verdict.[98]

When considering the freedom afforded to juries, generally decisions seem to turn on striking a desired balance between allowing jurors to perform their role of representing community values without constraint and ensuring that jurors do not make mistakes when evaluating evidence and reaching verdicts. The different approaches to procedure in this area clearly reflect differing prioritization of discretion and oversight influenced by culture and context. However, more precise articulation of goals may be helpful in facilitating the design of more effective procedures. For example, clearer differentiation between situations in which discretion is appropriate and situations in which there is a clear interpretation that is correct and should not be deviated from may facilitate procedure to maximize

[94] Thaman, 'Spain Returns to Trial by Jury' (n 16) 356.

[95] Jimeno-Bulnes, 'Jury Selection and Jury Trial in Spain' (n 61) 585–96.

[96] SC Thaman, 'Europe's New Jury Systems: The Cases of Spain and Russia' (1999) 62(2) Law and Contemporary Problems 233, 251.

[97] ibid 251–52.

[98] *Taxquet v Belgium* App no 926/05 (ECtHR, 13 January 2009).

appropriate discretion while also correcting mistakes and misconceptions. It is also important to note that while differences in underlying presumptions do not necessarily underlie different approaches in this area, there remains a significant degree of reliance on potentially unjustified assumptions in the design of procedures. For example, some systems seem to base procedure on the presumption that 'decision trees', 'question trails', and 'routes to verdict' can reduce the impact of mistakes and misconceptions without influencing decision-making in negative ways.

Conclusions

When jurisdictions choose to regulate juries in different ways, this may be due to different priorities meaning that they want juries to function differently and / or different context meaning regulation will have a different effect. However, this examination of different procedures and the presumptions underlying those procedures suggests that even when jurisdictions are relatively aligned in their priorities and lack obvious explanatory differences in context, different presumptions can result in the adoption of different legislation. This analysis reinforces the point that regulation surrounding the jury is often based on opinion (which can vary by jurisdiction) rather than scientific reality (which does not vary by jurisdiction, although note that reality may lead to different outcomes in different jurisdictions where context differs in relevant ways). For example, all jurisdictions want an impartial jury, but jurisdictions differ in terms of whether they presume that an impartial jury is best achieved by random selection or through legal processes that allow more control over jury composition.

This chapter has identified two key deficiencies underlying current regimes which explain differences in approach that do not appear to be justified from a scientific perspective. First, there is a lack of precise articulation of how we want juries to operate, which hampers the ability of policymakers to draw on evidence to design policy facilitating that operation. This lack of precision likely stems from the fact that law and legal procedure have traditionally been designed and justified normatively rather than empirically. This reality leaves space for differing interpretation and for procedures to be justified on the basis of normative argument rather than robust evidence. However, in modern society, as demands grow for the jury to evolve into a more sophisticated instrument, empirical as well as normative justification is crucial. It is therefore important to define precise benchmarks against which jury function can be assessed—we need to know exactly how the jury *should* be functioning. In the next chapter, I will attempt to develop some precise benchmarks relating to the function of the modern jury, which are intended to be general enough to apply across multiple jurisdictions.

The second deficiency identified in this chapter is the lack of strong empirical evidence underlying current procedure. Robust empirical examination of the jury is needed in order to inform regulation. Juries are complex decision-making bodies, and the way in which they work can be examined scientifically. In the same way as we know that applying oil to the engine of a car minimizes friction in the engine and reduces breakdowns, we can know how changes to procedure are likely to influence the jury. Current research provides some insight into how interventions might influence jury function, for example how *voir dire* influences the make-up of juries. However, in some areas (eg research relating to jury size) conflicting evidence means that essentially any position might be justified based on evidence. Relatedly, the range of influences on juries means that some findings may be confined to their own facts. These considerations underscore the importance of a robust evidence base relating to juries, underpinned by a theoretical model that can tie together existing literature to highlight not only what is likely to influence juries, but also when, why, and how that influence is likely to occur. The second part of this book will be devoted to developing such a model.

3
The Role of the Modern Jury

Introduction

In the previous chapters, I suggested that the jury needs to be strategically regulated to ensure that it functions in a way that furthers the goals of the criminal justice system. The first step in designing a jury system that furthers goals is to identify what those goals are. In this chapter, I move on to look more closely at what society demands of the jury today, with the intention of being broad enough to cover jury systems generally, primarily in the common law context. I suggest that while the focus of jury critique and reform during the eighteenth and early nineteenth centuries was ensuring fair procedure for the defendant (a result of historical development that had created a one-sided trial favouring the prosecution before that time; see Chapter 1), the last two centuries have seen increasing demand for the development of a more sophisticated jury with the ability to respond to evidence and integrate community judgment in ways that are rational from a scientific perspective and avoid the influence of misconceptions and biases. I discuss how this demand requires us to rethink how we conceptualize and assess jury decision-making.

I suggest that in this context it is helpful to more clearly delineate the role of the jury as a 'scientific' fact-finder, and the role of the jury as a democratic community decision-maker. In the fact-finding role the jury determines descriptive facts (non-normative, contingent facts),[1] primarily whether a defendant engaged in a particular act (or less often an omission) with a particular mindset. Descriptive facts relate to objective external reality—there is a right or wrong answer independent of jury opinion, although it is not always clear what that answer is. There is therefore a relatively clear 'target' for the jury to aim at. However, limitations of evidence and normative principles in the criminal justice system mean that even in the fact-finding role the jury should not be assessed against their ability to consistently hit this target. Instead, the jury should arrive at a level of confidence relating to relevant descriptive facts that is appropriately influenced by evidence, constrained by normative principles. Secondly, the jury has a democratic role in interpreting the law and in integrating community judgment—given what members of the jury believe happened and their confidence in that belief, should the defendant be found

[1] See M Greenberg, 'On Practices and the Law' (2006) 12(2) Legal Theory 113, 114.

How Juries Work. Rebecca K. Helm, Oxford University Press. © Rebecca K. Helm 2024.
DOI: 10.1093/9780191948107.003.0003

to have broken the law? Answering this question can involve interpreting legal standards, making normative judgments, and/or applying community conscience relating to the law. Here, although the target that the jury should be aiming for is different, the jury still has a target to aim for. They should make decisions that represent values of the community, constrained by normative principles and factual accuracy. I conclude by highlighting the difficulty in designing an instrument to achieve these distinct goals, and by noting the need for strong evidence-based procedure surrounding jury trial to ensure that the jury is well positioned to function optimally.

Section I: Modern Criticism of the Jury

A good place to start in considering how the jury might be failing to meet the needs of today's society is to examine criticisms of jury performance. Criticisms of the jury often focus on the failure of juries to 'get it right', meaning the failure to convict guilty people (and, less often, the conviction of factually innocent people).[2] In 1928, just over a decade before the abolition of all-citizen juries in France, François Lombard, a prominent liberal jurist, described the French jury as having been 'beaten and battered' by 'those who want to replace a justice of "impression" with a truly rational and scientific one'.[3] These criticisms were partly anchored in citizen unease about a high number of acquittals (particularly for certain classes of defendant).[4] While juries in other jurisdictions have survived, many have continued to be plagued by accusations of inaccuracy in factual judgments.[5] Much of this sentiment was captured by American historian Carl Becker when he stated:

> Trial by jury, as a method of determining facts, is antiquated and inherently absurd—so much so that no lawyer, judge, scholar, prescription-clerk, cook, or mechanic in a garage would ever think for a moment of employing that method for determining the facts in any situation that concerned him . . . certainly in this age, when fact-finding has become very nearly an exact science, some better method could be devised for determining the guilt or innocence of a person accused of a crime.[6]

[2] See eg Z Bankowski, 'The Jury and Reality' in M Findlay and P Duff (eds), *The Jury Under Attack* (Butterworths 1988).
[3] F Lombard, *Les jurés. Justice représentative et représentation de la justice* (L'Harmattan 2000) 272.
[4] ibid.
[5] See M Findlay and P Duff (eds), *The Jury Under Attack* (Butterworths 1988).
[6] C Becker, *Freedom and Responsibility in the American Way of Life* (Vintage Books 1945) 81–82.

Two more specific criticisms can substantiate these types of accusation by highlighting clear deficiencies in juror decision-making—one based on deficits in juror understanding and one based on juror bias.

Deficits in understanding

Many concerns are rooted in the status of juries as non-experts, who are susceptible to misunderstanding and failure to weigh evidence appropriately—Glanville Williams once asserted that 'it is an understatement to describe a jury . . . as a group of twelve men of average ignorance'.[7] Concerns over the understanding of the jury are not entirely unfounded. Empirical research shows that juries can have difficulties understanding both legal standards and case evidence. Demonstrated errors include misunderstanding of legal concepts and standards,[8] mistakes in the interpretation of complex evidence,[9] and a likely influence of inaccurate beliefs based on common sense (rather than scientific) reasoning.[10] These difficulties are unsurprising given that jurors, as complete novices, are making judgments about complex aspects of law, science, statistics, and human behaviour. The potential for confusion and mistakes in jury decision-making was illustrated by Professors Valerie Hans and Neil Vidmar in their description of the case of Normal Perl, a lawyer who stood trial in the 1980s on charges of fraud and conspiracy. When jurors were interviewed after the case it became clear that matters that should not have been discussed had been discussed and jurors' analysis of the relevant charges was contrary to the law and to judicial instructions. One juror is reported to have said: 'You can't really disregard what the judge tells you to when the trial lasts so long, because you can't remember what thing you were supposed to forget'.[11] Some

[7] G Williams, *The Proof of Guilt: Study of the English Criminal Trial* (Stevens & Sons Ltd 1963) 271–72.

[8] See DU Strawn and RW Buchanan, 'Jury Confusion: A Threat to Justice' (1976) 59(10) Judicature 478; F Strier, 'The Educated Jury: A Proposal for Complex Litigation' (1997) 47(1) DePaul Law Review 49, 52–54; B Saxton, 'How Well Do Jurors Understand Jury Instructions—A Field Test Using Real Juries and Real Trials in Wyoming' (1998) 33 Land & Water Law Review 59; J Koehler, 'Train our Jurors' in G Gigerenzer and C Engel (eds), *Heuristics and the Law* (MIT Press 2006) 11. See also C Davies, 'Vicky Pryce Faces Retrial After Jury "fails to grasp basics"' *The Guardian* (20 February 2013) <www.theguardian.com/uk/2013/feb/20/vicky-pryce-retrial-jury> accessed 6 June 2013 for a case in which a retrial was ordered after the jury failed to grasp the basics of the task assigned to them.

[9] J Koehler, 'The Psychology of Numbers in the Courtroom: How to Make DNA-Match Statistics Seem Impressive or Insufficient' (2001) 74 Southern California Law Review 1275, 1277.

[10] SM Kassin and others, 'On the "General Acceptance" of Eyewitness Testimony Research: A New Survey of the Experts' (2001) 56(5) American Psychologist 405; TR Benton and others, 'Eyewitness Memory is Still Not Common Sense: Comparing Jurors, Judges and Law Enforcement to Eyewitness Experts' (2006) 20(1) Applied Cognitive Psychology: The Official Journal of the Society for Applied Research in Memory and Cognition 115; RK Helm, 'Evaluating Witness Testimony: Juror Knowledge, False Memory, and the Utility of Evidence-Based Directions' (2021) 25(4) The International Journal of Evidence & Proof 264; BH Bornstein and E Greene, *The Jury Under Fire* (OUP 2017) chs 5 and 6.

[11] VP Hans and N Vidmar, 'Jury Competence: Twelve People of Average Ignorance' in VP Hans and N Vidmar, *Judging the Jury* (Springer 1986) 113–29.

evidence also suggests that juror problems with understanding are compounded by a lack of attention being paid to the trial process—for example reports describe jurors falling asleep during trial.[12]

Criminal justice systems have attempted to resolve problems with comprehension and understanding in some areas by allowing expert testimony to be given in court, providing jurors with the necessary knowledge to understand evidence. However, because of their lack of background knowledge jurors may struggle to use expert evidence appropriately—they may be unable to properly critique expert evidence,[13] or to appropriately weigh competing expert evidence in adversarial systems.[14] This lack of expertise and resulting lack of comprehension are likely to cause particular problems in cases involving complex evidence. One reporter recently described being on a jury in a fraud case in which 'much of the evidence was a total mystery'.[15] These types of criticism have led to suggestions that juries should not be hearing cases involving particularly complex evidence at all, specifically in the context of fraud.[16]

Knowledge, beliefs, and bias

Another root of the criticisms of the jury is bias that has been described as apparent in jury decisions.[17] The predominant existing model of jury decision-making, the

[12] See eg I Hayes, 'Trial Discharged After Juror Fell Asleep 15 Minutes Into Case' *The Irish Times* (13 February 2017) <www.irishtimes.com/news/crime-and-law/courts/criminal-court/trial-discharged-after-juror-fell-asleep-15-minutes-into-case-1.2973978> accessed 6 June 2023; S Day, 'Jury Discharged in Izabela Dauti's Manslaughter Trial After Juror Fell Asleep' *Andover Advertiser* (15 May 2018) <www.andoveradvertiser.co.uk/news/16226687.jury-discharged-izabela-dautis-manslaughter-trial-juror-fell-asleep/> accessed 6 June 2023; J Evans, 'Juror Kicked Off Sex Case After Falling Asleep While Considering Verdict' (*WalesOnline*, 23 October 2019) <www.walesonline.co.uk/news/wales-news/juror-fell-asleep-sex-case-17130300> accessed 6 June 2023; Y Khorram, 'Third Juror Dismissed in Elizabeth Holmes Trial After Found Playing Sudoku' *CNBC* (22 October 2021) <www.cnbc.com/2021/10/22/third-juror-dismissed-in-trial-of-theranos-founder-elizabeth-holmes-.html> accessed 6 June 2023; P Hirwani, 'Johnny Depp v Amber Heard Jurors "Fell Asleep" During Testimony, Stenographer Says' *The Independent* (7 June 2022) <www.independent.co.uk/news/world/americas/johnny-depp-jurors-asleep-testimony-amber-heard-b2095391.html> accessed 6 June 2023.

[13] See eg *R v Sally Clark* [2003] EWCA Crim 1020; RK Helm, VP Hans, and VF Reyna, 'Trial by Numbers' (2017) 27(1) Cornell Journal of Law and Public Policy 107, 116–18; Bornstein and Greene (n 10) ch 7.

[14] Strier, 'The Educated Jury' (n 8) 54.

[15] S Jenkins, 'Our Jury System is in Crisis, So Why Not Abolish Jury Trials' *The Guardian* (22 January 2021) <www.theguardian.com/commentisfree/2021/jan/22/justice-system-crisis-abolish-jury-trials-covid> accessed 6 June 2023.

[16] The Fraud Trials Committee Report (The Roskill Report) (1986) suggested that the jury be replaced by a panel of two experts and two lay judges in complex fraud trials. See N Monaghan, 'Who Should Try "Complex Fraud Trials"? Reconsidering the Composition of the Tribunal of Fact 30 Years after Roskill' in C Monaghan and N Monaghan (eds), *Financial Crime and Corporate Misconduct: A Critical Evaluation of Fraud Legislation* (Routledge 2020).

[17] See eg LJ Curley, I Dror, and J Munro, 'Juries are Subject to All Kinds of Biases When it Comes to Deciding on a Trial' (*The Conversation*, 28 February 2022) <https://theconversation.com/juries-are-subject-to-all-kinds-of-biases-when-it-comes-to-deciding-on-a-trial-176721> accessed 7 June 2023.

Story Model, posits that jurors make decisions by constructing potential narratives from case evidence and matching the best-fitting narrative to a legal verdict.[18] Jurors are thought to draw on their own knowledge and beliefs in this process, for example in deciding how to weigh case evidence and in assessing the likelihood of competing narratives representing the truth. In some ways, this influence of existing knowledge and beliefs is an inherent part of the jury process and has historically been viewed as one of the benefits of the criminal law jury. It certainly was when jurors were drawn from the communities in which crimes occurred and were largely self-informing (see Chapter 1). However, there is clear potential for the utilization of personal knowledge and beliefs to result in undesirable biases having an influence in the jury trial process.

First, jurors may have explicit bias against groups of victims or defendants that will result in biased judgments against those groups, and systematic inequalities in trial outcomes. For example, if jurors hold racist beliefs, these can be reflected in their decisions.[19] This possibility was considered by the European Court of Human Rights (ECtHR) in the case of *Sander v United Kingdom*.[20] In that case, the applicant was a British national of Asian origin who had been convicted of fraud. During his trial, a juror had sent a note to the trial judge expressing concerns that other members of the jury had made racist remarks and jokes and therefore did not appear impartial. That juror felt concern that the rest of the jury would convict the defendant not on the evidence but on the basis of being Asian. The ECtHR ruled that the actions of the judge, specifically in failing to discharge the jury following these accusations, breached the right of the defendant to a fair trial.[21] The Supreme Court in the United States of America (USA) has also grappled with the risk of racial bias in juries. In the case of *Pena-Rodriguez v Colorado*, the applicant, who was Hispanic, had been convicted of unlawful sexual conduct.[22] After the trial, two jurors informed the applicant's lawyer that one of the other jurors made racially biased statements about the applicant and his alibi witness, essentially suggesting they lacked credibility because they were Hispanic. The Supreme Court held that where a juror makes it clear that racial animus is a significant motivating factor in their decision to convict, the trial court can consider whether the juror's statement has compromised the defendant's rights (although note that not every comment

[18] N Pennington and R Hastie, 'Explaining the Evidence: Tests of the Story Model for Juror Decision Making' (1992) 62(2) Journal of Personality and Social Psychology 189.

[19] For a fuller discussion of the role of race in jury decision-making, see G Daly and R Pattenden, 'Racial Bias and the English Criminal Trial Jury' (2005) 64(3) The Cambridge Law Journal 678; MK Thompson, 'Bias on Trial: Toward an Open Discussion of Racial Stereotypes in the Courtroom' (2018) 5 Michigan State Law Review 1243.

[20] *Sander v United Kingdom* App no 34129/96 (2001) 31 EHRR 44.

[21] For press commentary on the case, see C Dyer, 'Juror's Racist Jokes Denied Asian Defendant a Fair Trial' *The Guardian* (10 May 2000) <www.theguardian.com/uk/2000/may/10/race.world> accessed 7 June 2023.

[22] *Pena-Rodriguez v Colorado* 580 US (2017) <www.oyez.org/cases/2016/15-606> accessed 7 June 2023.

indicating racial bias will meet this criterion). Jury racial bias may also be more subtle than it was in these cases, influencing juror judgment without explicitly being mentioned and even outside the conscious awareness of jurors themselves, for example as a result of implicit bias or stereotyping. There is evidence of this influence both in mock jury work[23] and in systematic evaluation of the outcomes in real cases.[24]

Another clear allegation of bias that has been levelled against the jury is that decisions can be influenced by problematic beliefs, including those informed by gender norms and stereotypes. This accusation is seen most clearly in cases involving rape and other forms of sexual assault where research suggests a risk that prejudicial, stereotyped, and false beliefs about sexual offences (known as rape myths) are negatively influencing judgments.[25] These beliefs include, among other things, associating delays in reporting,[26] a lack of physical resistance during an assault,[27] and intoxication of a complainant[28] with low complainant credibility. Importantly, this influence is thought to persist even when relevant myths are explicitly debunked.[29] Although some recent work, specifically in the context of England and Wales, has raised questions about whether a sufficient number of jurors endorse rape myths for that endorsement to be a problem,[30] the weight of evidence continues to demonstrate at least a risk that rape myths are influencing juries.[31] On that basis, legal directions seeking to minimize the influence of myths

[23] For reviews, see TL Mitchell and others, 'Racial Bias in Mock Juror Decision-Making: A Meta-Analytic Review of Defendant Treatment' (2005) 29(6) Law and Human Behavior 621; JS Hunt, 'Race, Ethnicity, and Culture in Jury Decision Making' (2015) 11(1) Annual Review of Law and Social Science 269.

[24] S Demuth and D Steffensmeier, 'Ethnicity Effects on Sentence Outcomes in Large Urban Courts: Comparisons Among White, Black, and Hispanic Defendants' (2004) 85(4) Social Science Quarterly 994; C Thomas, *Are Juries Fair?* (Ministry of Justice Research Series 1/10, February 2010) (this study analysed decisions in Crown Court trials and found small differences in verdict based on defendant ethnicity—a 63 per cent conviction rate for white and Asian defendants, and a 67 per cent conviction rate for Black defendants, though note case type and evidence strength could not be controlled for and could have explained or masked differences).

[25] F Leverick, 'What Do We Know About Rape Myths and Juror Decision Making?' (2020) 24(3) The International Journal of Evidence & Proof 255. Although see J Chalmers, F Leverick, and V Munro, 'Why The Jury is, and Should Still Be, Out on Rape Deliberation' (2021) 9 Criminal Law Review 753; C Thomas, 'The 21st Century Jury: Contempt, Bias, and the Impact of Jury Service' (2020) 11 Criminal Law Review 987.

[26] D Brereton, 'How Different are Rape Trials? A Comparison of the Cross-Examination of Complainants in Rape and Assault Trials' (1997) 37(2) The British Journal of Criminology 242.

[27] T Temkin and B Krahé, *Sexual Assault and The Justice Gap: A Question of Attitude* (Bloomsbury Publishing 2008).

[28] A-M Wall and RA Schuller, 'Sexual Assault and Defendant/Victim Intoxication: Jurors' Perceptions of Guilt 1' (2000) 30(2) Journal of Applied Social Psychology 253.

[29] KR Klement, BJ Sagarin, and JJ Skowronski, 'Accusers Lie and Other Myths: Rape Myth Acceptance Predicts Judgments Made About Accusers and Accused Perpetrators in a Rape Case' (2019) 81(1–2) Sex Roles: A Journal of Research 16.

[30] Thomas, 'The 21st Century Jury' (n 25).

[31] E Daly and others, 'Myths about Myths? A Commentary on Thomas (2020) and the Question of Jury Rape Myth Acceptance' (2022) 7(1) Journal of Gender Based Violence 1; Chalmers, Leverick, and Munro (n 25).

are now utilized in a range of jurisdictions.[32] The potentially harmful impact of these beliefs on jury decisions has also been reported in the press and has led to calls for the replacement of the jury in rape trials.[33] In fact, partially on this basis, a 2021 review in Scotland suggested that trial by judge alone should be considered in sexual offence cases.[34] Similar problematic beliefs in other areas of law, for example relating to domestic violence, are likely to be important, but have received less consideration.[35]

More generally, other pre-existing viewpoints that jurors may have—resulting from pretrial publicity,[36] political opinions,[37] perceived prevalence of alleged events,[38] perceived 'appropriate' emotions for victims and defendants,[39] and moral judgments relating to trial participants[40]—are likely to feed into jury verdicts, at least in cases where there is no clear answer based on conclusive evidence, for example DNA or closed-circuit television (CCTV). The clear evidence of bias and prejudice in society feeding into legal determinations by juries has led to criticism of the jury and, as noted above, even suggestions that getting rid of juries may be the best way to ensure justice.[41]

[32] See eg *R v Miller* [2010] EWCA Crim 1578; Crown Court Compendium (June 2023) Part 1: Jury and Trial Management and Summing Up, Section 20 'Sexual Offences' <https://www.judiciary.uk/wp-content/uploads/2023/06/Crown-Court-Compendium-Part-I-June-2023-updated-Feb-2024.pdf>accessed 3 May 2024; J Quilter, L McNamara, and M Porter, 'New Jury Directions For Sexual Offence Trials in New South Wales: The Importance of Timing' (2022) 46(3) Criminal Law Journal 138.

[33] See eg J Bindel, 'Juries Have No Place in Rape Trials. They Simply Can't Be Trusted' *The Guardian* (21 November 2018) <www.theguardian.com/commentisfree/2018/nov/21/juries-rape-trials-myths-justice> accessed 5 June 2023.

[34] Scottish Courts and Tribunals Service, 'Improving the Management of Sexual Offence Cases. Final Report from the Lord Justice Clerk's Review Group' (2021) <www.scotcourts.gov.uk/docs/default-source/default-document-library/reports-and-data/Improving-the-management-of-Sexual-Offence-Cases.pdf?sfvrsn=6> accessed 7 June 2023. For a similar discussion in England and Wales, see Law Commission, *Evidence in Sexual Offences Prosecutions: A Consultation Paper* (Law Com No 259, 2023) 600–17.

[35] J Peters, 'Measuring Myths about Domestic Violence: Development and Initial Validation of the Domestic Violence Myth Acceptance Scale' (2008) 16(1) Journal of Aggression, Maltreatment & Trauma 1; N Yamawaki and others, 'Perceptions of Domestic Violence: The Effects of Domestic Violence Myths, Victim's Relationship With Her Abuser, and the Decision to Return to Her Abuser' (2012) 27(16) Journal of Interpersonal Violence 3195; C Policastro and BK Payne, 'The Blameworthy Victim: Domestic Violence Myths and the Criminalization of Victimhood' (2013) 22(4) Journal of Aggression, Maltreatment & Trauma 329.

[36] LexisNexis, 'A Non-Biased Jury: Do They Really Exist?' <www.lexisnexis.co.uk/research-and-reports/bar/a-non-biased-jury-do-they-really-exist.html> accessed 7 June 2023.

[37] DM Kahan and D Braman, 'The Self-Defensive Cognition of Self-Defense' (2008) 45 American Criminal Law Review 1.

[38] RK Helm and B Growns, 'Prevalence Estimates as Priors: Juror Characteristics, Perceived Base Rates, and Verdicts in Cases Reliant on Complainant and Defendant Testimony' (2022) 36(4) Applied Cognitive Psychology 891.

[39] See eg MR Rose, J Nadler, and J Clark, 'Appropriately Upset? Emotion Norms and Perceptions of Crime Victims' (2006) 30 Law and Human Behavior 203.

[40] AM Sood, 'Motivated Cognition in Legal Judgments—An Analytic Review' (2013) 9 Annual Review of Law and Social Science 307.

[41] Scottish Courts and Tribunals Service (n 34). See also Law Commission of New Zealand, *The Justice Response to Victims of Sexual Violence, Criminal Trials and Alternative Processes* (2015) <www.lawcom.govt.nz/sites/default/files/projectAvailableFormats/NZLC-R136-The-Justice-Response-to-Victims-of-Sexual-Violence.pdf> accessed 7 June 2023.

Implications of criticisms

There is clear evidence that juror misunderstandings (relating to both law and evidence) and bias could be feeding into legal judgments, substantiating criticisms that juries are failing to consistently 'get it right'. However, what it means to get it right on a more precise level is not as clear as these criticisms suggest. In order to design a sophisticated instrument with the maximum potential to 'get it right' it is necessary to first define in precise terms what 'getting it right' looks like (rather than just what it does not look like).[42]

We need to isolate precise characteristics that judgments by juries should have rather than just the qualities they should not have. The obvious suggestion here is that judgments as to guilt should be accurate in that people who have committed crimes (sometimes referred to as people who are factually guilty) should be convicted and people who have not committed crimes (sometimes referred to as people who are factually innocent) should be acquitted. However, the various roles of the jury and the complexity of making judgments about events in the past mean that defining the way in which the jury should function is more complicated than that suggestion implies.

Section II: Defining the Goals of the Jury

Difficulties with evaluating jury judgments stem partly from the fact that juries have at least two ideological foundations—as fact-finders and as representatives of the community and community conscience.[43] Separating the role that the jury has in fact-finding (the fact-finding role) from the role that the jury has as a representative of community conscience (the democratic role) is helpful in defining the goals of the jury, due to fundamental differences in function and methods of evaluation in each role.

The fact-finding role

In its fact-finding role, the jury seeks to make determinations relating to descriptive facts (non-normative, contingent facts)—primarily what a defendant did and what their mindset was when they did it—based on evidence presented at trial. In some ways, the goals of the jury in this function may be seen as clear since there is,

[42] See also P Darbyshire, 'The Lamp That Shows That Freedom Lives—Is it Worth the Candle?' [1991] Criminal Law Review 740.

[43] For a discussion of ideological premises underlying trial by jury, see P Duff and M Findlay, 'Jury in England—Practice and Ideology' (1982) 10(3) International Journal of the Sociology of Law 253.

at least to some extent, a clear target for the jury to aim for—external reality (what actually happened). However, suggesting that the jury should be assessed against its ability to determine external reality is an oversimplification. As a preliminary point it is important to note that the jury should make decisions based on evidence. A jury that reaches a high number of verdicts that correspond to external reality but only as a result of chance (eg because of convicting all defendants when few innocent defendants are brought to trial) would be a meaningless legal instrument.[44] How the jury should make decisions based on evidence is considered below.

First, on a basic level, limitations of evidence mean that it is sometimes impossible to determine what happened in the past. Juries will always be limited by the evidence available to prove or disprove a particular allegation, so even the perfect jury may not be able to make accurate determinations relating to what happened in the past. The jury can therefore only realistically seek to respond appropriately to evidence—assigning probative value accurately. Assigning probative value accurately will not necessarily lead to knowing what happened in the past, but rather can inform an appropriate level of confidence as to what happened in the past given the evidence available. Broadly, confidence in conclusions as to whether something happened should correspond to the likelihood of the evidence having been produced if that thing happened as opposed to if it did not happen. A jury should be completely confident in a particular account of what happened where the evidence they are seeing could only have occurred if the account is correct. They should be roughly 50 per cent confident in a particular account of what happened where the evidence they are seeing is equally likely to have occurred if the account is correct as if the account is not correct (although of course they are unlikely to think in precise percentages). So, where evidence is presented that could only have occurred had a particular event occurred (eg reliable and clear CCTV evidence could only show a defendant stabbing a victim if the defendant did in fact stab the victim) the jury can have complete confidence in that event having occurred. But where evidence presented could have occurred in more than one way (eg an eyewitness account stating that a defendant stabbed a victim could have occurred because the eyewitness did see the defendant stab the victim or because the eyewitness was mistaken or lying) the jury must accurately assess the likelihood of the evidence having occurred under differing versions of events (most importantly under the prosecution version of events). If the evidence is equally likely to have been produced if the event occurred as alleged by the prosecution as if it did not, the jury should conclude that they cannot be sure what happened with any degree of certainty. This answer is the 'right' one, regardless of what actually happened. Therefore, the goal of the jury in this regard should be *to arrive at a level of confidence relating to descriptive facts that is appropriately influenced by evidence,*

[44] On the need for the jury to decide cases rationally, see *R v Young* (1995) QB 324.

meaning that probative value is assigned to evidence accurately. This goal will result in maximum correspondence with external reality in the determination of descriptive facts given the limitations of evidence.

Secondly, the suggestion that jury performance can be assessed by its ability to determine external reality artificially detaches the epistemological function of the jury from normative principles relating to how that function is performed. Directly equating judgments of what happened with correct jury judgment neglects the fact that other considerations in addition to external realities are important in the judgment of juries. Legal conclusions made by the jury are the product of their consideration of often complex evidence that has been 'filtered' through the trial and the laws of evidence and procedure.[45] The task of the jury is not the same as the task of the detective, because the jury's task is also complicated by normative principles that dictate how the search for what happened should be conducted in the criminal justice setting (which do not only concern how to reach the outcome that reflects external reality). As Professor Zenon Bankowski stated: 'One cannot see getting the truth as a separate value, rather it must be seen in the context of a procedure where all the different moral, pragmatic, and logical strands are inextricably intertwined and the justification is of the procedure as a whole.'[46] Important principles that should govern the search for truth are engrained in legal systems. As a result, jury judgments should not be assessed against their correspondence with external reality at all costs, but rather should cohere with external reality to the extent possible, given relevant normative principles and their importance (adhering to a coherence theory of truth). Existing research has sought to identify normative principles that should underscore the criminal justice process.[47] In his work on the criminal process, Professor Andrew Ashworth has outlined a general framework of twelve ethical principles and rights that is helpful to consider for this purpose.[48] These principles and rights include: (1) the right to be treated with humanity and without degradation; (2) the right of victims to compensation; (3) the right of innocent persons not to be convicted; (4) the right to be treated fairly and without discrimination; (5) the right to be presumed innocent; (6) the principle of legality (sometimes referred to as the rule of law, requiring the law to state clearly and in advance the body of rules and exceptions relating to the rights and powers that may be taken over individuals during the criminal process); (7) reasonable grounds for arrest and detention; (8) the right to be brought before a court; (9) the right to prepare a proper defence; (10) the right of the victim to respect in the criminal process; (11) the right to trial within a reasonable time; and (12) the principle of equality of arms.

[45] Bankowski (n 2).

[46] ibid 18.

[47] See eg A Ashworth, *The Criminal Process: An Evaluative Study* (OUP 1994); L Zedner and J V Roberts (eds), *Principles and Values in Criminal Law and Criminal Justice: Essays in Honour of Andrew Ashworth* (OUP 2012).

[48] Ashworth (n 47) 57–67.

Two of these principles are likely to be particularly important in constraining the fact-finding function of the jury (note that other principles may also be important—these two are chosen as particularly relevant in this context). First, the presumption of innocence requires the jury to disregard potentially probative information. For example, while the fact that a person is in court and charged with a crime increases the probability that they are guilty of the crime (when compared with other citizens in society), the presumption asks jurors to disregard this information and to give no weight to the fact that the defendant is suspected by the prosecution and has been brought to trial. Secondly, the right to be treated fairly and without discrimination should require the jury to disregard discriminatory generalizations even where those generalizations could be probative on average. For example, consider the recent reports that men who make allegations of coercive control are not believed.[49] Imagine that in reality men *are* less likely to be the victims of coercive control. Victim gender could be probative in ascertaining how likely it was that coercive control had occurred because any given man would be less likely to be a victim than any given woman. The alleged behaviour would be more common and therefore more probable if alleged against a female victim.[50] Despite this, the right to be treated fairly and without discrimination requires the jury to avoid reliance on such generalizations.

Combining the epistemological role of the jury, with its limitations discussed earlier in this section, and relevant normative principles, the goal of the jury in its fact-finding role can be defined as *arriving at a level of confidence relating to descriptive facts that is appropriately influenced by evidence, constrained by relevant normative principles including the presumption of innocence and the right to be treated fairly and without discrimination.* Once the jury has reached a level of confidence relating to descriptive facts in this way, it should move on to determine whether its level of confidence in particular descriptive facts is sufficient for a finding of legal liability. This judgment is made through the democratic role of the jury.

The democratic role

In its democratic role, the jury represents community conscience in the criminal justice process. This function is fulfilled primarily through the exercise of discretion in interpreting the law and applying the law to facts. Today, this exercise of discretion has two clear forms.

[49] J Rees, 'Coercive Control: Male Victims Say They Aren't Believed' *BBC News* (17 August 2021) <www.bbc.co.uk/news/uk-wales-58233300> accessed 18 August 2021.

[50] Helm and Growns (n 38).

First, juries have a role in exercising social judgment in their application of the law—the jury themselves define and interpret many legal terms. Juries are asked to interpret legal concepts such as 'gross negligence' for gross negligence manslaughter, 'grievous' for grievous bodily harm, 'actual' for actual bodily harm, and even 'intention'. For example, considering the meaning of intention in the United Kingdom (UK) House of Lords (now the Supreme Court), Lord Bridge stated that:

> the golden rule should be that, when directing a jury on the mental element necessary in a crime of specific intent, the judge should avoid any elaboration or paraphrase of what is meant by intent, and leave it to the jury's good sense to decide whether the accused acted with the necessary intent.[51]

In some cases the jury is explicitly given 'moral elbow room' in finding intention.[52] While a person shooting a victim and knowing it was virtually certain they would die but with the primary objective of stealing property probably should be found to have an intention to kill, a doctor prescribing birth control to a person aged under sixteen and knowing that it was virtually certain that it would encourage them to have sex probably should not be found to have an intention to encourage underage sex.[53] Even the standard of proof (eg 'beyond reasonable doubt,' or being 'sure') is a principle that inherently requires jury interpretation, rather than being scientific. Juries must exercise their judgment in determining whether a particular level of confidence constitutes sufficient proof to meet the relevant standard and to convict a defendant. These judgments require community interpretation, may be influenced by a complex range of factors, and cannot necessarily be dictated by formal and prescriptive legal rules.

Other legal terms explicitly call for the incorporation of normative judgments into legal judgments. For example, in England and Wales the definition of dishonesty, a *mens rea* requirement for finding liability in many property law offences, provides that a defendant should be found to be dishonest (in the absence of a statutory provision applying) where their conduct was dishonest by the standards of ordinary decent people.[54]

In many cases the community may not have a clear answer as to how relevant terms should be interpreted and applied to a case prior to considering the behaviour as a group through the jury process. To put it another way, a community viewpoint on a specific fact pattern may not exist until the community have deliberated

[51] *R v Moloney* [1985] AC 905, 926.

[52] J Horder, 'Intention in the Criminal Law—A Rejoinder' (1995) 58 Modern Law Review 678, 687.

[53] See eg *Gillick v West Norfolk and Wisbech AHA* [1985] UKHL 7. Although that case was a civil law case, the fact pattern presented is relevant for the criminal law, see J Child and D Ormerod, *Smith, Hogan, and Ormerod's Essentials of Criminal Law* (3rd edn, OUP 2019) 101–02.

[54] *Ivey v Genting Casinos (UK) Ltd t/a Crockfords* [2017] UKSC 67; *R v Barton* [2020] EWCA Crim 575 (confirming the applicability of *Ivey* in the criminal law).

on that fact pattern via jury deliberation—community standards can be thought of as inseparable from the process of creating those standards through community deliberation since people will not have considered specific fact patterns in detail prior to being asked to consider those fact patterns.[55] In this context it is very hard to assess whether an answer the jury has reached is 'right' independently of jury judgment.

Secondly, juries have an implicit power (jury equity or nullification), through which they can return a not guilty verdict even where they believe that a defendant is technically guilty. Through this power, juries can essentially inoculate law that is not in accordance with community values. A good example of this inoculation taking place is in the context of the USA just before the American Civil War, where juries refused to convict abolitionists who had violated fugitive slave laws by helping slaves.[56] There have been several far more recent examples of these powers potentially being exercised in the UK context. Four protestors (known as the 'Colston Four') who pulled down a statue of a former slave owner and threw it into a river were found not guilty of criminal damage,[57] and three Extinction Rebellion activists (the 'Shadwell Three') who climbed on a train or glued themselves to a train platform were found not guilty of obstructing trains or carriages on the railway[58] (although note that neither of these is necessarily a clear-cut example of jury nullification since the defendants in each case did argue that they had a legal defence or even multiple legal defences).

These exercises of discretion and subjectivity in jury judgment help to situate criminal offences within society's morality, which cannot be captured in clear rules and can evolve over time.[59] This grounding of the criminal law in morality is particularly important given the social stigma associated with criminal conviction.[60]

[55] See RK Helm, 'The Challenge of Factual Hard Cases for Self Incrimination Regimes' (forthcoming); L Zaibert, 'Figuring Things Out, Morally Speaking' (2021) 96(4) Philosophy 553, 560–61.

[56] See A McKnight, 'Jury Nullification as a Tool to Balance the Demands of Law and Justice' (2013) 4 Brigham Young University Law Review 1103.

[57] See eg M Boyd, '"Colston 4 Are the Latest of Many Proud Brits Acquitted for Smashing Things Up"' *The Mirror* (6 January 2022) <www.mirror.co.uk/news/uk-news/colston-4-latest-many-proud-25875384> accessed 8 June 2023; D Gayle, 'Colston Four Acquittal Raises Doubts About 10-Year Jail Term Proposal' *The Guardian* (6 January 2022) <www.theguardian.com/law/2022/jan/06/colston-four-acquittal-raises-doubts-about-10-year-jail-term-proposal> accessed 8 June 2023; thesecretbarrister, 'Do the Verdicts in the Trial of the Colston 4 Signal Something Wrong With Our Jury System? 10 Things You Should Know' (*The Secret Barrister*, 6 January 2022) <https://thesecretbarrister.com/2022/01/06/do-the-verdicts-in-the-trial-of-the-colston-4-signal-something-wrong-with-our-jury-system-10-things-you-should-know/> accessed 8 June 2023; B Bloch, 'Petition to Re-Try the "Colston 4" Gains Over 12k Signatures' *Bristol Post* (7 January 2022) <www.bristolpost.co.uk/news/bristol-news/petition-re-try-colston-4-6454957> accessed 8 June 2023.

[58] Z Blackler, 'First XR Jury Trial of 2022 Begins for Shadwell 3' (*Extinction Rebellion*, 11 January 2022) <https://extinctionrebellion.uk/2022/01/11/first-xr-jury-trial-of-2022-begins-for-shadwell-3/> accessed 8 June 2023.

[59] See eg CR Sunstein, 'Discerning Blue from Purple: How Prevalence Affects What is Perceived as Normal' (2023) 44(3) Evolution and Human Behavior 250.

[60] A Choo, *Abuse of Process and Judicial Stays of Criminal Proceedings* (Clarendon Press 1993) 13.

It also makes it impossible to say objectively whether a defendant is guilty or not prior to jury deliberation, at least in more complex cases.

In this context, it is clearly not right to say that the jury can exercise their discretion in any way they like. The question of what it means to 'get it right' is complicated, but there remains a target for juries to aim for. As detailed in Chapter 1, the democratic role of the jury is a role in bringing community conscience into the legal process.[61] Therefore, the decisions reached by the jury should reflect the viewpoint of the community rather than idiosyncrasies of a particular jury or the viewpoints of particularly dominant individuals on the jury.[62] Put simply, the jury should reach the determination that the community as a whole would have reached, had they deliberated on a particular fact pattern. As with the fact-finding role, this goal is constrained by normative principles that are fundamental to the criminal justice process. Important normative principles relevant to the democratic role of the jury (taken from Ashworth's framework, described above) include the right of innocent persons not to be convicted, the right to be treated fairly and without discrimination, and the principle of legality (as above, other principles may also be important—these three are chosen as particularly relevant in this context). The right of innocent persons not to be convicted requires that when the members of the jury compare their confidence in descriptive facts to the standard of proof, they should interpret the standard of proof in a way that does not result in the systematic conviction of innocent people. The right to be treated fairly and without discrimination requires that biasing or discriminatory views (eg racist or sexist views) should not feed in to jury judgments even where they are held by the community as a whole. The principle of legality requires that the factors that are likely to influence the jury in interpreting the law should be reasonably predictable in advance to avoid criminalizing behaviour where it was unclear at the time that such behaviour would be criminal. Importantly, the jury should also be constrained in this role by the need for factual accuracy—where the community hold viewpoints that are based on misconceptions these should be corrected for in exercising judgment. So, for example, where community opinion is based on endorsement of rape myths, this influence should be corrected for so that it is not reflected even in the democratic decision-making process.[63] The goal of the jury in its democratic role can therefore be defined as *making decisions that represent values of the community, constrained by normative principles including the right of*

[61] See eg M Spruill and V Hans, 'Trial by Jury: Psychological Research Contributions to an Enduring Legal Institution' in R Hollander-Blumoff (ed), *Research Handbook in Law and Psychology* (Edward Elgar forthcoming).

[62] This reflection of community viewpoint is also necessary for the rule of law, which requires predictability in the application of law and therefore consistency across fact-finders, see eg J Waldron, 'The Rule of Law' (*Stanford Encyclopedia of Philosophy*, 2016) <https://plato.stanford.edu/Entries/rule-of-law/> accessed 8 June 2023.

[63] See eg T Brooks, 'The Right to Trial by Jury' (2004) 21(2) Journal of Applied Philosophy 197, 202–04.

innocent persons not to be convicted, the right to be treated fairly and without discrimination and the principle of legality, and by factual accuracy.

Conclusions: Measuring Jury Performance

As detailed in Chapter 1, the jury has developed in accordance with tradition and normative legal principles rather than through precise testing to assess whether it delivers desirable outcomes. Much jury procedure currently used evolved at a time when the outcomes the jury was seeking to achieve may have been different from what they are today, and examination of the different evolutions of jury systems in different jurisdictions (conducted in Chapter 2) highlights how systems have developed based on disputable evidence and opinions rather than robust scientific standards and investigation. As commentators have noted, the emergence of the jury trial is more of a historical accident than a conscious decision.[64] This development is, to some extent, at odds with modern demands for a sophisticated jury system. In order to develop such a system, it is necessary to clearly outline the goals of the jury, and to design evidence-based procedure surrounding jury trial to maximize attainment of those goals.

I have suggested that when defining the goals of the jury it is helpful for us to separate two distinct judgments made by the jury—the fact-finding role, an objective role in determining descriptive facts, and the democratic role, a role in determining whether, given what happened (and the level of certainty in that judgment about what happened), the law has been broken. Importantly, these two judgments are judgments of different types, and success in achieving each of them should be measured differently. Success in the first role (the fact-finding role) can be defined as *arriving at a level of confidence relating to descriptive facts that is appropriately influenced by evidence, constrained by relevant normative principles including the presumption of innocence and the right to be treated fairly and without discrimination.* Success in the second role (the democratic role) can be defined as *making decisions that represent values of the community, constrained by normative principles including the right of innocent persons not to be convicted, the right to be treated fairly and without discrimination and the principle of legality, and by factual accuracy.*

It is important to note that achieving these goals represents a challenge. Consider scientific instruments. Such instruments are designed with one goal in mind—the search for truth. The goals of the jury are inherently more complex. The jury must seek to make judgments that cohere with truth (both in terms of descriptive facts relating to what happened in the past and in terms of the viewpoints

[64] ibid.

of the community), but in a way that is constrained by a range of normative principles.[65] Determinations can be complex and value-laden in a way which scientific determinations are not. Importantly, while in some respects the way in which we as humans make decisions is consistent with the goals of the jury, in other respects the way that we make decisions is clearly in conflict with how the jury should function. These realities underscore why the jury is uniquely well placed to make legal decisions, but also the need for a careful and precise infrastructure surrounding the jury to ensure appropriate function. In the remainder of this book, I will draw on psychological theory and empirical work to conduct a scientific examination of how jurors and juries are likely to function as decision-makers, and how evidence-based procedure can enhance their ability to achieve the goals identified above.

[65] For a discussion of combining evidence with normative judgment in another context, see T Greenhalgh and J Russell, 'Evidence-Based Policy Making: A Critique' (2009) 52(2) Perspectives in Biology and Medicine 304.

4

Juror Decision-Making Models: Existing Models and a New Representation-Based Framework

Introduction

Juries are decision-making bodies composed of a group of individual lay decision-makers. To understand how juries function it is necessary to understand the psychology underlying how these decision-makers evaluate evidence, and how these evaluations are combined to reach an overall group verdict. Existing research in behavioural sciences provides insight into both individual and group decision-making generally, and in a legal context (juror and jury decision-making). This insight is an important starting point in understanding how juries work, not only in terms of what influences decisions but also *why and how* certain variables have their influence, which is crucial to truly understanding the jury and assessing the normative desirability of influences on it.

In this chapter, I focus on models of juror decision-making—assessing existing models and developing a new theory-based model. Models of juror decision-making are an important starting point for understanding how juries work, since (as will be discussed in Chapter 8) juror decisions are highly predictive of jury decisions. I begin by providing an overview of existing models of juror decision-making, with a particular focus on two cognitive models—the Story Model and the Director's Cut Model. I outline empirical support for these models, but also highlight key limitations of the models in providing a full explanation of how jurors work that can be useful in critiquing their function against normative goals. I then propose a new theory-based model with the potential to be helpful in developing our understanding of how jurors and juries work and, importantly, the factors that influence them. Specifically, I introduce and outline Fuzzy-Trace Theory (FTT), a psychological theory of memory and decision-making, and combine FTT with Fuzzy Logic (FL), an approach to computing based on degrees of truth rather than a true/false dichotomy, to develop a new model of juror decision-making, focused on attribution of meaning (the Representation-Based Model). I then review the ways in which people develop intuitions and beliefs that feed into attribution of meaning and discuss what that development can tell us about

How Juries Work. Rebecca K. Helm, Oxford University Press. © Rebecca K. Helm 2024.
DOI: 10.1093/9780191948107.003.0004

juror decision-making. I conclude by noting benefits and risks related to the assignment of meaning in the juror decision-making process, and by describing how the Representation-Based Model can provide a framework through which much existing work on juror decision-making can be better understood, and influences on jurors evaluated.

Section I: Existing Juror Decision-Making Models

Probability-based models

Juror decision-making involves what is known as reasoning under uncertainty, or probabilistic reasoning: drawing conclusions about the likelihood of uncertain events. A range of existing work has sought to understand how jurors draw these conclusions. Relatively early models of this decision-making attempted to use probability theory to describe reasoning processes of jurors. Most notably, probability theorists have proposed using Bayes' theorem to describe reasoning in legal cases.[1] According to Bayes' theorem, jurors should adopt an initial degree of belief as to guilt (the prior probability, represented on a 'mental meter'), which is then logically updated by each new individual unit of information or evidence in a multiplicative process to form a new probability estimate that represents the conditional probability of guilt given the evidence (a posterior probability). This posterior probability can then be updated again if more information is available. When the posterior probability is final (ie there is no more evidence to update it with), it should be compared to a decision threshold (eg beyond reasonable doubt, also represented on the 'mental meter'). If the posterior probability is higher than the decision threshold, a defendant should be found guilty. Other related models, including algebraic models[2] and stochastic models,[3] have also attempted to model juror decision-making through the estimation and combination of probabilities.[4] For example, Thomas and Hogue's process model of juror decision-making (a stochastic model) describes jurors summing the weight of evidence from evidentiary sources with the weight of evidence from non-evidentiary sources once both have reached a critical point where the weight of evidence from that source becomes

[1] R Hastie, 'Introduction' in R Hastie (ed), *Inside the Juror: The Psychology of Decision Making* (CUP 1993) 11–17.

[2] R Hastie, 'Algebraic Models of Juror Decision Processes' in R Hastie (ed), *Inside the Juror: The Psychology of Decision Making* (CUP 1993).

[3] N Kerr, 'Stochastic Models of Juror Decision Making' in R Hastie, *Inside the Juror: The Psychology of Decision Making* (CUP 1993).

[4] For more details and summaries of these models, see R Hastie, *Inside the Juror: The Psychology of Decision Making* (CUP 1993); DJ Devine, *Jury Decision-Making: The State of the Science* (NYU Press 2012).

fixed. This value is then compared to the threshold value required for a guilty verdict.[5]

These mathematical models (sometimes called probability-based approaches)[6] are now often viewed as being relatively prescriptive (describing what jurors should do) rather than descriptive (describing what jurors actually do) for a number of reasons. Jurors are unlikely to assign precise values to evidence and, even where jurors are given precise values, they are unlikely to be able to integrate them into decisions in a way that is mathematically rational.[7] Thus, even if decisions reflect these types of process qualitatively, they are unlikely to do so quantitatively. Secondly, these models are generally inconsistent with juror reports of their own experiences. When jurors describe how they reached a decision, they do not talk about assigning numerical values to individual pieces of evidence.[8] Thirdly, these models are not consistent with modern psychological theory, suggesting that human decision-making is contextual rather than precise.[9] Finally, these models are inconsistent with empirical evidence relating to juror decision-making. For example, research suggests that the weight jurors give to evidence may not be independent of other evidence and is instead dependent on the incorporation of the evidence in overarching narratives.[10]

The Story Model

Cognitive models have drawn on research and theory in psychology in order to provide verbal accounts of how jurors make decisions that are thought to be more realistic representations of underlying cognitive processes than probability-based models. The leading cognitive model of juror decision-making is known as the Story Model. The Story Model draws on earlier literature in memory and language comprehension, highlighting the nature of human comprehension as a largely

[5] EA Thomas and A Hogue, 'Apparent Weight of Evidence, Decision Criteria, and Confidence Ratings in Juror Decision Making' (1976) 83(6) Psychological Review 442; Kerr (n 3).

[6] M Vorms and D Lagnado, 'Coherence and Credibility in the Story-Model of Jurors' Decision-Making: Does Mental Simulation Really Drive the Evaluation of the Evidence?' in A Nepomuceno-Fernández and others (eds), *Model-Based Reasoning in Science and Technology; Inferential Models for Logic, Language, Cognition and Computation* (Springer 2018).

[7] See eg T Shengelia and D Lagnado, 'Are Jurors Intuitive Statisticians? Bayesian Causal Reasoning in Legal Contexts' (2020) 11 Frontiers in Psychology 519262.

[8] N Pennington and R Hastie, 'Juror Decision-Making Models: The Generalization Gap' (1981) 89(2) Psychological Bulletin 246.

[9] See eg W Kintsch, *The Representation of Meaning in Memory* (1st edn, Psychology Press 1974); RC Schank and RP Abelson, *Scripts, Plans, Goals and Understanding: An Inquiry into Human Knowledge Structures* (1st edn, Psychology Press 1977); T Trabasso and P van den Broek, 'Causal Thinking and the Representation of Narrative Events' (1985) 24(5) Journal of Memory and Language 612.

[10] N Pennington and R Hastie, 'A Cognitive Theory of Juror Decision Making: The Story Model' (1991) 13 Cardozo Law Review 519; N Pennington and R Hastie, 'Explaining the Evidence: Tests of the Story Model for Juror Decision Making' (1992) 62(2) Journal of Personality and Social Psychology 189.

constructive process.[11] This research highlights the importance of narratives (or story-telling) in comprehension.[12] More broadly, related research has shown the importance of narratives in learning—people seem to learn and understand information effectively when it is incorporated in narrative form.[13] Essentially, the Story Model predicts that jurors construct a causal model to explain the available facts and then base subsequent decisions on that causal model (as opposed to valuing each piece of evidence individually and combining probative value extracted from each piece of evidence). This prediction has been supported by a range of empirical evidence.[14]

According to the Story Model, jurors make decisions in three stages. First, they evaluate case evidence through narrative construction.[15] Evidence will be valued more highly when it fits within an overarching narrative.[16] Narratives are thought to be constructed by drawing on trial evidence itself (eg statements made by witnesses), world knowledge about similar events (eg knowledge about similar crimes that have taken place), and knowledge about story structures (eg knowledge that actions are often motivated by goals). Some potential components of the story will come directly from the facts (eg witness evidence shows that a defendant was very drunk, or that the victim had insulted the defendant) while other components are the result of inferences made by the juror as a result of their reasoning and experience (eg because the defendant was very drunk, the defendant is more likely to have been violent, or because the victim had insulted the defendant, the defendant was likely to have been angry). Different jurors will create different narratives as a result of different underlying knowledge and beliefs (eg one juror may conclude that drinking alcohol would have made the defendant more likely to have offended as a result of increased unpredictability and violence, while another may conclude it would have made the defendant less likely to have offended as a result of impaired capacity). Where jurors have not received enough information in the case to create a complete story (ie where evidence is ambiguous), their own knowledge is likely

[11] Kintsch (n 9); Schank and Abelson (n 9).

[12] P van den Broek and M Gustafson, 'Comprehension and Memory for Texts: Three Generations of Reading Research' in SR Goldman, AC Graesser, and P van den Broek (eds), *Narrative Comprehension, Causality, and Coherence: Essays in Honor of Tom Trabasso* (Routledge 1999) 15–34.

[13] See eg C Witherall and N Noddings (eds), *Stories Live Tell: Narrative and Dialogue in Education* (Teachers' College Press 1991) 279–80:

> [W]e learn from stories. More important, we come to understand—ourselves, others, and even the subjects we teach and learn. Stories engage us . . . Stories can help us to understand by making the abstract concrete and accessible. What is only dimly perceived at the level of principle may become vivid and powerful in the concrete. Further, stories motivate us. Even that which we understand at the abstract level may not move us to action, whereas a story often does.

[14] Devine (n 4) ch 2.

[15] Stories involve human action sequences connected by relationships of physical and intentional causality—a chain of events connected by causal relationships; see Trabasso and van den Broek (n 9).

[16] Pennington and Hastie, 'Explaining the Evidence' (n 10).

to have a more significant role in gap-filling.[17] Importantly, the resulting story (informed by evidence), rather than evidence itself, is what is said to inform a verdict.

Jurors may construct more than one possible narrative. The narrative that they ultimately accept and their confidence in it are thought to be determined by reference to coverage (the extent to which the narrative accounts for the evidence presented at trial) and coherence (consisting of completeness—the extent to which the story has all necessary 'parts', plausibility—the extent to which the story is consistent with knowledge of events in the real world, and consistency—the extent to which the story does not contain internal contradictions).[18] If more than one narrative has good coverage and coherence (described as narratives lacking uniqueness), uncertainty is expected to result.[19] Finally, the accepted narrative and a juror's confidence in it are thought to be compared to verdict categories (usually guilty or not guilty). A guilty verdict will be delivered where there is a sufficiently good fit between the accepted narrative and associated confidence and the guilty verdict category (eg being 'sure' of defendant guilt), otherwise a default verdict of not guilty would be expected. Empirical research has provided support for the Story Model over mathematical models of jury decision-making. For example, research has shown that the rated importance of trial evidence is strongly related to the causal role of the evidence in the narrative associated with a person's verdict, and that presenting evidence in an order to encourage construction of a particular narrative leads more people to reach verdicts consistent with that narrative.[20]

The Story Model remains widely accepted as the most realistic representation of how jurors work and therefore must be considered and taken seriously in any new representation of juror decision-making.[21] However, it does have limitations in terms of providing a full explanation of how juries work that can be useful in critiquing their function against normative goals.

First, the model lacks a clear description of how jurors assess and value evidence, independently of its incorporation into narratives or evaluations of narratives. The model, and associated empirical work, show that the weight given to evidence is likely to be influenced by how it fits into narratives. For example, mock jurors are more likely to remember and use evidence that fits in with the predominant narrative.[22] However, clearly, the strength of evidence itself is highly relevant to how stories are developed and evaluated, and some evidence may be strong enough that the story has to form around the facts which that evidence establishes. For

[17] ibid.
[18] ibid.
[19] Pennington and Hastie, 'A Cognitive Theory of Juror Decision Making' (n 10).
[20] N Pennington and R Hastie, 'Explanation-Based Decision Making: Effects of Memory Structure on Judgment' (1988) 14(3) Journal of Experimental Psychology: Learning, Memory, and Cognition 521; Pennington and Hastie, 'Explaining the Evidence' (n 10).
[21] See eg Devine (n 4) ch 2.
[22] Pennington and Hastie, 'Explaining the Evidence' (n 10).

example, DNA evidence showing a defendant was at the scene of a crime may be convincing enough independently of a narrative that it drives the evaluation of the narrative, rather than the opposite. Despite this reality, the current model gives no clear description of how jurors evaluate the strength of evidence independently of the story. As a result, the model can appear circular. The best story is selected based on the weight of evidence, and the weight of evidence is evaluated by reference to its fit in the story.[23] Of course, both of these things can be true to some extent, but presumably jurors also evaluate the weight of evidence at least somewhat independently of a broader narrative, as well as being influenced by the narrative. For example, the value jurors give to testimony of an eyewitness placing a defendant at the scene of a crime may be a product of both cues in the testimony itself (eg the confidence of the witness[24]), and the fit of the testimony in an overarching narrative (eg evidence suggesting the defendant had a motive to commit the crime). The current Story Model provides little insight into the former type of judgment.

Secondly, the Story Model is limited in directly accounting for factors that have been shown to influence the decisions jurors reach and how they reach them. This limitation relates more to the utility of the model in fully understanding how juries work than to how effectively it does what it intends to do, which is to describe the general process through which jurors make decisions. However, juror decision processes and the conclusions reached through them can be influenced by a range of factors, and understanding those factors is important in understanding how juries work in practice. Work applying the Story Model recognizes one of these influences—the order of presentation of case evidence—which it has been shown can influence the narratives jurors construct and related verdicts.[25] Research has also shown a range of other factors that can influence the verdicts jurors reach. One of these factors is emotion, which research suggests can have an impact on evidence evaluation and verdict choice. In the legal context specifically, evidence suggests that the influence of negative emotion (and in particular anger) on juror decisions is likely to be prejudicial in the context of a criminal trial.[26] This influence on the jury is often recognized by legal procedural rules. For example, in the federal system in the United States of America (USA), relevant evidence may be found to be unfairly prejudicial and inadmissible under federal law[27] if it would likely provoke an emotional response from the jury.[28]

[23] Vorms and Lagnado (n 6).

[24] N Brewer and A Burke, 'Effects of Testimonial Inconsistencies and Eyewitness Confidence on Mock-Juror Judgments' (2002) 26(3) Law and Human Behavior 353.

[25] Pennington and Hastie, 'Explaining the Evidence' (n 10) 193.

[26] DA Bright and J Goodman-Delahunty, 'Gruesome Evidence and Emotion: Anger, Blame, and Jury Decision-Making' (2006) 30(2) Law and Human Behavior 183; N Nuñez and others, 'Negative Emotions Felt During Trial: The Effect of Fear, Anger, and Sadness on Juror Decision Making' (2015) 29(2) Applied Cognitive Psychology 200.

[27] Federal Rules of Evidence, r 403.

[28] *S v Harry* 20 F Supp 3d 1196 (DNM 2014).

Thirdly, the model does not give meaningful insight into how jurors interpret qualitative terms in legal standards—a key part of the role of the jury (eg was particular conduct dishonest, or is confidence in the verdict sufficient to meet the standard of proof).[29] The last stage in the posited decision-making process does involve matching what happened to the criteria for relevant verdict alternatives (eg for a finding of murder jurors should be sure that the defendant killed another person with the intention to kill them or cause them grievous bodily harm). At this point in the process, the model provides that jurors may have to reason about whether a circumstance in the story constitutes a good match to required circumstances. However, little detail is provided on how jurors engage in reasoning surrounding the interpretation of legal terms (both the standard of proof and more broadly), and what ultimately influences their decisions. For example, how do jurors determine whether someone has been 'dishonest'?

The Director's Cut Model

Relatively recently, Dr Dennis Devine has incorporated some basic ideas of the Story Model into the 'Director's Cut' Model of juror decision-making, which seeks to integrate and extend existing knowledge on juror decision-making.[30] According to that model, jurors form an initial representation of a trial prior to hearing evidence, based on scripts, stereotypes, and any information available to them (eg resulting from pretrial publicity and opening statements) (note that this representation may also involve feelings or emotions relating to the case, such as a desire to blame someone for a tragedy that has occurred). The features of jurors themselves (including juror race, gender, socio-economic status, and trust in the legal system) and trial participants (including defendant race, gender, socio-economic status, prior criminal history, physical attractiveness, and display of emotion) will likely be important in forming this initial representation. Case evidence is then thought to be added to this initial representation in order to update it and translate it into a mental model which is drawn on to evaluate the plausibility of story explanations offered by the prosecution and the defence. The plausibility of these explanations is thought to be evaluated in terms of their scope (the richness of evidence and detail in the story); credibility (the believability of story elements); and singularity (being the only story that evidence converges on, rather than one of more possible stories). Based on this evaluation of the plausibility of story explanations, jurors will (1) favour the prosecution's story, (2) favour an alternative story offered by the defence, (3) be unable to choose between two or more stories which seem equally

[29] See also KM Clermont, 'Standards of Proof Revisited' (2009) 33(3) Vermont Law Review 469.
[30] Devine (n 4) ch 8.

plausible, or (4) be unable to formulate any story that provides an accurate account of the evidence. They will go into deliberations in one of these four states.

The Director's Cut Model supplies important detail not provided by the Story Model, in particular into the specific features of jurors themselves and trial participants that can influence how narratives are constructed (primarily through influencing the initial representation of the evidence). It also incorporates a role of emotion which, as noted above, is not explicitly accounted for by the Story Model. However, according to the Director's Cut Model, the influence of juror features and emotion are (at least largely) confined to their impact on an initial representation prior to hearing trial evidence. The model therefore does not provide a good explanation for research showing that evidence itself can be interpreted differently by different jurors (even outside the context of a trial) and the fact that evidence itself can trigger emotion that can influence verdict.[31] Similarly to the Story Model, the Director's Cut Model is limited in its consideration of how jurors evaluate individual pieces of evidence. The model proposes that jurors evaluate the prosecution's story by reference to the trustworthiness or believability of major evidentiary elements (as well as the scope and singularity of the story). A premise of the model is that assertions will be accepted as true unless (1) the assertion comes from a witness who is not seen as credible, (2) the assertion is incompatible with existing juror beliefs, or (3) the assertion is disputed by a credible source. Where evidence conflicts, the model presumes that either 'the most credible source could be believed, or the number of credible sources behind each assertion could be considered'.[32] However, in-depth consideration is not given to what influences how jurors interpret individual pieces of evidence, and, more specifically, what leads jurors to determine which source is most credible. Finally, as with the Story Model, the Director's Cut Model does not give meaningful consideration to how jurors interpret qualitative terms in legal standards.

Section II: FTT, FL, and the Importance of Mental Representation

Applying new psychological theory and a new type of logic to understanding juror decision-making can help to inform a model that takes into account the strengths of previous models while also addressing the limitations discussed above. One empirically supported theory, which builds on (but is distinct from) the Story Model, and which makes predictions about how human decision-makers evaluate and apply evidence, is FTT.[33]

[31] Bright and Goodman-Delahunty (n 26).

[32] Devine (n 4) ch 8, 196.

[33] For some experimental and mathematical tests of the theory, see VF Reyna and B Kiernan, 'Development of Gist Versus Verbatim Memory in Sentence Recognition: Effects of Lexical Familiarity, Semantic Content, Encoding Instructions, and Retention Interval' (1994) 30(2) Developmental Psychology 178; VF Reyna and B Kiernan, 'Children's Memory and Metaphorical Interpretation'

Verbatim and gist-based representations and associated processing

FTT is a dual process theory of memory and decision-making.[34] According to the theory, when people hear information, they encode it in memory in two forms, as gist-based representations and as verbatim representations.[35] Gist-based representations capture the meaning of information in context (the essential substance of the information irrespective of exact words, images, or numbers), so encoding gist involves attaching meaning to information, which may differ from person to person. Importantly, the influences on the particular gist attached to information may be both conscious and unconscious. Verbatim representations capture the precise surface form of the information in a superficial way. Imagine an expert witness testifying that the false report probability relating to a DNA match (ie the chance of mistakenly misclassifying non-matching samples as matching, for example as the result of testing error) is approximately 1 in 450. Jurors would encode this specific information 'a 1 in 450 chance of a matching error' (a verbatim representation), but also the gist of that information for them, which might be 'a low chance of a matching error' (a gist-based representation). These representations are thought to be encoded roughly at the same time, but to be encoded, stored, and retrieved separately from one another.[36]

When a person retrieves information to make a decision, they are likely to rely more on a particular type of representation (either gist or verbatim). Reliance on gist-based representations supports fuzzy (yet advanced) processing of information relying on fewer dimensions of information where possible to reach a decision

(1995) 10(4) Metaphor and Symbol 309; CJ Brainerd, VF Reyna, and C Aydin, 'Remembering in Contradictory Minds: Disjunction Fallacies in Episodic Memory' (2010) 36(3) Journal of Experimental Psychology: Learning, Memory, and Cognition 711; JC Corbin and others, 'How Reasoning, Judgment, and Decision-Making are Colored by Gist-Based Intuition: A Fuzzy-Trace Theory Approach' (2015) 4(4) Journal of Applied Research in Memory and Cognition 344; RK Helm and VF Reyna, 'Fuzzy-Trace Theory: Memory and Decision-Making in Law, Medicine, and Public Health' in B Logie and others (eds), *Memory in Science for Society: There is Nothing as Practical as a Good Theory* (OUP 2023) 93.

[34] Note that memory is about more than memorization and is often recognized as important in decision-making. See eg MR Dougherty, AM Franco-Watkins, and R Thomas, 'Psychological Plausibility of the Theory of Probabilistic Mental Models and the Fast and Frugal Heuristics' (2008) 115(1) Psychological Review 199; R Ratcliff and G McKoon, 'The Diffusion Decision Model: Theory and Data for Two-Choice Decision Tasks' (2008) 20(4) Neural Computation 873; TJ Pleskac and JR Busemeyer, 'Two-Stage Dynamic Signal Detection: A Theory of Choice, Decision Time, and Confidence' (2010) 117(3) Psychological Review 864; LJ Schooler and R Hertwig, 'How Forgetting Aids Heuristic Inference' (2005) 112(3) Psychological Review 610.

[35] CJ Brainerd and VF Reyna, 'Fuzzy-Trace Theory: Dual Processes in Memory, Reasoning, and Cognitive Neuroscience' in HW Reese and R Kail (eds), *Advances in Child Development and Behaviour* (Academic Press 2001); VF Reyna, 'A New Intuitionism: Meaning, Memory, and Development in Fuzzy-Trace Theory' (2012) 7(3) Judgment and Decision-Making 332.

[36] For specific models and experiments differentiating retrieval from storage of memories, see VF Reyna and CJ Brainerd, 'Fuzzy-Trace Theory: An Interim Synthesis' (1995) 7(1) Learning and Individual Differences 1; CJ Brainerd, VF Reyna, and ML Howe, 'Trichotomous Processes in Early Memory Development, Aging, and Neurocognitive Impairment: A Unified Theory' (2009) 116(4) Psychological Review 783.

(often described as more intuitive decision-making), and reliance on verbatim representations supports precise and detail-oriented analysis.[37] Which representations a person is likely to rely on, and how they draw on information encoded in memory to make decisions, depends on a number of factors. Importantly, FTT predicts that reliance on gist-based as opposed to verbatim representations when making decisions is developmentally advanced, and while children rely more on verbatim representations, adults will rely on gist-based representations where possible.[38] Thus, the decision-making process in adults does not involve superficial consideration of precise information (as, for example, solving mathematical problems might do), but a meaningful process integrating context, intuitions (feelings about what seems true) and beliefs (convictions about what is true) in the form of gist-based representations. For example, when adults evaluate evidence they are not engaging in a mathematical exercise with precise rules (eg an expert with more than ten years of experience is automatically more reliable than an expert with less than ten years of experience, or expert credentials equals the sum of years of experience, level of training, and endorsement in the field), but rather are representing pieces of information in a meaningful way and combining them to form an overall representation (eg combining years of experience with other relevant information in a qualitative way in order to inform an overall impression of an expert as a very reliable witness, a reasonably reliable witness, or an unreliable witness).

Generally, reliance on gist-based representations is thought to facilitate mature and informed decision-making in applied contexts, where good decisions often pivot on simple qualitative insights.[39] The relative superiority and developmentally advanced nature of this more intuitive processing can be illustrated clearly by experimental work drawing on FTT in the context of diagnosing patients with cardiac disease.[40] That work suggested that more experienced doctors relied more on intuition than less experienced doctors (evidenced by processing less information

[37] VF Reyna, 'How People Make Decisions That Involve Risk: A Dual-Processes Approach (2004) 13(2) Current Directions in Psychological Science 60.

[38] VF Reyna and BA Mills, 'Theoretically Motivated Interventions for Reducing Sexual Risk Taking in Adolescence: A Randomised Controlled Experiment Applying Fuzzy-Trace Theory' (2014) 143(4) Journal of Experimental Psychology General 1627; Y Kwak and others, 'The Rational Adolescent: Strategic Information Processing During Decision-Making Revealed by Eye Tracking' (2015) 36 Cognitive Development 20; CM White, M Gummerum, and Y Hanoch, 'Adolescents' and Young Adults' Online Risk Taking: The Role of Gist and Verbatim Representations' (2015) 35(8) Risk Analysis 1407. For reviews of work demonstrating reliance on gist rather than verbatim representations of information, see VF Reyna, 'Reasoning, Remembering, and Their Relationship: Social, Cognitive, and Developmental Issues' in ML Howe, CJ Brainerd, and VF Reyna (eds), *Development of Long-Term Retention* (Springer-Verlag 1992) 103–27; Reyna and Brainerd, 'Fuzzy-Trace Theory: An Interim Synthesis' (n 36).

[39] See eg Reyna and Mills (n 38); Kwak and others (n 38); White, Gummerum, and Hanoch (n 38).

[40] VF Reyna and FJ Lloyd, 'Physician Decision Making and Cardiac Risk: Effects of Knowledge, Risk Perception, Risk Tolerance, and Fuzzy Processing' (2006) 12(3) Journal of Experimental Psychology: Applied 179. Relatedly, see M Raoelison, VA Thompson, and W De Neys, 'The Smart Intuitor: Cognitive Capacity Predicts Intuitive Rather Than Deliberative Thinking' (2020) 204 Cognition 104381.

and making sharper all-or-none distinctions rather than explicitly considering a range of criteria in detail) and were also better at discriminating levels of risk.

Although adults are thought to generally rely on gist-based representations, their tendency to rely on gist-based or verbatim representations can also be influenced by the accessibility of each of those representations in memory, and the requirements of a task itself. Cues in questions and the granularity required in responses can push people to rely more on verbatim representations than they would otherwise. For example, a question asking people to remember exact wording or numerical information will trigger more reliance on verbatim representations. People may also be forced to rely more on verbatim representations where gist-based representations do not distinguish between decision options (eg choosing between two options that both have the gist of being 'good' or that both have the gist of being 'reliable').[41] However, it is important to note that gist-based representations are more stable than verbatim representations over time, and people may be forced to rely on gist-based representations when verbatim representations are no longer available in memory, regardless of the task.[42] Where people rely on gist-based representations and verbatim representations are not accessible, people can have false memory for gist-consistent but verbatim-inconsistent stimuli even where they are attempting to retrieve verbatim representations (as in Deese-Roediger-McDermott (DRM) lists, described below).[43]

Errors and cognitive biases associated with gist

Although reliance on gist is thought to be developmentally advanced, this reliance can also lead to errors, and systematic deviations from rational decision-making (cognitive biases), in predictable situations. Increases in gist-based errors and cognitive biases with age provide support for the predicted developmental trajectory from reliance on verbatim to reliance on gist, and relatedly the prediction that adults will generally rely on gist-based representations. For example, consider the DRM false memory paradigm.[44] In that paradigm, participants are presented with a list of words that share semantic relations with each other (eg sofa, rocking, sitting, table, recliner . . .). In subsequent tests, participants are asked whether original word lists contained particular words, including words that were presented

[41] VF Reyna and CJ Brainerd, 'Dual Processes in Decision Making and Developmental Neuroscience: A Fuzzy-Trace Model' (2011) 31(2–3) Developmental Review 180; Reyna, 'A New Intuitionism' (n 35).

[42] Kintsch (n 9); Reyna and Kiernan, 'Development of Gist Versus Verbatim Memory' (n 33); Reyna and Kiernan, 'Children's Memory and Metaphorical Interpretation' (n 33).

[43] CJ Brainerd and others, 'Conjoint Recognition and Phantom Recollection' (2001) 27(2) Journal of Experimental Psychology: Learning, Memory, and Cognition 307.

[44] HL Roediger and KB McDermott, 'Creating False Memories: Remembering Words Not Presented in Lists' (1995) 21(4) Journal of Experimental Psychology: Learning, Memory, and Cognition 803.

on the original list, unpresented and unrelated words (eg bike), and unpresented words that are semantically related to those on the original lists (eg chair). People often falsely remember the semantically related words as having been presented.[45] According to FTT, this false memory is a result of gist-based processes. Put simply, people rely on the gist of items on the list rather than specific items, which leads them to accept the semantically related words (which have the same or similar gist) as having been presented.[46] This tendency to accept semantically related words can be counteracted by drawing on verbatim memory for exactly what was presented, which will demonstrate the gist-consistent item was not presented (through a process known as recollection rejection). However, the deterioration of verbatim memory over time makes people particularly susceptible to gist-related false memories even when tasks seek to cue verbatim representations.[47] Crucially, false memories for semantically related words (including on accessible lists for children) have been shown to increase from childhood to adulthood even when child-normed lists are utilized, supporting FTT's assertion that while children tend to rely on verbatim representations, adults tend to rely on gist-based representations.[48]

In the decision-making context, similar developmental reversals can be seen in a cognitive bias associated with reliance on gist-based representations—risky-choice framing effects.[49] Risky-choice framing effects refer to changes in preference in risk-taking problems depending on how the problem is framed. These problems typically ask people to choose between a sure but less favourable outcome (the sure choice), and the chance of a better outcome and chance of a worse outcome (the risky choice). Generally, people show a cognitive bias such that when a problem is framed as a gain (eg a choice between winning £50 for sure or a 50 per cent chance of £100 and 50 per cent chance of nothing), they are more likely to select the sure choice than when the same problem is framed as a loss (eg being given £100 and having a choice between losing £50 for sure or a 50 per cent chance

[45] See eg ibid; JH Coane and others, 'Manipulations of List Type in the DRM Paradigm: A Review of How Structural and Conceptual Similarity Affect False Memory' (2021) 12 Frontiers in Psychology 668550.

[46] VF Reyna and F Lloyd, 'Theories of False Memory in Children and Adults' (1997) 9(2) Learning and Individual Differences 95; Brainerd and others (n 43).

[47] For more information on the constructs of FTT's memory model, termed conjoint recognition, see Brainerd and others (n 43); CJ Brainerd, VF Reyna, and AH Mojardin, 'Conjoint Recognition' (1999) 106(1) Psychological Review 160.

[48] CJ Brainerd, VF Reyna, and SJ Ceci, 'Developmental Reversals in False Memory: A Review of Data and Theory (2008) 134(3) Psychological Bulletin 343; CJ Brainerd, VF Reyna, and E Zember, 'Theoretical and Forensic Implications of Developmental Studies of the DRM Illusion' (2011) 39(3) Memory & Cognition 365.

[49] VF Reyna and SC Ellis, 'Fuzzy-Trace Theory and Framing Effects in Children's Risky Decision Making' (1994) 5(5) Psychological Science 275; VF Reyna and F Farley, 'Risk and Rationality in Adolescent Decision Making: Implications for Theory, Practice, and Public Policy' (2006) 7(1) Psychological Science in the Public Interest 1; VF Reyna and others, 'Neurobiological and Memory Models of Risky Decision Making in Adolescents Versus Young Adults' (2011) 37(5) Journal of Experimental Psychology: Learning, Memory, and Cognition 1125.

of losing £100 and a 50 per cent chance of losing nothing).[50] According to FTT, this effect occurs as a result of reliance on the least precise gist, because the simple gist that is extracted (ie some money or none) creates framing differences. In the gain frame, the gist of decision options is likely to be winning something versus maybe winning something and maybe winning nothing, while in the loss frame the gist of decision options is likely to be losing something versus maybe losing something and maybe losing nothing, creating a preference for the sure option in the gain frame and the risky option in the loss frame.[51] Consistent with FTT's predictions that framing effects result from reliance on gist, and reliance on gist increases with age, research has shown that framing effects increase with age.[52]

The importance of meaning to gist-based representations means that reliance on gist also makes people susceptible to the influence of other heuristics and cognitive biases associated with intuition (discussed later in this chapter), that lead to mistakes and an influence of rationally irrelevant factors on decision-making. To give a simple example, the verbatim representation of the number 10 (provided it is remembered correctly) will always be 10. However, the gist-based representation of that number can be biased by context, intuitions, and beliefs that can change whether that number is encoded as 'small', 'medium', or 'large'.

The relationship between intuition and 'hot' and 'cold' influence

As well as incorporating the role of mental representations in decision-making, FTT accounts for a range of other factors than can influence decisions, combining concepts of meaning from psycholinguistics with notions of reflection and impulsivity from traditional dual process theories.[53] But while traditional dual process theories sometimes associate intuitive thinking with impulsive or emotional thinking,[54] FTT maintains that impulsivity and intuition are not similar processes, and affect decision-making differently: 'FTT would not categorize unconscious intuitions of experts with impulsive choices of children.'[55] So, while adults are expected to rely on intuition in the form of gist, this reliance does not represent a primitive process, and can be thoughtful, considered, and advanced. As a result, so called 'hot' influences (eg emotion) and 'cold' influences (eg reflection as opposed

[50] A Kühberger, M Schulte-Mecklenbeck, and J Perner, 'The Effects of Framing, Reflection, Probability, and Payoff on Risk Preference in Choice Tasks' (1999) 78(3) Organizational Behavior and Human Decision Processes 204.

[51] A Kühberger and C Tanner, 'Risky Choice Framing: Task Versions and a Comparison of Prospect Theory and Fuzzy-Trace Theory' (2010) 23(3) Journal of Behavioral Decision Making 314, 318.

[52] Reyna and Ellis (n 49).

[53] See eg D Kahneman, *Thinking, Fast and Slow* (Macmillan 2011).

[54] See eg JSBT Evans and KE Stanovich, 'Dual-Process Theories of Higher Cognition: Advancing the Debate' (2013) 8(3) Perspectives on Psychological Science 223.

[55] VF Reyna and others, 'Development of Risky Decision Making: Fuzzy-Trace Theory and Neurobiological Perspectives' (2015) 9(2) Child Development Perspectives 122.

to impulsivity) have a separate impact on decisions from reliance on gist-based (meaningful) or verbatim (precise and superficial) representations.[56]

Importantly, these influences have the potential to change the specific gist that is encoded and relied on. Because encoding gist involves attaching meaning to evidence, this encoding can be influenced by a range of factors, including emotion. First, the gist of a stimulus will often include a valence that may be assigned consciously or unconsciously. For example, trial participants might be encoded as good/bad or better/worse people.[57] Importantly, the valence assigned to information is often a result of interpreting its gist, for example, that an act was committed intentionally with malice (which is an inference that goes beyond verbatim facts). Hence, new information that conflicts with encoded valence may be downplayed because it does not fit a pre-established gist.[58] Secondly, feeling states or discrete emotions can infuse the gist representation of a stimulus, particularly where the stimulus is ambiguous.[59] In fact, this impact of feeling states is important and adaptive. Being driven by feelings relating to a stimulus can help people to navigate through the world, for example by sensing potential danger.[60] However, the effect can be misleading where the gist assigned to a stimulus is impacted by incidental feeling states—for example, research has shown that medical symptoms may be interpreted differently by those feeling them depending on the incidental mood that they are in.[61] Thirdly, impulsivity may also lead to encoding a misleading gist of a stimulus, through failure to engage with information that is relevant to the meaning of that stimulus. In addition to influencing the gist representation from a stimulus, factors including emotion and impulsivity are likely to have independent (and potentially related) influences on decisions. For example, high levels of arousal can reduce inhibition, and result in a lack of behavioural regulation (eg through jumping to conclusions or engaging in tempting but negative behaviours).[62]

[56] ibid.

[57] For work showing how the valence of stimuli can influence decision-making, see FX Gibbons, M Gerrard, and DJ Lane, 'A Social Reaction Model of Adolescent Health Risk' in J Suls and KA Wallston (eds), *Social Psychological Foundations of Health and Illness* (Blackwell Publishing 2003) 107–36.

[58] MH Farrell, MA Murphy, and CE Schneider, 'How Underlying Patient Beliefs Can Affect Physician-Patient Communication About Prostate-Specific Antigen Testing' (2002) 5(3) Effective Clinical Practice 120; P Slovic and others, 'Affect, Risk, and Decision Making' (2005) 24(4S) Health Psychology S35. For a discussion, see SE Rivers, VF Reyna, and B Mills, 'Risk Taking Under the Influence: A Fuzzy-Trace Theory of Emotion in Adolescence' (2008) 28(1) Developmental Review 107.

[59] N Schwarz and GL Clore, 'How Do I Feel About It? Information Functions of Affective States' in K Fiedler and J Forgas (eds), *Affect, Cognition and Social Behavior* (Hogrefe International 1998) 44–62; JP Forgas, 'Feeling and Doing: Affective Influences on Interpersonal Behavior' (2002) 13(1) Psychological Inquiry 1.

[60] P Slovic and others, 'Risk As Analysis and Risk as Feelings: Some Thoughts About Affect, Reason, Risk, and Rationality' (2004) 24(2) Risk Analysis: An International Journal 311, 313; Rivers, Reyna, and Mills (n 58).

[61] P Salovey and D Birnbaum, 'Influence of Mood on Health-Relevant Cognitions' (1989) 57(3) Journal of Personality and Social Psychology 539.

[62] Rivers, Reyna, and Mills (n 58).

Section III: FTT, FL, and Representation in Jury Decision-Making

It is worth noting that FTT and the Story Model are related due to their recognition of the importance of meaning in human decision-making, and an FTT-informed model can retain many of the core concepts introduced by the Story Model. In fact, results supporting the Story Model's account of juror decision-making, combined with related findings in psycholinguistics, were part of the impetus for FTT.[63] (Although FTT also departs from core constructs of the Story Model.)[64] Work applying FTT to jury decision-making in the context of juror damages awards has suggested that gist constitutes the core or central meaning of a story—the take-home message of the constructed narrative.[65] However, FTT extends the Story Model by introducing the broader concept of independent mental representations of verbatim and gist. In this way, FTT provides greater insight than existing models into how jurors are likely to assess individual pieces of evidence, independently of their incorporation in the narrative (as well as through their incorporation in the narrative). Thus, applying FTT to the context of criminal adjudication results in new predictions relating to juror decision-making.

Importantly, reliance on gist as opposed to verbatim is not just predicted for numerical evidence, but also applies to evidence more broadly. For example, in the context of defendant or complainant testimony, jurors are unlikely to rely on exact words or phrases said by the witness, but rather on a meaningful interpretation of what was important or salient about the testimony (eg it was generally consistent, or it contained a particular meaningful inconsistency or some particular meaningful inconsistencies).

Jurors rely on meaningful and not precise representations of evidence and trial participants

The gist of the narrative (the 'story') connects all of the dots together and is the highest level of gist. However, gist is not just the end product of a deliberative

[63] See VP Hans and VF Reyna, 'To Dollars from Sense: Qualitative to Quantitative Translation in Jury Damage Awards' (2011) 8 Journal of Empirical Legal Studies 120, 132.

[64] See discussion of constructivism in VF Reyna and CJ Brainerd, 'Fuzzy-Trace Theory: Some Foundational Issues' (1995) 7(2) Learning and Individual Differences 145–62, for example.

[65] Hans and Reyna (n 63). Note that work drawing on FTT in the civil law context provides support for the importance of meaning in the jury decision-making process, see VF Reyna and others, 'The Gist of Juries: Testing a Model of Damage Award Decision Making' (2015) 21(3) Psychology, Public Policy, and Law 280; VP Hans, RK Helm, and VF Reyna, 'From Meaning to Money: Translating Injury into Dollars' (2018) 42(2) Law and Human Behavior 95; RK Helm and others, 'Numeracy in the Jury Box: Numerical Ability, Meaningful Anchors, and Damage Award Decision Making' (2020) 34(2) Applied Cognitive Psychology 434; VP Hans and others, 'Guiding Jurors' Damage Award Decisions: Experimental Investigations of Approaches Based on Theory and Practice' (2022) 28(2) Psychology, Public Policy, and Law 188.

process but is extracted throughout the process from the evidence presented to jurors, and also from other meaningful elements of the trial process, including the trial participants themselves—jurors represent each *piece* of evidence and each trial participant in a gist-based and a verbatim-based way and also sub-categories of evidence in gist-based and verbatim-based ways.[66] Jurors are representing pieces of information in a meaningful way and combining these meaningful representations to form an overall representation. So, for example, years of experience may have a different impact on an evaluation of an expert depending on the specific experience of the expert, broad trends in the relevant field, and the expert's productivity at different points during their time in the field. These factors will likely be combined in a qualitative way based on juror intuitions and beliefs, rather than in a precise or mathematical way, and different jurors may weigh different factors differently.

Similarly, when a juror is told that there is a 1 in 450 false report probability (as discussed above), they are likely to rely not on this precise number in their decision-making but on the gist that there is a very low risk of a false report. This integrates the exact information with the meaningful interpretation of the juror that, in that context, 1 in 450 represents a low chance (note that 1 in 450 may not be considered low in all contexts, for example when considering risk of death, or even in the context of a DNA match to a person in a database of many individuals, where the small chance of a match may add up over multiple individual DNA comparisons). This prediction has support in existing work in which jury pool member estimates of the probability of a defendant being guilty did not differ between conditions in which there was a zero false report probability, a 1 in 10,000 false report probability, and a 1 in 100 false report probability (all were likely encoded as essentially nil chance in the context of the case).[67] Similarly, research examining likelihood ratios (ratios that may be given by forensic scientists comparing the likelihood of obtaining a piece of evidence if the prosecution case were true with the likelihood of obtaining the evidence given an alternative proposition), has shown that jurors' estimates of the probability of guilt do differ when ratios change categorically (eg from weak to moderate to strong) but not within categories.[68]

So, a story is one kind of gist, but gist-based representations of individual pieces of evidence and trial participants are also important, as they will influence the overall gist or 'story' on which a juror relies. As demonstrated above, the gist-based representations of evidence encoded will be the result of jurors assigning meaning to evidence. The meaning jurors assign to evidence will be influenced not only by

[66] Kintsch (n 9).

[67] WC Thompson, SO Kaasa, and T Peterson, 'Do Jurors Give Appropriate Weight to Forensic Identification Evidence?' (2013) 10(2) Journal of Empirical Legal Studies 359.

[68] See also, more generally, EA Wilhelms, L Fraenkel, and VF Reyna, 'Effects of Probabilities, Adverse Outcomes, and Status Quo on Perceived Riskiness of Medications: Testing Explanatory Hypotheses Concerning Gist, Worry, and Numeracy' (2018) 32(6) Applied Cognitive Psychology 714.

the evidence itself but also by the context surrounding it at trial, and by juror intuitions and beliefs.[69] Similarly, jurors will represent trial participants in a gist-based way, such as being 'good' or 'bad', 'honest' or 'dishonest'. For example, a juror who believes witnesses are inconsistent when they lie may encode the testimony of a witness who is inconsistent as dishonest and therefore unreliable. Thus, the role of juror beliefs (or knowledge) is not in being directly combined with evidence to form narratives (per the Story Model), but rather is in influencing relevant meaningful representations that are encoded—influencing the gist-based representations of evidence and trial participants that jurors rely on when constructing narratives.

FTT's predictions relating to reliance on gist-based representations is consistent with, and can explain, findings in empirical work relating to the Story Model. For example, empirical work has shown that mock jurors have a tendency to falsely remember evidence consistent with the overall narrative but that was not presented (ie was not part of the evidence they saw) as having been presented (ie as having been part of the evidence they saw).[70] This effect is a classic false memory effect of the type described above in relation to DRM lists, explained by reliance on gist-based representations in memory. (The precise relationship between semantic consistency and memory judgments depends on factors such as delay and retrieval cues.)[71] People will rely on the gist of evidence rather than verbatim representations when asked to recall evidence, and as a result they are susceptible to incorrectly reporting that gist-consistent information was given, particularly in the absence of a verbatim memory to trigger recollection rejection.[72]

Jurors evaluate narratives in an intuitive (gist-based) way

It is also important to note that this FTT-informed framework has implications for the construction and evaluation of narratives themselves. Where a person is relying on more gist-based representations (as most adults are thought to do), they would be expected to rely on gist-based processing (discussed above). As a result, they would be expected to construct narratives in a fuzzy and contextual way, integrating evidence intuitively to form story-like narratives (in a similar way to that

[69] On knowledge in gist, see VF Reyna and MB Adam, 'Fuzzy-Trace Theory, Risk Communication, and Product Labeling in Sexually Transmitted Diseases' (2003) 23(2) Risk Analysis 325; SJ Blalock and VF Reyna, 'Using Fuzzy-Trace Theory to Understand and Improve Health Judgments, Decisions, and Behaviors: A Literature Review' (2016) 35(8) Health Psychology 781.

[70] Pennington and Hastie, 'Explanation-Based Decision Making' (n 20).

[71] See VF Reyna and AL Titcomb, 'Constraints on the Suggestibility of Eyewitness Testimony: A Fuzzy-Trace Theory Analysis' in DG Payne and FG Conrad (eds), *A Synthesis of Basic and Applied Approaches to Human Memory* (Lawrence Erlbaum Associates 1996).

[72] Brainerd and others (n 43). See also CJ Brainerd and VF Reyna, 'Fuzzy-Trace Theory, False Memory, and the Law' (2019) 6(1) Policy Insights from the Behavioral and Brain Sciences 79.

expected by the Story Model). However, FTT also makes clear that adults would be unlikely to assess narratives against criteria in a scientific or clearly rational way (although the benchmarks suggested by the Story Model may be important in informing intuition where they are relevant in a particular context). Instead, adults would be expected to make relatively intuitive judgments about narrative fit. These judgments, as gist-based judgments, may be informed by logically probative factors such as those suggested by the Story Model, but the relative importance given to each factor may vary depending on context, and evaluations may also be distorted in predictable ways.

Jurors rely on meaningful representations of legal standards

According to FTT, legal standards will also be represented in both a gist-based and verbatim-based way. The resulting role of subjectivity in the interpretation of legal standards is not recognized by existing models, perhaps due to the presumption that legal standards are akin to scientific ones, and 'guilty' and 'innocent' are clear concepts that exist independently of legal judgment. Recognizing the potential subjectivity of legal standards and outcomes is important in understanding how jurors interpret legal standards and how they apply them to case facts. In the context of legal standards, reliance on gist would be expected to lead to a more meaning-based process asking the extent to which legal standards and defendant behaviour match each other in meaningfully important ways. So, does their level of confidence meaningfully resemble or feel like something they would characterize as 'being sure' or 'beyond reasonable doubt'? And do the attributes of the behaviour match those required by legal standards in ways that are meaningful for jurors?

A form of logic known as FL, which recognizes that often concepts that are treated as dichotomous can more appropriately be assessed on a spectrum, can provide insight that is important in understanding why the assignment of meaning to legal standards is necessary, and what the assessment of behaviour against legal standards is likely to look like. FL is a form of logic that allows for intermediate values in traditionally dichotomous categorizations.[73] So, while traditional logic (Boolean logic) uses what are known as 'crisp sets'—true/false, high/low, guilty/not guilty—FL allows reality to fall somewhere in the middle of these categorizations. So, a fact cannot only be completely true or completely false, but it can also be somewhere in between—a statement and its opposite can both be true to a degree. A statement is not necessarily true or false, but it can have degrees of truth from ranging from 0 'totally false' to 1 'totally true', with partial truth (or intermediate

[73] LA Zadeh, 'Fuzzy Sets' (1965) 8 Information and Control 338.

degrees of truth) in between.[74] One motivation for FL is to deal with the problem of vagueness, illustrated by what is known as the Sorites paradox. This paradox can be illustrated by the following example:[75]

(1) 10^{100} is a huge number.
(2) If n is a huge number, then $n - 1$ is also huge.

If this logic is repeated many times, we end up with the conclusion that 1 is a huge number. FL can deal with the paradox by recognizing that (2) may be almost true but not fully true—as n gets smaller, (2) becomes less and less true.[76]

FL has the potential to be useful in understanding and modelling how juries work, as it can help to model the vagueness in this judgment. In the same way that height forms a continuum, meaning that we cannot always clearly conclude objectively whether a specific person is 'tall', behaviours form a continuum so we cannot always clearly conclude that a specific behaviour meets a certain legal standard (eg is 'dishonest'). For example, imagine a person finding a £50 bank note on the floor of a supermarket and choosing to keep it after first looking around and trying to locate the owner. They might be considered honest to a degree but also dishonest to a degree. Then imagine a person who did the same but with a wad of ten £50 bank notes. They would likely be considered more dishonest. Then imagine a person who did the same but proactively approached people in the area asking if the money was theirs. They would likely be considered more honest. Therefore, a decision-maker must engage in detailed consideration of (1) what is meaningful in increasing or decreasing the extent to which behaviour is dishonest, and (2) what level of dishonesty is required to be sufficient for a finding of legal liability. The law does not provide guidance here, and instead relies on juror judgments. As a result, assessments inherently involve consideration of meaning and cannot be made relying on verbatim representations. Thus, while the final guilt judgment of the jury must be dichotomous (either guilty or not guilty), underlying factual realities and underlying factual judgments are likely to be more complex (as Professor Kevin Claremont has stated, 'The world of black or white is a special, extreme case of the world shaded in grays').[77]

Therefore, in addition to jurors having a natural tendency to rely on gist, (part of) the task required of them pushes for reliance on gist—they often cannot match the law and their favoured narrative in a superficial way (as in a game of snap, for

[74] R Cintula, 'Fuzzy Logic' (*Stanford Encyclopaedia of Philosophy*, 11 November 2011) <https://plato.stanford.edu/entries/logic-fuzzy/> accessed 13 June 2023. Note that FL also has mechanisms for determining the truth value of compound propositions, but these do not translate well into the legal context and are not considered here.

[75] ibid.

[76] ibid.

[77] KM Clermont, 'Death of Paradox: The Killer Logic Beneath the Standards of Proof' (2013) 88(3) Notre Dame Law Review 1061, 1084.

example, where cards clearly match one another). Rather, jurors must compare the overlap between their narrative and confidence in it to a focal case of a breach of the law, in order to determine whether their belief in what the defendant did and their confidence in that belief are a sufficient match to that focal case in ways that are meaningful in context. The question is more about meaningful overlap (how much overlap is perceived, and how much overlap is necessary) than it is about matching.

Section IV: A New Representation-Based Model of Juror Decision-Making

Model visualization

FTT and the reasoning discussed above can inform a new model of juror decision-making (the Representation-Based Model), similar in many respects to the Story Model, but recognizing the importance of representations of information rather than information itself in human decision-making, and the nature of applying legal standards as a complex process assessing meaningful similarity and overlap rather than simple matching. A framework for the Representation-Based Model (illustrating the material discussed above) is shown in Figure 4.1.

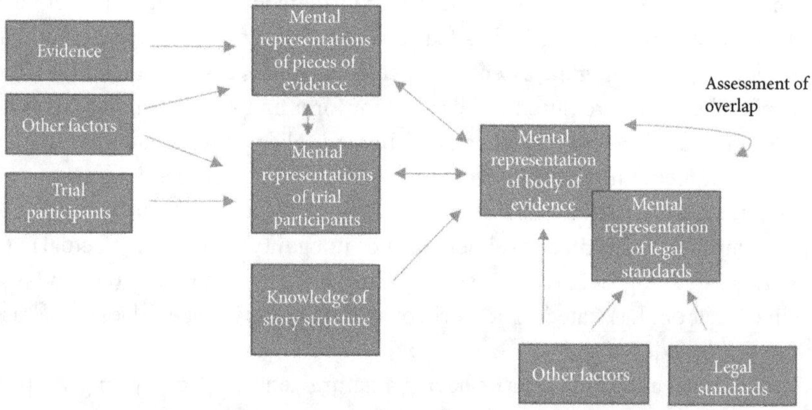

Figure 4.1 Representation-based model of juror decision-making

Central to this model is the importance not only of evidence, trial participants, the body of evidence, and legal standards, but of the ascription of meaning to these constructs by jurors in the form of gist-based representations—which can be influenced by a range of factors. This role of meaningful representations has important consequences for understanding juror decision-making. One of those consequences is that it is vital to understand the factors that are likely to influence how jurors ascribe meaning to each construct (ie the other factors included in Figure 4.1).

As noted above, the ascription of meaning is driven by jurors using context alongside their own intuitions and beliefs to interpret information. In order to understand relevant intuitions and beliefs and how they might interact with context, it is important to understand how human intuition and beliefs are formed, how they influence decision-making (including evidence evaluation), where they improve decision-making, and where they may be susceptible to error.

Understanding intuitions and beliefs underlying representations

In the context of juror decision-making, relevant intuitions and beliefs generally result from instincts and experience as humans, rather than from formal education, since juror decision-making relies on lay knowledge rather than discipline-specific expertise (with expertise being provided at trial where it is deemed necessary). Understanding sources of intuitions and beliefs is important in evaluating their reliability and their role in juror decision-making. Here I will discuss three related sources of intuitions and beliefs: ingrained tendencies (including heuristics and biases), observations of frequency and connections, and statements of others.

Ingrained tendencies (including heuristics and biases)

Some intuitions and beliefs that we have as humans are partly a result of tendencies that are ingrained in us which can change how we interpret and apply information (including context). These tendencies include heuristics (mental shortcuts) and cognitive biases (predictable deviations from rational decision-making). Although heuristics and cognitive biases can be adaptive, they are 'highly imperfect' and have the potential to lead to mistakes in and irrational influences on decision-making.[78]

One example of a tendency that can underlie intuitions and beliefs is the tendency that we have as humans to overweight negative information (a cognitive bias known as the negativity bias in psychology). An explanation that has been given for this bias is evolutionary. Essentially, negative events are more threatening than positive events are beneficial (eg avoiding death, a negative event, is the most important factor from an evolutionary perspective).[79] This tendency may be helpful from a survival perspective but has the potential to be misleading in terms of the allocation of probative value.

[78] D Kahneman and G Klein, 'Conditions for Intuitive Expertise: A Failure to Disagree' (2009) 64(6) American Psychologist 515, 521–22.

[79] See P Rozin and EB Royzman, 'Negativity Bias, Negativity Dominance, and Contagion' (2001) 5(4) Personality and Social Psychology Review 296.

Another example of a tendency that can underlie intuitions and beliefs is the tendency to be influenced by irrelevant information received prior to making a decision (known as anchoring bias—a form of priming).[80] Put simply, information given prior to making a decision (even where irrelevant to the decision) can serve as an anchor which then biases the information that comes to mind when considering that decision.[81] This effect does not occur consciously. Rather, the information feeds into judgment outside of conscious awareness.

Other examples of heuristics and cognitive biases that appear to be ingrained in human cognition and which underlie intuitions and beliefs are confirmatory bias (seeking out and crediting evidence that is consistent with existing hypotheses),[82] motivated cognition (interpreting evidence in a way that is consistent with existing opinions),[83] identity-protective cognition (interpreting evidence in a way that is consistent with the opinion of an in-group),[84] attribute framing (being influenced by whether a particular characteristic is framed in a positive or negative light),[85] 'halo effects' (where positive/negative interpretations of a person in one area lead to more positive/negative interpretations of that person in another area),[86] and some illogical impacts of emotion (discussed above).

Observations of frequency and connections

How we learn through observing frequency and connection

The majority of our intuitions and beliefs are gained through learning purely by living in society, and much of this learning is done unconsciously. As Professor Duncan Watts has noted, humans can learn about social environments seemingly by 'osmosis', 'more or less without even knowing that we're doing it'.[87] A key mechanism through which we learn from our environment is by making observations about frequency, and the frequency with which multiple things are connected. For example, at a very simple level, a child would learn that the word 'spoon' refers to a spoon by noting that people say the word 'spoon' far more often when they are

80 See Reyna and others, 'The Gist of Juries' (n 65); Hans, Helm, and Reyna (n 65).

81 Kahneman and Klein (n 78) 521.

82 KA Carlson and JE Russo, 'Biased Interpretation of Evidence by Mock Jurors' (2001) 7(2) Journal of Experimental Psychology: Applied 91.

83 AM Sood, 'Motivated Cognition in Legal Judgments—An Analytic Review' (2013) 9 Annual Review of Law and Social Science 307; VF Reyna, 'A Scientific Theory of Gist Communication and Misinformation Resistance, With Implications for Health, Education, and Policy' (2021) 118(15) Proceedings of the National Academy of Sciences, e1912441117.

84 DM Kahan, H Jenkins-Smith, and D Braman, 'Cultural Cognition of Scientific Consensus' (2011) 14(2) Journal of Risk Research 147.

85 E Gamliel and H Kreiner, 'Applying Fuzzy-Trace Theory to Attribute-Framing Bias: Gist and Verbatim Representations of Quantitative Information' (2020) 46(3) Journal of Experimental Psychology: Learning, Memory, and Cognition 497.

86 SM Laham and JP Forgas, 'Halo Effects' in RF Pohl, *Cognitive Illusions: Intriguing Phenomena in Judgment, Thinking and Memory* (2nd edn, Routledge 2017).

87 D Watts, *Everything is Obvious: Once You Know the Answer* (Atlantic Books 2011) 7.

holding a spoon than when they are holding other objects.[88] This learning through connections continues throughout life. Put simply, we learn what is common and rare in our environment, which can influence our expectations about the future and, relatedly, about the most plausible way to interpret ambiguous evidence. For example, if people tend to encounter healthy organic food more often than non-healthy organic food they are likely to have a bias towards believing that a novel organic food is healthy.[89] Or, to give another example, people tend to encounter truth more often than lies and therefore generally have a bias towards believing a novel statement that they are told is true (known as the 'truth bias').[90]

Learning through observations of frequency and connections may also be linked to adaptive heuristics that influence intuitions and beliefs. Generally, scenarios that have occurred in the past, and particularly that happen frequently, are more likely to happen again than scenarios which have not. For example, generally a person who has behaved violently in the past is more likely to behave violently in the future. This reality likely underlies a variety of adaptive heuristics that help people navigate their environment quickly and easily. For example, people tend to accept claims or explanations as true more often when they are easier for them to imagine (a tendency known as the simulation heuristic),[91] and ease of imagination is likely linked to previous experience. More generally, we are more likely to accept claims that we can process fluidly, probably because things we can process fluidly are usually consistent with what we have observed previously and are therefore more likely to be correct.

In addition, frequency is likely to have an important role in our subjective judgments of the morality of behaviour of others—for example, what conduct is dishonest (and what conduct is sufficiently dishonest to justify the imposition of legal liability). As Professor Cass Sunstein has noted: 'whether conduct counts as unethical depends on what conduct is on people's viewscreens'—conduct may be seen as ethical when surrounded by terrible behaviour but unethical when surrounded by good behaviour.[92]

Assessing learning through frequency and connection

Learning through observing frequency and connections has key advantages, and often leads to the successful acquisition and application of knowledge. As we learn

[88] RM Hogarth, *Educating Intuition* (University of Chicago Press 2001) 81.

[89] S Perkovic and J Lund Orquin, 'Implicit Statistical Learning in Real-World Environments Leads to Ecologically Rational Decision Making' (2018) 29(1) Psychological Science 34.

[90] CNH Street, 'ALIED: Humans as Adaptive Lie Detectors' (2015) 4(4) Journal of Applied Research in Memory and Cognition 335.

[91] D Kahneman and A Tversky, *The Simulation Heuristic* (Stanford University 1981). In the legal context, see KE Niedermeier, NL Kerr, and LA Messé, 'Jurors' Use of Naked Statistical Evidence: Exploring Bases and Implications of the Wells Effect' (1999) 76(4) Journal of Personality and Social Psychology 533.

[92] C Sunstein, 'Discerning Blue from Purple: How Prevalence Affects What is Perceived as Normal' (2023) 44(3) Evolution and Human Behavior 250.

from experience it shapes our expectations for society and our interpretations of evidence in ways that are often appropriate and probative. In the example above, the child would successfully learn the meaning of the word 'spoon'. Learning from connections and frequency can allow us to account for subtle distinctions that we may not fully understand but which allow us to function effectively in society. For example, learning the subtleties of how people behave in particular social situations allows us to conform our behaviour in order to feel comfortable in social environments, and learning the cues related to people or areas most frequently associated with crime allows us to maximize our chances of being safe. However, there are also limitations associated with learning developed in this way.

Perhaps most importantly, when we learn through this type of experience, we learn what is likely to be connected but not *why* those things are connected. People end up associating a range of things without necessarily being able to articulate why or how those things are associated. This reality is problematic as it results in intuitions and beliefs that are informed by general rules (ie generalizations), which has the potential to be harmful for at least two reasons. First, it can result in intuitions and beliefs based on damaging stereotypes and proxies since people and things can end up being judged based on averages rather than individual consideration. For example, people in a community may come to associate others of a particular ethnicity with crime and as a result have a bias towards judging an innocent person of that ethnicity as likely to have committed a crime. Secondly, it can lead to inaccurate application of learning to non-experienced contexts where existing experience does not apply.[93] For example, a person may learn that they have good memory for faces by frequently remembering faces. However, if they only have experience with seeing people from the same ethnic group as them, they may inappropriately generalize their face recognition ability to groups that they do not have experience with, not knowing that their facial recognition ability is influenced by ethnicity.[94] In the case of judgments relating to morality, experience of what is common in one community may not translate well to what is common in another community, meaning someone from a community with a high level of good behaviour may judge someone from a community with a high level of poor behaviour against ethical standards that the person cannot reasonably be expected to have known about or complied with.

We can also fail to appropriately learn from frequency and connections when we do not have representative experience and effective feedback.[95] In the absence of these factors we are vulnerable to not truly knowing which things tend to be

[93] Hogarth (n 88) 83–86.
[94] CA Meissner and JC Brigham, 'Thirty Years of Investigating the Own-Race Bias in Memory for Faces: A Meta-Analytic Review' (2001) 7(1) Psychology, Public Policy, and Law 3.
[95] Hogarth (n 88) 87–90.

connected. In the case of representative experience, inaccurate intuitions and beliefs may result from skewed reporting on media platforms (eg towards unusual high-profile events) and polarized information consumption.[96] In the case of feedback, inaccurate intuitions and beliefs may result from mistakes relating to our own experience. For example, we can only accurately learn about how often we remember faces where we receive feedback on whether our memory for particular faces is correct. If we only base our beliefs about ability on experience in the absence of feedback we could be misled, for example if we think that we remember a face but actually what we have is a false memory.

Statements of others

People also develop intuitions and beliefs as a result of what they are told by others, particularly where those people are viewed as reliable authority figures. What we learn from others can have a direct impact on our intuitions and beliefs and can also impact those intuitions and beliefs through impacting the experiences that we have. For example, a parent may tell a child to be wary of a particular type of person and, as a result, the child may avoid that type of person and never gain experience that is insightful as to whether being wary of that type of person is logical.[97] Of course, relying on information from others rather than learning from one's own experience presents a risk of misunderstanding and misconception, and, perhaps even more importantly, the spread of misunderstanding and misconception in communities and even through generations.

Importantly, perceptions of who is trustworthy and therefore who is learned from can be influenced by a range of factors other than true trustworthiness of the source. For example, research suggests that a cognitive bias known as 'identity-protective cognition', introduced above, leads to people being more likely to believe an expert who is espousing an opinion that is consistent with (as opposed to inconsistent with) the opinion of their cultural group rather than rationally evaluating credentials and knowledge.[98] This effect is thought to occur, sometimes unconsciously, as a result of a need that we have to protect ourselves (eg from estrangement from an in-group). The current reality of polarized consumption of information mentioned above is also relevant here—we become in danger of sitting in echo chambers and somewhat automatically believing people whom we are predisposed to believe.[99]

[96] See eg PM Napoli, 'What if More Speech is No Longer the Answer? First Amendment Theory Meets Fake News and the Filter Bubble' (2018) 70(1) Federal Communications Law Journal 55; C Lombardi, 'The Illusion of a "Marketplace of Ideas" and the Right to Truth' (2019) 3(1) American Affairs 198.

[97] ibid 87.

[98] Kahan, Jenkins-Smith, and Braman (n 84).

[99] For discussion, see RK Helm and H Nasu, 'Regulatory Responses to "Fake News" and Freedom of Expression: Normative and Empirical Evaluation' (2021) 21(2) Human Rights Law Review 302.

Intuitions and beliefs in juror decision-making

Identifying and evaluating sources of intuitions and beliefs that are likely to feed into mental representations is important in deciphering how jurors are likely to work. The discussion above highlights how our experience in society may be beneficial in understanding society, and in accounting for subtle cues relating to behaviour in society that may interact with each other in various ways. However, it also highlights risks as to where intuitions and beliefs may be misleading generally, or misleading specifically in the context of factual judgments that should be reached 'beyond a reasonable doubt'. The discussion highlights four primary ways in which intuitions and beliefs that feed into representations can be misleading: where they result from the operation of heuristics and cognitive biases, where they result from inappropriate generalizations, where they arise in the absence of representative experience and effective feedback, and where they are formed as the result of reliance on a statement of a particular person rather than as the result of experience or investigation. Intuitions and beliefs that fall into one of these categories, as with intuitions and beliefs more generally, are likely to feed into representations underlying juror decisions and have the potential to compromise the effective function of the jury according to the criteria outlined in Chapter 3. They must therefore be understood and accounted for by legal procedure.

Conclusions

In this chapter I have suggested that juror ascription of meaning to pieces of evidence, trial participants, the body of evidence, and legal standards, in the form of gist-based representations, is central to understanding the juror decision-making process. Meaning that is ascribed to pieces of evidence, trial participants, the body of evidence, and legal standards will result from combining context and juror intuitions and beliefs with information itself. These intuitions and beliefs are likely to result from the operation of ingrained tendencies (including heuristics and cognitive biases), observations of frequencies and connections, and/or believing statements made by others. This ascription of meaning is advanced and necessary to incorporate nuances of evidence into legal decision-making. However, the centrality of meaning to gist-based representations means that representations may be influenced by intuitions and beliefs susceptible to error as a result of the operation of heuristics and cognitive biases, inappropriate generalizations, the absence of representative experience and effective feedback, or being formed as the result of reliance on a statement of a particular person rather than as the result of experience or investigation.

Through accounting for the importance of meaningful representations of evidence, trial participants, the body of evidence, and legal standards, the Representation-Based Model provides a helpful framework which can bring together much existing work on juror decision-making in a way that has the potential to be helpful in guiding both future research and policy. In the next three chapters, I examine how relationships between juror decisions and juror characteristics (Chapter 5), case characteristics (Chapter 6), and legal standards and procedures (Chapter 7) can be explained by the relationships between each of these factors and the assignment of meaning. Through exploring ways in which various factors in each of these categories may influence the assignment of meaning, I provide new insight into influences on juror verdict preferences. I then draw on this insight to examine the normative acceptability of influences on jurors and to begin to consider factors that need addressing in order to promote optimal jury function.

5
Juror Characteristics

Introduction

Existing research, including both experimental work and examination of real jury decisions, has shown that verdict preferences are determined not only by case evidence, but also by the characteristics of the jurors who evaluate that evidence. Understanding the juror characteristics that are associated with legal decisions, and causal pathways that can explain those associations, gives important insight into intuitions and beliefs underlying juror decision-making. The Representation-Based Model outlined in the previous chapter suggests that juror characteristics have the potential to feed directly and indirectly into juror representations of individual pieces of evidence, trial participants, the body of evidence, and legal standards, specifically where juror characteristics influence intuitions and beliefs which underlie those representations (given that juror characteristics clearly do not influence evidence, trial participants, or legal standards themselves).

In this chapter I identify literature demonstrating associations between juror characteristics and verdicts and examine how these associations can be explained by relationships between juror characteristics and the meaning assigned to evidence, trial participants, the body of evidence, and legal standards (ie through differences in relevant representations). Seven distinct characteristics will be considered, grouped under two headings: (1) *juror attitudes, beliefs, and experiences* including political opinions (including authoritarianism), legal attitudes (including legal system trust), case-specific beliefs, and experiences, and (2) *individual differences and demographics* including need for cognition and cognitive processing, gender, and race. Based on this examination I assess the normative desirability of relationships between juror characteristics and verdicts against the criteria outlined in Chapter 3. I conclude by drawing on this examination to briefly assess what these relationships tell us about how jurors work and, crucially, how jurors might work better.

Section I: Associations Between Juror Characteristics and Verdicts

Juror attitudes, beliefs, and experiences

A relatively large body of research demonstrates that juror attitudes and beliefs are related to their legal determinations, and group legal determinations following

How Juries Work. Rebecca K. Helm, Oxford University Press. © Rebecca K. Helm 2024.
DOI: 10.1093/9780191948107.003.0005

deliberations. The majority of this research has been conducted using mock juries, since it is typically not feasible to measure juror attitudes and perspectives in actual legal cases.

Political opinions

First, research has shown a relationship between political beliefs and decision-making in criminal trials. The clearest relationship between juror political beliefs and verdicts has been shown when examining *authoritarianism* (the extent to which a person values clear rules, social order, conventional norms, and strong leadership). Two meta-analyses in the United States (US) context considering mock jury work suggest a positive association between authoritarianism and guilty verdicts such that jurors who have higher levels of authoritarianism are more likely to find a defendant guilty (although both suggest the relationship between authoritarianism and verdicts is relatively modest).[1] Research has also provided support for this association at a jury (rather than juror) level, in that mock juries with greater proportions of jurors high in authoritarianism have been found to be more likely to convict in some contexts.[2] The relationship between authoritarianism and verdict may vary depending on case type—in one of the meta-analyses referred to above, the authors found the strongest relationship between authoritarianism and verdicts in homicide cases and capital trials, and a much weaker relationship in sexual assault cases.[3]

More generally, research across multiple jurisdictions has shown that a variety of juror political opinions are associated with different patterns in verdicts depending on case subject matter. This effect is generally in line with politically partisan values; for example, work has found that conservative jurors may be more willing than liberal jurors to accept a defence based on 'gay panic',[4] that political conservatism may be linked to not guilty verdicts in sexual assault trials,[5] and that jurors with more hierarchical and individualistic values may be more likely than jurors with more egalitarian and communitarian values to accept a self-defence argument in a case involving a commuter defending himself from a

[1] D Narby, B Cutler, and G Moran, 'A Meta-Analysis of the Association Between Authoritarianism and Jurors' Perceptions of Defendant Culpability' (1993) 78(1) Journal of Applied Psychology 34; D Devine and D Caughlin, 'Do They Matter? A Meta-Analytic Investigation of Individual Characteristics and Guilt Judgments' (2014) 20(2) Psychology, Public Policy, and Law 109.

[2] R Bray and A Noble, 'Authoritarianism and Decisions of Mock Juries: Evidence of Jury Bias and Group Polarization' (1978) 36(12) Journal of Personality and Social Psychology 1424. Although this finding has not been replicated in all contexts, see eg S Lundrigan, M Dhami, and K Muller-Johnson, 'Predicting Verdicts Using Pre-Trial Attitudes and Standard of Proof' (2016) 21(1) Legal and Criminological Psychology 95.

[3] Devine and Caughlin (n 1) 118.

[4] J Salerno and others, 'Excusing Murder? Conservative Jurors' Acceptance of the Gay-Panic Defence' (2015) 21(1) Psychology, Public Policy, and Law 24.

[5] N Taylor and J Joudo Larsen, *The Impact of Pre-Recorded Video and Closed Circuit Television on Testimony by Adult Sexual Assault Complainants on Jury Decision-Making: An Experimental Study* (Australian Institute of Criminology 2005).

drunk victim but less likely than those jurors to accept a self-defence argument in a case involving a woman defending herself from an abusive partner.[6] In a related context involving real decisions (specifically in the context of lay judges rather than jurors), an empirical study of the Gothenburg District Court in Sweden (where politically appointed lay judges known as *nämndemän* are used) found that convictions for young defendants and those with distinctly Arabic names increased when lay judges from a far-right party were assigned, whereas convictions in cases with a female victim increased when lay judges from a far-left party were assigned.[7]

Legal attitudes

A related but distinct factor that has been consistently found to be associated with verdicts is juror pretrial legal attitudes. Measures of pretrial legal attitudes have been developed, and their impact on juror verdicts examined in mock jury work. For example, the Juror Bias Scale (JBS) measures general pro-defence and pro-prosecution attitudes, through asking participants the extent to which they agree with a set of statements, such as 'defence lawyers don't really care about guilt or innocence, they are just in business to make money' and 'if a majority of evidence—but not all of it—suggests that the defendant committed the crime, the jury should vote not guilty'.[8] Another measure of juror attitudes is the Pre-Trial Juror Attitudes Questionnaire (PJAQ). This questionnaire measures the extent to which participants agree with statements across six subscales—conviction proneness (eg 'criminals should be caught and convicted by any means possible'); cynicism towards defence (eg 'in most cases where the accused presents a strong defence, it is only because of a good lawyer'); social justice (eg 'rich individuals are almost never convicted of their crimes'); racial bias (eg 'minorities only use the "race issue" when they are guilty'); system confidence (eg 'if a suspect runs from the police, then he probably committed the crime'); and innate criminality (eg 'once a criminal, always a criminal').[9] These measures have been shown to be predictive of juror decisions in a variety of jurisdictions and contexts. For example:

1. A mock jury study in Spain identified jurors as either prosecution biased or defence biased based on responses to the JBS and examined their

[6] D Kahan and D Braman, 'The Self-Defensive Cognition of Self-Defense' (2008) 45(1) American Criminal Law Review 1.

[7] S Anwar, P Bayer, and R Hjalmarsson, 'Politics in the Courtroom: Political Ideology and Jury Decision-Making' (2019) 17(3) Journal of the European Economic Association 834.

[8] S Kassin and L Wrightsman, 'The Construction and Validation of a Juror Bias Scale' (1983) 17(4) Journal of Research in Personality 423.

[9] L Lecci and B Myers, 'Individual Differences in Attitudes Relevant to Juror Decision Making: Development and Validation of the Pretrial Juror Attitude Questionnaire' (2008) 38(8) Journal of Applied Social Psychology 2010.

decisions both before and after group deliberations in a mock homicide case.[10] The study found that where case evidence favoured the prosecution, prosecution-biased and defence-biased jurors did not make different decisions, but where case evidence was ambiguous, prosecution-biased jurors were marginally more likely to find a defendant guilty, both before and after deliberations.

2. A mock jury study in England and Wales examined pretrial legal attitudes of jurors using the JBS and PJAQ (as well as a measure of authoritarianism and a measure of interpretations of the beyond reasonable doubt standard), and decisions of the same jurors in a residential burglary case.[11] Results showed significant positive correlations between the JBS and PJAQ and the verdict, such that more prosecution-friendly attitudes were associated with a higher likelihood of finding the defendant guilty.
3. A mock jury study in Australia examined pretrial attitudes in jurors using an amended subset of JBS items measuring attitudes relating to the probability of commission of an offence (in addition to other scales) and the decisions of jurors both before and after deliberations in a terrorism-related murder case.[12] Results showed a significant positive association between the bias measure and verdicts, such that jurors with more pro-prosecution attitudes relating to the probability of offence commission were more likely to find that the defendant was guilty. This effect persisted, and actually got stronger, after deliberations.
4. A small mock jury study in Canada examined attitudes towards the legal system using the PJAQ split into its subscales and mock juror decisions in murder and property offence cases that varied in defendant appearance (using either a face generally rated as more trustworthy, or a face generally rated as more untrustworthy).[13] Results showed that higher scores on the racial bias subscale of the PJAQ were associated with an increased probability of convicting the defendant even in light of exonerating evidence, specifically in cases involving an 'untrustworthy-looking' defendant. The authors concluded that untrustworthy faces may activate the influence of particular biases.

[10] L De La Fuente, EI De La Fuente, and J García, 'Effects of Pretrial Juror Bias, Strength of Evidence and Deliberation Process on Juror Decisions: New Validity Evidence of The Juror Bias Scale Scores' (2003) 9(2) Psychology, Crime & Law 197.

[11] Lundrigan, Dhami, and Mueller-Johnson (n 2).

[12] D Tait, 'Deliberating About Terrorism: Prejudice and Jury Verdicts in a Mock Terrorism Trial' (2011) 44(3) Australian and New Zealand Journal of Criminology 387.

[13] N Korva and others, 'Dangerous Decisions: Influence of Juror Attitudes and Defendant Appearance on Legal Decision-Making' (2013) 20(3) Psychiatry, Psychology and Law 384.

Case-specific beliefs

More case-specific attitudes and beliefs have also been found to be related to juror verdict decisions. In the sentencing context, research drawing on real juror interviews in the USA suggests that jurors who support the death penalty are more likely to find that a defendant should receive the death penalty in capital cases.[14] Importantly, beliefs associated with juror decisions can be inconsistent with established evidence or legal standards and research shows that these beliefs can continue to influence verdicts despite expert testimony.

This influence of likely erroneous or legally inconsistent beliefs has been shown in multiple contexts in mock jury research, for example: beliefs about insanity (such as 'I believe all human beings know what they're doing and have the power to control themselves' and 'I believe that people should be held responsible for their actions no matter what their mental condition') have been shown to be associated with verdicts in a case involving the insanity defence,[15] and with evaluations of relevant expert testimony;[16] beliefs relating to memory (such as 'a child eyewitness is more reliable than an adult eyewitness') have been shown to be associated with guilt judgments in trials involving witness testimony;[17] and endorsement of 'rape myths' (commonly held beliefs that are false, such as the idea that if a woman is wearing provocative clothing or has consumed alcohol she is partly to blame for her rape) have been associated with not guilty verdicts in sexual offence trials.[18]

Experiences

Finally, mock jury research has shown an association between the experiences of jurors and their judgments in legal cases. For example, one USA-based meta-analysis found that mock jurors with sexual abuse experiences (specifically those who were victimized themselves or knew other victims) assigned more guilt to defendants in sexual abuse cases.[19]

[14] T Eisenberg, S Garvey, and M Wells, 'Forecasting Life and Death: Juror Race, Religion, and Attitude Toward the Death Penalty' (2001) 30(2) Journal of Legal Studies 277.

[15] Michael V and others, 'Measuring Attitudes Toward the Insanity Defense in Venirepersons: Refining the IDA-R in the Evaluation of Juror Bias' (2009) 8(1) International Journal of Forensic Mental Health 62.

[16] See eg D Krauss and others, 'Mental State at Time of Offence in the Hot Tub: An Empirical Examination of Concurrent Expert Testimony in an Insanity Case' (2018) 36(3) Behavioral Sciences & the Law 358.

[17] T Neal and others, 'The Effects of Mock Jurors' Beliefs About Eyewitness Performance on Trial Judgments' (2012) 18(1) Psychology, Crime & Law 49.

[18] S Dinos and others, 'A Systematic Review of Juries' Assessment of Rape Victims: Do Rape Myths Impact on Juror Decision-Making?' (2015) 43(1) International Journal of Law, Crime and Justice 36.

[19] T Jones, B Bottoms, and M Stevenson, 'Child Victim Empathy Mediates the Influence of Jurors' Sexual Abuse Experiences on Child Sexual Abuse Case Judgments: Meta-Analyses' (2020) 26(3) Psychology, Public Policy, and Law 312.

Individual differences and demographics

Research has also provided insight into the relationships between individual differences and demographics in jurors and case verdicts. Several important relationships have emerged, as discussed below. Again, the majority of this research has been conducted using mock juries, due to the challenges of examining juror differences and demographics in real cases.

Need for cognition and cognitive processing

The relationship between juror education and verdicts remains unclear, with a number of studies finding no significant association between juror education and verdicts. A meta-analysis examining a range of mock jury work found no evidence for an association between juror education and verdicts,[20] and even work involving evaluations of relatively complex scientific evidence has not shown a relationship between education and verdicts.[21] However, work has demonstrated a link between related characteristics and verdicts. Importantly, research suggests that these related characteristics are distinct from education and intelligence, reflecting thinking dispositions.[22] One such characteristic is 'need for cognition', which refers to the tendency of a person to engage in and enjoy thinking. Research has identified a number of potential positive effects of high need for cognition in jurors. For example, mock jury research suggests jurors who are higher in need for cognition distinguish better between high and low-quality expert evidence,[23] that jurors with higher need for cognition are less influenced by negative pretrial publicity,[24] and that at least where the threat of bias is obvious, jurors high in need for cognition are more likely to overcome potential bias.[25]

Relatedly, research has drawn on insight from cognitive psychology to identify individual differences in the way that people process information and the relationship that this has with the decision-making of people acting as jurors. This research provides insight into how differences in cognitive processing in jurors may influence legal verdicts. One theory that has been used to provide insight into juror decision-making is Cognitive Experiential Self Theory (CEST). CEST is a dual-process theory that posits that information can be processed either in a

[20] Devine and Caughlin (n 1).

[21] J Koehler and others, 'Science, Technology, or the Expert Witness: What Influences Jurors' Judgments About Forensic Science Testimony' (2016) 22(4) Psychology, Public Policy, and Law 401.

[22] See eg K Stanovich, 'On the Distinction Between Rationality and Intelligence: Implications for Understanding Individual Differences in Reasoning' in KJ Holyoak and RG Morrison (eds), *The Oxford Handbook of Thinking and Reasoning* (OUP 2012) 433–55.

[23] See eg B McAuliff and M Kovera, 'Juror Need for Cognition and Sensitivity to Methodological Flaws in Expert Evidence' (2008) 38(2) Journal of Applied Social Psychology 385.

[24] C Ruva, 'The Impact of Pretrial Publicity and Need for Cognition on Mock-Jurors' Decisions and Deliberation Behavior' (2016) 6(1) International Journal of Psychology and Behavioral Sciences 20.

[25] D Wegener and others, 'Flexible Corrections of Juror Judgments: Implications for Jury Instructions' (2000) 6(3) Psychology, Public Policy, and Law 629.

rational way (with an emphasis on analysis, fact, and logic) or in an experiential way (with an emphasis on emotion and personal experience).[26] A series of experimental studies has provided empirical support for these constructs.[27] Mock jury research has examined the relationship between reliance on more rational or more experiential processing and juror decisions. The majority of this work has examined how manipulations of evidence presentation that trigger rational or experiential processing influence decisions. This work suggests that reliance on experiential processing leads to greater susceptibility to bias (eg based on the appearance of a defendant).[28] One mock jury study found a similar result looking specifically at the tendency of jurors to rely more on rational or experiential processing. Results showed a bias based on defendant attractiveness (as rated during pre-testing) in jurors relying more on experiential processing but not in jurors relying more on rational processing.[29]

Gender

The relationship between juror gender and verdict decisions is variable, with research suggesting that there is sometimes a relationship between juror gender and verdict, but that this relationship varies by case type.

A meta-analysis examining the influence of juror characteristics on case verdicts found that in mock jury studies using community residents or *venirepersons* (as opposed to students) as participants, there was no significant relationship between gender and verdicts.[30] However, studies in specific contexts have found a relationship between gender and verdicts. In some cases, women have been found to be more punitive; for example: a meta-analysis examining mock jury work in rape and child sexual abuse cases found that women were significantly more likely than men to vote for conviction;[31] mock jury research examining decisions in a case involving a defendant accused of actual bodily harm found that female jurors

[26] Note that the influence of emotion on case verdicts is discussed in detail in Chapter 4.

[27] See eg V Denes-Raj and S Epstein, 'Conflict Between Intuitive and Rational Processing: When People Behave Against Their Better Judgment' (1994) 66(5) Journal of Personality and Social Psychology 819; S Epstein and others, 'Individual Differences in Intuitive-Experiential and Analytical-Rational Thinking Styles' (1996) 71(2) Journal of Personality and Social Psychology 390. See also S Epstein, 'Integration of the Cognitive and the Psychodynamic Unconscious' (1994) 49(8) American Psychologist 709. Although, for conflicting evidence, see V Reyna and C Brainerd, 'Numeracy, Ratio Bias, and Denominator Neglect in Judgments of Risk and Probability' (2008) 18(1) Learning and Individual Differences 89.

[28] J Lieberman, 'Head Over the Heart or Heart Over The Head? Cognitive Experiential Self-Theory and Extralegal Heuristics in Juror Decision Making' (2002) 32(12) Journal of Applied Social Psychology 2526; D Krauss, J Lieberman, and J Olson, 'The Effects of Rational and Experiential Information Processing of Expert Testimony in Death Penalty Cases' (2004) 22(6) Behavioral Sciences & the Law 801.

[29] J Gunnell and S Ceci, 'When Emotionality Trumps Reason: A Study of Individual Processing Style and Juror Bias' (2010) 28(6) Behavioral Sciences and the Law 850.

[30] Devine and Caughlin (n 1).

[31] J Schutte and H Hosch, 'Gender Differences in Sexual Assault Verdicts: A Meta-Analysis' (1997) 12(3) Journal of Social Behavior and Personality 761.

were more likely to vote to convict the defendant at the start of deliberations (although note that deliberations had a greater impact on female jurors, and female jurors had lower conviction rates than male jurors did post-deliberation);[32] mock jury research examining an alleged father-perpetrated infanticide found that female jurors rendered more guilty verdicts than male mock jurors and perceived the defendant as having greater intent to kill his infant;[33] and mock jury research in Australia found female jurors to be more punitive in sentencing an Indigenous defendant than male jurors were.[34]

However, in other contexts research has found that men are more punitive. For example, one mock jury study examined juror decisions in a patricide case involving child sexual abuse allegations. Results indicated that women generally considered the defendant to be less responsible for the murder than men did.[35] In addition, studies examining mock juror decisions in death-penalty cases in the USA have found men to be more likely than women to choose the death penalty,[36] and female jurors to be more receptive to mitigation than male counterparts.[37]

Race

Research has shown that juror race is associated with differences in verdicts, particularly when juror race differs from defendant race.[38] A 2005 meta-analysis drawing on data from twenty-nine mock jury studies found evidence of a small outgroup bias—meaning that jurors were generally more likely to find a defendant guilty if the defendant was from a different racial group from them.[39] This meta-analysis found that racial bias in juror verdicts was stronger when jury instructions were not provided, and in older studies of decision-making (specifically studies conducted or published in the 1970s). Additional studies suggest that the relationship between juror race and legal decisions is moderated by context and crime. For example, a series of mock jury research studies has shown that juror bias against other racial groups is less marked in trials in which race is specifically brought up.[40]

[32] C Thomas, *Are Juries Fair?* (Ministry of Justice Research Series 1/10, February 2010) 19.

[33] B Bottoms and others, 'Gender Differences in Jurors' Perceptions of Infanticide Involving Disabled and Non-Disabled Infant Victims' (2011) 35(2) Child Abuse and Neglect 127.

[34] R ForsterLee and others, 'The Effects of Defendant Race, Victim Race, and Juror Gender on Evidence Processing in a Murder Trial' (2006) 24(2) Behavioral Sciences and the Law 179.

[35] T Haegerich and B Bottoms, 'Empathy and Jurors' Decisions in Patricide Trials Involving Child Sexual Assault Allegations' (2000) 24(4) Law and Human Behavior 421.

[36] C Beckham, B Spray, and C Pietz, 'Jurors' Locus of Control and Defendants' Attractiveness in Death Penalty Sentencing' (2007) 147(3) Journal of Social Psychology 285.

[37] T Brewer, 'Race and Jurors Receptivity to Mitigation in Capital Cases: The Effect of Jurors', Defendants', and Victims' Race in Combination' (2004) 28(5) Law and Human Behavior 529.

[38] A significant amount of related research has examined the impact of defendant and victim race on jury decision-making more generally; this research is considered in Chapter 6.

[39] T Mitchell and others, 'Racial Bias in Mock Juror Decision-Making: A Meta-Analytic Review of Defendant Treatment' (2005) 29(6) Law and Human Behavior 621.

[40] S Sommers and P Ellsworth, 'White Juror Bias: An Investigation of Prejudice Against Black Defendants in the American Courtroom' (2001) 7(1) Psychology, Public Policy, and Law 201; E Cohn

Mock jury research also suggests that where a crime is stereotypically associated with defendant race, racial bias is likely to be stronger.[41]

Out-group bias has been clearly demonstrated in the US context in capital cases, where research has demonstrated a clear association between juror race and verdicts. For example, one archival investigation examined racial composition and jury decisions in 340 US capital trials and found that the greater the proportion of white jurors to Black jurors, the more likely a Black defendant was to be sentenced to death, particularly if the victim in the case was white.[42] This finding has been supported by separate archival data.[43] The presence of out-group bias is particularly important where a particular racial group (eg white jurors) make up the majority of jurors, due to the differential impact that group is likely to have on deliberations.[44]

Section II: Explaining the Relationships Between Juror Characteristics and Verdicts

Paths through which juror characteristics influence verdicts

According to the Representation-Based Model suggested in the previous chapter, there are four primary routes through which differences in juror characteristics might result in systematically different verdicts: through influencing their mental representations of pieces of evidence, through influencing their mental representations of trial participants, through influencing their mental representations of the body of evidence, and through influencing their mental representations of legal standards (and, relatedly, the behaviour that falls within or outside those standards). Different juror characteristics are likely to be associated with some differences in beliefs and intuitions (and therefore differences in the assignment of meaning), for example as the result of differential experiences, group-membership, and information consumption. These differences have the potential to influence the operation of relevant heuristics and biases, the frequencies and connections that people will have observed, and the sources of information that people are

and others, 'Reducing White Juror Bias: The Role of Race Salience and Racial Attitudes' (2009) 39(8) Journal of Applied Social Psychology 1953.

[41] C Jones and M Kaplan, 'The Effects of Racially Stereotypical Crimes on Juror Decision-Making and Information Processing Strategies' (2003) 25(1) Journal of Basic and Applied Social Psychology 1.

[42] W Bowers, B Steiner, and M Sandys, 'Death Sentencing in Black and White: An Empirical Analysis of Jurors' Race and Jury Racial Composition' (2001) 3 University of Pennsylvania Journal of Constitutional Law 171.

[43] H Daudistel and others, 'Effects of Defendant Ethnicity on Juries' Dispositions of Felony Cases' (1999) 29 Journal of Applied Social Psychology 1314.

[44] See eg Eisenberg, Garvey, and Wells (n 14).

likely to trust. In this section, I will consider existing work demonstrating relationships between juror characteristics and the assignment of meaning to pieces of evidence, trial participants, the body of evidence, and legal standards, that can explain the identified associations between juror characteristics and verdicts.

Impacts on representation of evidence

A range of existing evidence suggests that jurors with different characteristics will evaluate pieces of evidence differently, for a range of reasons. It is important to note that, consistent with the Story Model, associations between juror characteristics and their evaluations of evidence (and their representations of evidence) will become more likely and stronger as that evidence becomes more ambiguous and, as a result, there is increasing room for differing interpretations of evidence. If evidence is very strong and clear or a fact pattern is a strong match to a legal standard, juror intuitions and beliefs are likely to align, regardless of juror characteristics.

Perhaps most obviously, jurors with different characteristics can have systematically different beliefs that are directly relevant to evidence evaluation. One area in which differential beliefs have been demonstrated is legal cases involving testimony from child complainants where sexual assault is involved. Researchers found that, on average, women held different beliefs then men about the credibility of children and that these differences in beliefs partly explained differences in verdicts in a case reliant on testimony from a child. Specifically, women believed that statements made by children were more reliable than men did, and this partially explained the fact that women were more likely to believe allegations made by a child complainant than men were.[45] Importantly, existing research suggests that the prevalence of problematic beliefs may differ based on demographics. For example, a body of research shows that men are more likely than women to believe 'rape myths'.[46]

Other more subtle influences, often impacting legal verdicts in ways that are outside of conscious awareness also have the potential to be important in explaining the role of juror characteristics. One type of belief that has been noted as important, particularly in the context of lay testimony evaluation, is belief as to the relative prevalence of events alleged by prosecution and defence witnesses (or, more specifically, a vague underlying impression of how common these events are, likely influenced by observations of frequency and connection).[47] In fact, the

[45] B Bottoms and others, 'Explaining Gender Differences in Jurors' Reactions to Child Sexual Assault Cases' (2014) 32(6) Behavioral Sciences and the Law 789.

[46] See eg KJ Russell and CJ Hand, 'Rape Myth Acceptance, Victim Blame Attribution, and Just World Beliefs: A Rapid Evidence Assessment' (2017) 37 Aggression and Violent Behavior 153.

[47] RK Helm and B Growns, 'Prevalence Estimates as Priors: Juror Characteristics, Perceived Base Rates, and Verdicts in Cases Reliant on Complainant and Defendant Testimony' (2022) 36(4) Applied Cognitive Psychology 891. See also RK Helm, 'Adaptive Lie Detection and Perceived Prevalence of False Reports in Evaluation of Sexual Offense Allegations' (2023) 13(1) Journal of Applied Research in Memory and Cognition 82.

prevalence of underlying alleged events is logically relevant to interpreting ambiguous evidence. Put simply, more prevalent events are more likely to explain ambiguous facts than less prevalent ones—neglecting this reality is a form of base rate neglect. In medical literature this sentiment has been captured by the phrase 'when you hear hooves think of horses not zebras'.[48] So, for example, in the context of sexual offences, if false allegations are very common, a particular allegation is more likely to be false, but if false allegations are very rare, a particular allegation is more likely to be true. Existing work has provided support for the idea that estimates of underlying prevalence influence legal verdicts, specifically in the context of testimony evaluation.[49] Importantly, in predictable situations, such estimates differ based on characteristics of people making those estimates. For example, research has shown that as people's political beliefs become more hierarchical, they tend to believe that the prevalence of false allegations is higher, and this higher rated prevalence leads them to more defence-friendly evaluations of testimony (and related verdicts) in cases involving sexual assault.[50] Different jurors may also have different intuitions informed by experience and information consumption that make it easier (or more difficult) for them to imagine a particular account being true (eg as a result of the stimulation heuristic discussed in the previous chapter). As a result, some jurors can be influenced by problematic factors even when they do not explicitly endorse related beliefs. For example, a juror who only has only learned about sexual assault through traditional media portrayal of assaults in which the victim fights back may not believe that victims of rape always fight back, but may still find it intuitively difficult to believe a victim who did not fight back, as a result of finding it hard to imagine a victim behaving in that way.

The way that jurors process and scrutinize evidence (influenced by individual differences, eg in need for cognition) has also been shown to impact how people represent evidence, and the probative value they ascribe to it.[51] A juror with low need for cognition may represent evidence in a way that is superficial or does not incorporate clear flaws or strengths in the evidence.

Research has also shown that the same evidence can be interpreted in different ways by people with different characteristics as a result of a cognitive bias known as identity-protective cognition, introduced in Chapter 4. Identity-protective cognition refers to a tendency to seek out and credit information supportive of

[48] See eg AM Hart and KS Moore, 'When You Hear Hoofbeats, Think Horses—But Be Prepared for Zebras' (2019) 15(6) Journal for Nurse Practitioners 10, 10.

[49] SM Kassin and others, '"I'd Know a False Confession if I Saw One": A Comparative Study of College Students and Police Investigators' (2005) 29(2) Law and Human Behavior 211; K Domagalski and others, 'Detecting Children's True and False Denials of Wrongdoing: Effects of Question Type and Base Rate Knowledge' (2020) 38(6) Behavioral Sciences & the Law 612; Helm (n 47). For more information on the role of base rates in evaluations of honesty more generally, see CNH Street, 'ALIED: Humans as Adaptive Lie Detectors' (2015) 4(4) Journal of Applied Research in Memory and Cognition 335.

[50] Helm and Growns (n 47).

[51] See eg McAuliff and Kovera (n 23).

self-defining values (in other words values that are supportive of the beliefs associated with the groups to which they belong).[52] This tendency means that, particularly in cases invoking self-defining values (eg that invoke issues relating to gender norms or mental health), jurors are likely to interpret evidence in a way that adheres to those values even when they are attempting to decide neutrally and in accordance with law. An influence of identity-protective cognition on verdicts has been empirically supported in the context of juror assessments of reasonableness. Mock jury research examining politically polarizing cases, specifically self-defence cases[53] and acquaintance-rape cases,[54] has used quantitative analyses to provide support for the contention that juror beliefs can influence verdicts through influencing the way that jurors perceive evidence. For example, in the self-defence case, structural equation models provided support for the prediction that political attitudes (as well as race, gender, and education) influenced fact perceptions (such as the belief that it was unreasonable for a woman to shoot her husband in self-defence as there were other ways that she could have protected herself) which then influenced the verdict.[55] Importantly, research specifically suggests that identity-protective cognition can influence evaluations of scientific evidence as well as more ambiguous factual judgments. Research on expert evidence more generally has shown that identity-protective cognition can influence interpretations of expert credibility, meaning that experts are more likely to be interpreted as credible when they are giving opinions that accord with self-defining values.[56] In the legal context this creates the potential that, at least in cases in which self-defining values are implicated, jurors may find experts who give evidence supporting the stance that is in line with their values more credible (and vice versa). For example, beliefs on whether a person should be held accountable for their actions regardless of mental state would be likely to influence views on the credibility of an expert giving evidence on psychological or neurological disorders in a case involving potential insanity. This influence of identity-protective cognition can explain relationships between demographics such as juror race or gender on decisions, as well the influence of attitudes. Specifically, experimental research suggests that identity-protective cognition may explain relationships between race and gender and decisions, since cultural attitudes and norms can feature race and gender differentiation.[57]

[52] D Kahan and others, 'Culture and Identity-Protective Cognition: Explaining the White-Male Effect in Risk Perception' (2007) 4(3) Journal of Empirical Legal Studies 465, 470.

[53] Kahan and Braman (n 6).

[54] D Kahan, 'Culture, Cognition, and Consent: Who Perceives What, and Why, in Acquaintance-Rape Cases' (2010) 158(3) University of Pennsylvania Law Review 729.

[55] Kahan and Braman (n 6).

[56] A Fragale and C Heath, 'Evolving Information Credentials: The (Mis)Attribution of Believable Facts to Credible Sources' (2004) 30(2) Personality and Social Psychology Bulletin 225; D Kahan, H Jenkins-Smith, and D Braman, 'Cultural Cognition of Scientific Consensus' (2011) 14(2) Journal of Risk Research 147.

[57] Kahan and others (n 52).

Impacts on representation of trial participants

Existing research also suggests that juror characteristics may influence the way they see and relate to trial participants (and therefore how they are likely to represent those trial participants in memory) and as a result influence their judgments. Importantly, representations of trial participants (which may differ based on juror characteristics) can influence evaluations of evidence, as well as having their own separable influence on verdicts. More generally, it is also important to note that liking a trial participant or seeing them in a positive light (eg for the reasons discussed below) is likely to lead to more positive representations about them more generally through cognitive biases known in psychology as 'halo effects'[58] (introduced in Chapter 4).

First, research shows that empathy with the victim or defendant in a case can bias a juror towards assigning meaning to ambiguous case facts in a favourable way towards that party.[59] For example, one mock jury study found that participants who empathized with rape victims (assessed by scores on the 'Rape Empathy Scale') placed less responsibility on victims in a case than those who did not, and were more likely to find an accused person guilty.[60] Differences in empathy can explain some of the associations described above, for example the association between gender and verdicts in child sexual assault cases. Specifically, mock jury research described above found that empathy (in addition to case-specific beliefs) mediated the identified relationship between juror gender and verdicts.[61] This finding suggests that at least one reason that women make more prosecution-friendly judgments in child sexual assault cases is that they have greater empathy for child victims that can lead them to interpret evidence in a sympathetic way towards them. Empathy may also be important in explaining the relationship between other characteristics and verdicts. In the case of race, research specifically suggests that out-group bias may be caused by reduced empathy for out-group members.[62]

Secondly, the culpable control theory of blame attribution, a theory based on a cognitive bias known as motivated cognition (introduced in Chapter 4), suggests that people's judgments about the morality of a trial participant can influence

[58] SM Laham and JP Forgas, 'Halo Effects' in RF Pohl, *Cognitive Illusions: Intriguing Phenomena in Judgment, Thinking and Memory* (2nd edn, Routledge 2017). Although see AC Austin and others, 'No Halo Effect For Sex Offenders: An Examination of the Effects of Appearance and Gender on the Public's Perception of Sex Offenders' (2013) 9(2) Applied Psychology in Criminal Justice 124.

[59] More generally empathy has been shown to have a substantial impact on decision-making and has also been shown to differ based on social group membership (eg race or gender); JD Weinberg and LB Nielsen, 'Examining Empathy: Discrimination, Experience, and Judicial Decisionmaking' (2011) 85(2) Southern California Law Review 313, 325–26.

[60] S Deitz and L Byrnes, 'Attribution of Responsibility for Sexual Assaults: The Influence of Observer Empathy and Criminal Occupation and Attractiveness' (1981) 108 The Journal of Psychology 17.

[61] Bottoms and others, 'Explaining Gender Differences in Jurors' Reactions' (n 46).

[62] J Johnson and others, 'Rodney King and O.J. Revisited: The Impact of Race and Defendant Empathy Induction on Judicial Decisions' (2002) 32(6) Journal of Applied Social Psychology 1208.

(and bias) their allocation of meaning to evidence, even where these judgments are not probative. Importantly, jurors are more likely to interpret evidence relating to blame-relevant facts against a defendant where that defendant is seen as deviating from what they consider to be acceptable behaviour in society. For example, in one study researchers found that participants were more likely to view a speeding driver as the primary cause of a car accident when the driver had been speeding home to hide drugs than when they had been speeding home to hide a gift.[63] This work is consistent with Professor Jonathan Haidt's moral foundations theory.[64] According to that theory, judgments that appear rational are often the result of initial impulses, which colour evaluations of evidence seen afterwards.

A perception of a trial participant as a bad or immoral person could easily lead jurors to assign meaning to that trial participant in a way that is consistent with that impression. Thus, judgments about the good or bad morality of the defendant and their behaviour have the potential to influence unrelated judgments. Importantly, these judgments about whether and to what extent behaviour deviates from what is acceptable may differ based not only on the behaviour but also on the juror judging the behaviour. For example, there is a significant body of research that demonstrates differences in moral and ethical reasoning based on gender. Put simply, research suggests that, on average, women tend to have stricter ethical standards and to view morally questionable behaviours as less permissible or ethical than men do.[65] Accordingly, differences in the way defendant character and morality is interpreted may partly explain relationships between juror characteristics and verdicts.

Impacts on representation of the body of evidence (narratives)

Different underlying intuitions and beliefs have the potential to contribute to differences in evaluation of potential narratives. For example, people who have experienced sexual assault themselves (disproportionately women) may find it easier to imagine sexual assault having occurred in the context of a case. This experience will be relevant to the attribution of meaning to narratives through heuristics that incorporate previous experience, such as the simulation heuristic (the tendency of

[63] M Alicke, 'Culpable Causation' (1992) 63(3) Journal of Personality and Social Psychology 368.

[64] Jonathan Haidt, *The Righteous Mind: Why Good People Are Divided by Politics and Religion* (Penguin 2013).

[65] See eg GR Franke, DF Crowne, and DF Spake, 'Gender Differences in Ethical Perceptions of Business Practices: A Social Role Theory Perspective' (1997) 82 Journal of Applied Psychology 920; SC Borkowski and YJ Ugras, 'Business Students and Ethics: A Meta-Analysis' (1998) 17 Journal of Business Ethics 1117; SH Glover and others, 'Gender Differences in Ethical Decision Making' (2002) 17(5) Women in Management Review 217; AC McCabe, R Ingram, and M Conway Dato-on, 'The Business of Ethics and Gender' (2006) 64 Journal of Business Ethics 101; JA Kennedy and LJ Kray, 'Who is Willing to Sacrifice Ethical Values for Money and Social Status? Gender Differences in Reactions to Ethical Compromises' (2013) 5(1) Social Psychological and Personality Science 52; AJ Kennedy, LJ Kray, and G Ku, 'A Social-Cognitive Approach to Understanding Gender Differences in Negotiator Ethics: The Role of Moral Identity' (2017) 138 Organizational Behavior and Human Decision Processes 28.

people to believe events are more likely to have happened where they are easier to imagine; introduced in Chapter 4).

Impacts on representation of legal standards

Research also confirms that the characteristics of jurors can influence their representations of legal standards. First, juror characteristics may influence their perceptions about whether behaviour meets the legal criteria (specifically the *mens rea*) required for a particular offence, especially where legal standards contain terms requiring subjective interpretation (eg dishonesty, materiality, reasonableness).[66] This influence occurs because people's intuitions and beliefs surrounding these standards may differ systematically based on their own experiences and demographics, and the information they consume. For example, research suggests that on average ethical standards differ by gender, as noted above. Recent research specifically examined how interpretations of particular behaviour as being dishonest differed based on the age and gender of those interpreting the behaviour (although note that this research was conducted in the guilty plea context where the tendency to self-blame or accept blame is also important). That work examined whether participants considered picking up money left on the floor to be dishonest (both with and without attempts to find the owner and involving various sums of money). Broadly, female participants were more likely to interpret behaviour as dishonest than male participants,[67] and older participants were more likely to interpret behaviour as dishonest than younger participants. Thus, what legal standards really mean, and the behaviours that satisfy them, will sometimes differ based on the characteristics of jurors applying those standards, particularly where the standards require subjective interpretation.

Secondly, juror characteristics may influence their representations of the standard of proof.[68] The way people interpret standards may well differ based on their own intuitions and beliefs relating to risk and the level of risk of (1) wrongful conviction, and (2) future offending. People with more authoritarian views, for example, may well disagree that society should be willing to risk ten guilty defendants going free rather than one innocent person being convicted. The influence of these viewpoints may arise as the result of cognitive biases such as motivated cognition, rather than as the result of conscious manipulation of legal standards. Some experimental work has found that gender, age, and education level do not

66 See Kahan and Braman (n 6).

67 This finding is consistent with work in business ethics suggesting that, at least in that context, women tend to have more stringent ethical standards than men; see eg WA Weeks and others, 'The Effects of Gender and Career Stage on Ethical Judgment' (1999) 20(4) Journal of Business Ethics 301 (finding that in the majority of vignettes studied women adopted a stricter ethical stance than their male counterparts); McCabe, Ingram, and Conway Dato-on (n 65) (finding that, on average, men view bribery as more ethical than women do). See also Borkowski and Ugras (n 65).

68 JB Weinstein and I Dewsbury, 'Comment on the Meaning of "Proof Beyond a Reasonable Doubt"' (2006) 5(2) Law, Probability and Risk 167.

significantly influence interpretations of beyond reasonable doubt outside of the context of a specific legal fact pattern.[69] However, in other contexts, researchers have found differences in interpretations of the standard by gender. For example, one study found that male students had stricter interpretations of beyond reasonable doubt in the context of a hypothetical rape case than female students.[70] It is likely that the impact of juror characteristics on interpretations of standards of proof will depend on the case type involved, and the extent to which their characteristics are associated with seeking prioritization of crime control over the avoidance of wrongful conviction in that particular area.

Normative acceptability of relationships between juror characteristics and verdicts

Understanding the causal pathways through which juror characteristics are likely to be linked with verdicts is important in assessing the normative desirability of relationships between juror characteristics and verdicts, and more broadly in assessing the normative appropriateness of juror function. Crucially, understanding these pathways can help to inform procedure to maintain normatively desirable influences on decisions and to reduce normatively problematic influences on decisions. Broadly, the discussion above suggests that differences in how jurors assign meaning resulting from differences in underlying intuitions and beliefs explain differences in decisions based on juror characteristics. The normative desirability of these impacts can be assessed against the goals for the jury introduced in Chapter 3 of this book.

As a preliminary matter, it should be noted that some juror characteristics, such as need for cognition, can make jurors more capable of scrutinizing evidence, and can be seen as beneficial in the jury decision process through improving the ability of jurors to arrive at well-reasoned conclusions. In fact, as noted in Chapter 2, a concern in England and Wales in requiring unanimity in jury verdicts while opening up jury participation widely in the community was that less able jurors would be able to prevent convictions. However, requiring special qualifications for people to serve as jurors is generally considered to undermine the representativeness of the jury which is highly beneficial for reasons that will be discussed below, and therefore the role of differences in ability will not be considered in depth here.[71]

[69] K Mueller-Johnson, MK Dhami, and S Lundrigan, 'Effects of Judicial Instructions and Juror Characteristics on Interpretations of Beyond Reasonable Doubt' (2018) 24(2) Psychology, Crime & Law 117.

[70] S Nagel, 'Bringing the Values of Jurors in Line With the Law' (1979) 63(4) Judicature 189.

[71] For discussion of juries selected based on specific experience in the US context, see GP Du Bois Jr, 'Desirability of Blue Ribbon Juries' (1961) 13(4) The Hastings Law Journal 479; MA Fisher, 'Going for the Blue Ribbon: The Legality of Expert Juries in Patent Litigation' (2000–01) 2 Columbia Science and Technology Law Review 1; JC Oldham, *Trial by Jury: The Seventh Amendment and Anglo-American Special Juries* (NYU Press 2006).

The fact-finding role

In Chapter 3, success in the fact-finding role is defined as *arriving at a level of confidence relating to descriptive facts that is appropriately influenced by evidence, constrained by relevant normative principles including the presumption of innocence and the right to be treated fairly and without discrimination.* In terms of the extent to which the influence of a range of intuitions and beliefs that differ by juror characteristics is desirable, it is necessary to determine whether these intuitions and beliefs are likely to be probative in making judgments relating to descriptive facts, and whether their influence is consistent with the presumption of innocence and the right to be treated fairly and without discrimination .

In terms of making judgments relating to descriptive facts there are some cases in which a diverse range of juror experience is likely to maximize the extent to which juries are appropriately influenced by evidence (ie the appropriate allocation of probative value to evidence). This is most likely to be the case where there is not a scientific answer to a question, and insight is best gained through experience that jury members are likely to have, for example, 'most people would not view a particular action as indicative of consent', or 'most people would interpret a particular unwanted physical advance as threatening'. As described in Chapter 4, as creatures in an incredibly complex environment, people learn from experience. People learn what is common in the environment they are in, and, put simply, being part of a complex environment can be the best way to understand it. Differing viewpoints of jurors with a diverse range of experiences can therefore be beneficial in some ways in reaching informed decisions representative of reality, through what might be termed collective wisdom (although it should be noted that this is only the case if these differing viewpoints are each represented appropriately during jury deliberations, an issue that will be considered in Chapter 8 of this book). However, in other cases the application of diverse viewpoints may be harmful. For example, certain intuitions or beliefs that jurors may hold are widely accepted scientifically to be false or discriminatory. These include beliefs such as 'all human beings know what they're doing and have the power to control themselves', 'child witnesses are always more reliable than adult witnesses', and 'if a woman was really raped, she would resist physically'. Such viewpoints do not contribute helpfully to legal decision-making and it is important to seek to reduce their influence. Where there is an objectively right answer and some community members may disagree with it, it is important that clear education is given to jurors to correct misconceptions and to ensure that misconceptions are not driving legal decision-making (and thus undermining appropriate allocation of probative value). Even where there is not an objectively right answer, it is important to identify misconceptions likely to be held by some jurors that have the potential to feed into decision-making. Discussion in Chapter 4 as to when intuitions and beliefs are susceptible to inaccuracy is helpful in identifying cases in which some of the diverse intuitions and beliefs held by jurors may be harmful.

First, where jurors do not have sufficiently relevant experience and are left to generalize from other contexts in their evaluations of evidence, the beliefs and intuitions of those jurors are susceptible to inaccuracy. For example, consider cases where jurors who have never experienced sexual assault judge whether a complainant's reaction to being assaulted undermines their credibility. Scientific research shows that reactions to such assaults can be predictably counterintuitive—for example freezing rather than fighting back can be a natural response to being assaulted.[72] This type of insight is not likely to be gained through deliberation of people with no experience of being assaulted (although it may be gained through the insight of a juror with experience of assault). Secondly, diverse experience is unlikely to facilitate appropriate allocation of probative value where that experience of jurors has not been accompanied by feedback and therefore jurors will not have learned from their experience appropriately.

A good example of a potential flaw in current procedure where legal systems often presume collective experience produces good judgment is in the evaluation of witness memory evidence. Legal systems, including the system in England and Wales, have left evaluation of this evidence largely to the jury (and excluded expert evidence) on the basis that humans have their own experiences of memory and thus can be expected to have their own expertise in this area which can be usefully pooled during deliberations. However, in fact a variety of research shows that while people have experience of memory this experience does not necessarily facilitate accurate knowledge relating to memory of others, since different people have different memory ability and can find different things memorable.[73] In fact, own experience of memory can actually be misleading rather than helpful in evaluating the memories of others.[74] Put simply, while memory of self is within our own experience, memory of others is not, and these two things have the potential to differ significantly. Therefore, drawing on own experience of memory to evaluate the memory of others can represent problematic generalization. In addition, although people get some feedback on the operation of memory (eg they will know whether they are conscious of remembering something), there are predictable areas where people will not have received feedback and therefore knowledge may be particularly poor. For example, people who experience false memories are often unlikely to know that their memory is false—usually, they will believe that what they remember is true. Thus, many of us will have relatively little knowledge relating to false memory and when and why it might occur. In these situations, scientific insight rather than diverse opinions is likely to facilitate the most appropriate allocation of probative value to evidence.

[72] See eg BP Marx and others, 'Tonic Immobility as an Evolved Predator Defense: Implications for Sexual Assault Survivors' (2008) 15(1) Clinical Psychology: Science and Practice 74.

[73] Helm and Growns (n 47).

[74] ibid.

In addition, it should be noted that generalizing from experience may also compromise the right to be treated fairly and without discrimination where jurors from a particular group generalize knowledge relating to their group (eg individuals of their own race) to another group (eg individuals of another race) inappropriately. For example, generalizing learning on own race memorability to cross-race memorability fails to account for the cross-race effect in memory and may lead to an inappropriately high level of belief in cross-race identifications, with potentially discriminatory outcomes.[75] Even where juror experience does facilitate the appropriate allocation of probative value to evidence, the utilization of this experience should be viewed as undesirable where it results in unfairness or discrimination against particular trial participants. For example, as noted in Chapter 3, even if men are less likely than women to be victims of certain offences, the testimony of male complainants should not be discounted on this basis. It is therefore important to identify and reduce the influence of any potentially discriminatory beliefs and intuitions.

Cognitive biases influencing the assignment of meaning, the impact of which is demonstrated in several of the associations between characteristics and verdicts, also have the potential to undermine appropriate allocation of probative value to evidence (through facilitating the influence of logically irrelevant context), to result in unfairness and discrimination against certain trial participants, and to undermine the presumption of innocence. In some cases, the impact of these cognitive biases may be reduced by the deliberation process; however, in other cases, cognitive biases, particularly where those biases are likely to have influenced the majority of jurors in similar ways, are susceptible to spread (see Chapter 8). The influences of cognitive bias may be particularly harmful in a number of situations. For example, where the identity of a defendant (or complainant) is distinct from the identities held by the majority of members of the jury, identity-protective processes could lead to a tendency for the jury to decide against the defendant (or complainant), unrelated to probative evidence. To some extent, minority representation on the jury might account for this problem in the case of discrimination against a defendant, however this protection will only occur where unanimity is required in the jury (or where the minority group make up more jurors than can dissent for a majority verdict to pass or can convince the majority jurors of their viewpoint). It might be that in cases invoking particularly political or contentious issues involving clear polarization, extra consideration should be given to jury composition and voting requirements to ensure an unbiased jury. Care is also needed to reduce the impact of empathy (or a lack of empathy) with trial participants, and the perceived morality of trial participant behaviour (at least when

[75] See RK Helm and ER Spearing, 'The Role of Race in Evaluations of Memory: Insensitivity to the Cross-Race Effect and Inaccuracy in Cross-Race Identification Evaluation' (forthcoming).

this judgment is not probative in the legal determination jurors are being asked to make) on the assignment of meaning.

The democratic role

In Chapter 3, success in the democratic role is defined as *making decisions that represent values of the community, constrained by normative principles including the right of innocent persons not to be convicted, the right to be treated fairly and without discrimination and the principle of legality, and by factual accuracy*. In this part of the process, diverse viewpoints from the community are likely to facilitate accurate judgment in terms of reaching the determination the community as a whole would have made. In achieving this goal, the differences between jurors actually represent strengths, with each juror contributing a unique perspective, allowing the jury to construct community judgment relating to specific individual fact patterns. The question of the extent to which views of the community are adequately represented in a group of jurors is, however, important to consider. Of course, as jury size increases the jury becomes more representative of the population, and an important question in this regard is the extent to which the viewpoints of twelve people are likely to accurately reflect the viewpoint of the community as a whole (were the community as a whole to consider the question). Consideration is given to this question in Chapter 8, examining jury deliberations.

It should be noted that any influence of beliefs or intuitions that introduce discrimination or unfairness against a particular trial participant or which introduce factual misconceptions into the decision-making process should also be considered problematic. For example, the endorsement of rape myths (eg that if a woman is wearing provocative clothing or has consumed alcohol she is partly to blame for her rape) should not be brought into the process even where they reflect views in the wider community and even where any influence occurs unconsciously (eg as the result of the simulation heuristic). Avoiding the influence of these factors is a challenge, particularly where their influence may occur outside of conscious awareness. Finally, cognitive biases that lead to beliefs as to levels of risk relating to wrongful conviction and future offending being unconsciously incorporated into the meaning assigned to the standard of proof have the potential to undermine the right of innocent persons not to be convicted, and therefore to be problematic.

Conclusions

A range of juror characteristics have been associated with verdicts, and research suggests that a number of causal paths create these associations. These paths appear to be rooted in predictable and systematic differences in juror intuitions and beliefs. Some of these causal paths are normatively desirable—a range of intuitions and beliefs can, in some cases, result in appropriate evaluation of evidence, particularly where appropriate evaluation is facilitated by viewpoints of, and experience in, the community. However, some intuitions and beliefs held by jurors have the potential to undermine the ability of the jury to arrive at a level of confidence relating to descriptive facts that is appropriately responsive to evidence, as well as to undermine important normative principles. The beneficial influence of diverse juror intuitions and beliefs should be distinguished from harmful influences resulting from misunderstanding, inappropriate generalization, and cognitive biases, including biases resulting from identity-protective cognition, empathy, and legally irrelevant judgments about the morality of trial participants and their behaviours. Interventions to improve jury function must target these harmful influences without jeopardizing the positive impact of the range of juror perspectives contributing to ultimate jury decisions.

6
Case-Level Characteristics

Introduction

Juries are tasked with interpreting case evidence and reaching findings of fact based on that evidence. It is therefore not surprising that the evidence presented to them is central to both individual juror and collective jury decision-making. Despite critiques showing various influences on jurors, strength of the evidence in a case likely remains the most significant influence on jury decisions across many case types (and, in addition, where the evidence is clearly very strong or very weak, for example in cases involving clear closed-circuit television or reliable DNA evidence that provide clear answers on contested points, other influences on the jury are likely to be limited). However, case characteristics can also influence juries in ways not related (or at the very least not directly related) to the strength of evidence. For example, jury decisions can be influenced by the race of the victim and defendant, by emotions invoked by case evidence, and by pretrial publicity. The Representation-Based Model outlined in Chapter 4 suggests that characteristics of a case have the potential to feed directly into juror representations of evidence, trial participants, the body of evidence (narratives), and legal standards, not only through evidence itself, but also through influencing intuitions and beliefs which underlie relevant representations more broadly. This influence can be both rational and irrational.

In this chapter I identify literature demonstrating associations between case characteristics and verdicts and examine how these associations can be explained by relationships between case characteristics and the meaning assigned to evidence, trial participants, the body of evidence, and legal standards (ie through differences in relevant representations). I first consider case evidence itself, and then other important case characteristics including victim and defendant characteristics, emotional evidence, and pretrial publicity. Based on this examination, I assess the normative desirability of relationships between case characteristics and verdicts against the criteria outlined in Chapter 3. I conclude by briefly discussing what these relationships can tell us about how jurors work and how they might work better.

How Juries Work. Rebecca K. Helm, Oxford University Press. © Rebecca K. Helm 2024.
DOI: 10.1093/9780191948107.003.0006

Section I: Associations Between Case-Level Characteristics and Verdicts

Case evidence

A wide variety of empirical research has examined the impact of case evidence on juror verdicts. This research includes examination of verdicts in both real cases and in mock trial work. Ultimately, and unsurprisingly, the strength of case evidence has generally been shown to be an important predictor of juror verdicts across case types. In research examining real cases, generally juror responsiveness to evidence strength has been measured by examining agreement between juror evaluation of evidence and ratings given by experts (specifically lawyers and/ or judges). For example, one study examined post-trial questionnaire data from judges, lawyers, and jurors in 179 criminal jury trials in Indianapolis in the United States of America (USA).[1] Strength of evidence ratings were obtained by asking the two lead lawyers and the judge to rate the strength of the case against the defendant. Results showed significant and substantial positive correlations between juror verdicts and strength of evidence ratings, such that when the prosecution's evidence was rated as stronger by lawyers and the judge, a guilty verdict from the jury was more likely. Another study found a similar result using data from 357 trials across the USA, collected by the United States National Center for State Courts.[2] Mock jury research has been able to adopt a different approach using randomized control trials—essentially giving different jurors or juries identical case facts, but with a particular piece of evidence that is varied to be scientifically strong or weak. That research confirms that generally jurors are more likely to convict in cases where evidence is stronger than in cases where evidence is weaker.[3] Recent research has also shown that jurors are likely to respond appropriately to variations in expert credentials.[4]

Of course, this ability of jurors to be responsive to evidence strength is reliant on jurors being able to assign appropriate probative value to evidence. Research suggests that generally jurors can do this even in cases involving relatively complex

[1] D Devine and others, 'Strength of Evidence, Extraevidentiary Influence, and the Liberation Hypothesis: Data from the Field' (2009) 33(2) Law and Human Behavior 136.

[2] T Eisenberg and others, 'Judge-Jury Agreement in Criminal Cases: A Partial Replication of Kalven and Zeisel's *The American Jury*' (2005) 2(1) Journal of Empirical Legal Studies 171.

[3] See eg ME Martín and others, 'The Influence of Sample Type, Presentation Format, and Strength of Evidence on Juror Simulation Research' (2007) 13(2) Psychology, Crime, & Law 139 (Spain); B Klettke, AC Graesser, and MB Powell, 'Expert Testimony in Child Sexual Abuse Cases: The Effects of Evidence, Coherence and Credentials on Juror Decision Making' (2010) 24 Applied Cognitive Psychology 481 (USA).

[4] KA Martire, G Edmond, and D Navarro, 'Exploring Juror Evaluations of Expert Opinions Using the Expert Persuasion Expectancy Framework' (2020) 25(2) Legal and Criminological Psychology 90.

evidence, such as statistical evidence.[5] For example, research on random match probabilities (RMPs, the probability of finding a DNA match to a crime scene in someone who is randomly sampled) found that evaluations of evidence did vary appropriately when the RMP was varied (ie more weight was given to a DNA match when the RMP was lower).[6]

However, research also highlights areas in which juries might struggle to assign appropriate value to evidence, and thus might fail to appropriately represent it and account for it. First, jurors may make mistakes where complex evidence is hard to understand and evaluate. Research has highlighted a risk that jurors are unable to consistently distinguish high-quality forensic evidence from what has been termed 'junk-science'. For example, one mock jury study in the US context presented opposing expert testimony on memory to jurors in a mock child sexual abuse case.[7] The study found that although jurors could distinguish between valid and invalid research, they were not always sensitive to other factors that weakened the strength of evidence. Ultimately, jurors may struggle to understand complex evidence and, relatedly, may be misled by evidence given by experts. This danger can be illustrated by the real case of Sally Clark in England. Clark was convicted of murdering her two infant sons partly on the basis of evidence given by a paediatric pathologist named Dr Roy Meadows, who testified in her case that the chances of having two children die from cot death was 'one in 73 million' and the equivalent of backing an 80 to 1 outsider in the Grand National four years running and winning each time.[8] Following her conviction by jury, experts from the Royal Statistical Society raised serious concerns about the use of statistics in the case,[9] and eventually her conviction was quashed.[10] A number of other convictions were also quashed on the same basis.[11]

Secondly, mock jury research suggests that even if jurors can accurately identify strengths of evidence independently of case information, this accuracy may be compromised by the influence of context in some criminal cases. Mock jury

[5] See RK Helm, VP Hans, and VF Reyna, 'Trial by Numbers' (2017) 27(1) Cornell Journal of Law and Public Policy 107, 112.

[6] WC Thompson, SO Kaasa, and T Peterson, 'Do Jurors Give Appropriate Weight to Forensic Identification Evidence?' (2013) 10(2) Journal of Empirical Legal Studies 359. See also DL Faigman and AJ Baglioni Jr, 'Bayes' Theorem in the Trial Process: Instructing Jurors on the Value of Statistical Evidence' (1988) 12 Law and Human Behavior 1; BC Smith and others, 'Jurors Use of Probabilistic Evidence' (1996) 20(1) Law and Human Behavior 49. Although see also WC Thompson and others, 'Perceived Strength of Forensic Scientists' Reporting Statements About Source Conclusions' (2018) 17(2) Law, Probability and Risk 133.

[7] LM Levett and M Bull Kovera, 'The Effectiveness of Opposing Expert Witnesses for Educating Jurors About Unreliable Expert Evidence' (2008) 32(4) Law and Human Behavior 363.

[8] *R v Sally Clark* [2003] EWCA Crim 1020.

[9] Letter from the President of the Royal Statistical Society to the Lord Chancellor regarding the use of statistical evidence in court cases (23 January 2002) <https://rss.org.uk/RSS/media/File-library/Membership/Sections/2020/Sally-Clark-RSS-letter-2002.pdf> accessed 15 June 2023.

[10] *R v Sally Clark* (n 8).

[11] See *R v Angela Cannings* [2004] EWCA Crim 1; *R v Donna Anthony* [2005] EWCA Crim 952. See also *R v Angela Alison Gay and Ian Anthony Gay* [2006] EWCA Crim 820.

research suggests that case context can lead to significant inflation (or deflation) of the strength of evidence (specifically forensic evidence), particularly where the evidence is of a weak or ambiguous standard.[12] Another study found a similar result in the context of video-recorded eyewitness identifications (which are inherently open to multiple interpretations)—assessors could distinguish to some extent between accurate and inaccurate identifications in a neutral context, but this ability was wiped out in the context of a specific criminal case where other evidence influenced how the identifications were assessed.[13]

Research has also suggested that evidence strength may interact with extra-legal influences on decisions, such as juror characteristics or pretrial publicity. Specifically, research suggests that (consistent with the Story Model) extra-legal influences are most likely to influence juror decisions in cases where the evidence is weak or ambiguous. In such cases the lack of clear situational cues has the potential to lead to a greater influence of juror biases in interpretations of evidence (and potential inflation of the reliability of such evidence, when combined with case facts pointing towards guilt). This has been demonstrated, for example, in the context of murder trials and pretrial juror bias scores in a Spanish mock jury experiment[14] and interpretations of forensic science evidence in case context in a UK mock jury experiment.[15]

Jurors may also be susceptible to other cognitive errors or biases in interpreting case evidence that may compromise their ability to assign appropriate probative weight to it. Here I will give three examples, although there are many more. First, the way that information is framed can influence the value extracted from statistical evidence. One mock jury study found that jurors are more likely to be convinced by DNA evidence when RMPs are presented as probabilities (eg a 0.005 chance of a random match) than when they are framed as frequencies (eg a 5 in 1,000 chance of a random match).[16] Secondly, jurors are likely to be biased by initial impressions of a case and the strength of initial evidence seen (as well as juror characteristics detailed in Chapter 5). Research has shown that jurors have a tendency to interpret new evidence to support whichever verdict is tentatively favoured in a trial.[17] This bias is gist-based, is a form of what is known as confirmatory bias (introduced in

[12] L Smith, R Bull, and R Holliday, 'Understanding Juror Perceptions of Forensic Evidence: Investigating the Impact of Case Context on Perceptions of Forensic Evidence Strength' (2011) 56(2) Journal of Forensic Sciences 409.

[13] 'Case Information Biases Evaluations of Video-recorded Eyewitness Identification Evidence' Journal of Applied Research in Memory and Cognition (forthcoming).

[14] L De La Fuente, EI De La Fuente, and J García, 'Effects of Pretrial Juror Bias, Strength of Evidence and Deliberation Process on Juror Decisions: New Validity Evidence of the Juror Bias Scale Scores' (2003) 9(2) Psychology, Crime & Law 197.

[15] Smith, Bull, and Holliday (n 12).

[16] JJ Koehler, 'When are People Persuaded by DNA Match Statistics?' (2001) 25(5) Law and Human Behavior 493.

[17] K Carlson and JE Russo, 'Biased Interpretation of Evidence by Mock Jurors' (2001) 7(2) Journal of Experimental Psychology: Applied 91.

Chapter 4), and can occur independently of or in combination with other biases. Tentative impressions may be a result of the initial legal arguments in a case, or even pretrial publicity (see the section on pretrial publicity below for discussion). Finally, research suggests that jurors are susceptible to something known as the weak evidence effect—essentially people have a tendency to interpret evidence that is weakly supportive of one position as actually being counter to that position (eg evidence that is weakly supportive of guilt may be interpreted as providing some evidence of innocence).[18]

Other influences

Victim and defendant characteristics

A range of work has shown that victim and defendant characteristics that are legally irrelevant to a verdict can sometimes influence jurors. Here I will focus on research showing an influence of defendant and victim gender, race, and physical appearance to illustrate effects, although research has also found relationships between other defendant and victim characteristics and juror decisions.

In the context of gender, race, and physical appearance, research examining jury decisions has reached mixed conclusions. Essentially, work shows that these factors can impact juror decisions, but it has not yet provided clear insight into when this effect is likely to occur. A 1994 meta-analysis examining the effects of physical attractiveness, race, socio-economic status, and gender of defendants and victims on judgments of mock jurors concluded that defendants are generally disadvantaged in cases involving female victims, and that jurors are more likely to convict male defendants and those with low physical attractiveness, at least in certain types of cases.[19] That work found no significant impact of defendant or victim race on juror decisions, however a more recent meta-analysis examining racial bias specifically in mock juror decision-making suggested a small but significant out-group bias against defendants.[20] Some work has also suggested that both Black and white defendants are more likely to be found guilty by mock jurors when they are accused of crimes that are consistent with stereotypes relating to their race.[21]

Research also suggests that any impact of defendant and victim characteristics may be complex and depend on other trial participant characteristics and also

[18] KA Martire and others, 'The Expression and Interpretation of Uncertain Forensic Science Evidence: Verbal Equivalence, Evidence Strength, and the Weak Evidence Effect' (2013) 37(3) Law and Human Behavior 197.

[19] R Mazzella and A Feingold, 'The Effects of Physical Attractiveness, Race, Socio-Economic Status, and Gender of Defendants and Victims on Judgments of Mock Jurors: A Meta-Analysis' (1994) 24(15) Journal of Applied Social Psychology 1315.

[20] TL Mitchell and others, 'Racial Bias in Mock Juror Decision-Making: A Meta-Analytic Review of Defendant Treatment' (2005) 29(6) Law and Human Behavior 621.

[21] Mazzella and Feingold (n 19).

characteristics of jurors. For example, some research has found that defendants are more likely to be found guilty where the victim in their case is of a different race from them,[22] although note that other work has found the opposite, even in the same general area (cases involving sexual assault).[23] Another study in the context of child sexual assault cases found that male jurors (but not female jurors) rendered fewer guilty verdicts against a female defendant accused of molesting a boy than a female defendant accused of molesting a girl. Verdicts of both male and female jurors were not influenced by victim gender when the defendant was a man.[24] It is also important to note that impacts of race in particular may vary by jurisdiction due to differing attitudes and stereotypes in the general population.

Importantly, research has examined how any biasing impact of defendant and victim characteristics might be reduced. In the case of physical attractiveness, research has suggested that effects of physical attractiveness on juror evaluations may be attenuated or even reversed following jury deliberations.[25] Research in the North American context has also identified a range of factors that make it more likely that white jurors will be biased against Black defendants,[26] including pretrial publicity,[27] the absence of racially charged issues at trial,[28] the absence of judicial instructions to avoid sympathy or prejudice,[29] the crime being committed by an individual from a lower social class (blue-collar crime rather than white-collar crime),[30] and case facts being ambiguous.[31]

The majority of work examining the impact of defendant and juror characteristics on verdicts has been carried out in the USA. However, some recent work has examined potential racial bias in juries in England and Wales. This work looked specifically at verdicts of juries both in mock jury simulations and in real Crown Court cases. In mock jury simulations, all-white juries were given identical case facts which varied based on whether the defendant in the case was white or from

[22] See eg RW Hymes and others, 'Acquaintance Rape: The Effect of Race of Defendant and Race of Victim on White Juror Decisions' (1993) 133(5) The Journal of Social Psychology 627.

[23] BL Bottoms, SL Davis, and MA Epstein, 'Effects of Victim and Defendant Race on Jurors' Decisions in Child Sexual Abuse Cases' (2004) 34(1) Journal of Applied Social Psychology 1.

[24] JA Quas and others, 'Effects of Victim, Defendant, and Juror Gender on Decisions in Child Sexual Assault Cases' (2002) 32(10) Journal of Applied Social Psychology 1993.

[25] MW Patry, 'Attractive But Guilty: Deliberation and the Physical Attractiveness Bias' (2008) 102(3) Psychological Reports 727.

[26] SR Sommers, 'Race and the Decision Making of Juries' (2007) 12(2) Legal and Criminological Psychology 171.

[27] S Fein and others, 'Hype and Suspicion: The Effects of Pretrial Publicity, Race, and Suspicion on Jurors' Verdicts' (1997) 53(3) Journal of Social Issues 487.

[28] SR Sommers and PC Ellsworth, 'Race in the Courtroom: Perceptions of Guilt and Dispositional Attributions' (2000) 26(11) Personality and Social Psychology Bulletin 1367.

[29] JE Pfeifer and JRP Ogloff, 'Ambiguity and Guilt Determinations: A Modern Racism Perspective 1' (1991) 21(21) Journal of Applied Social Psychology 1713.

[30] RA Gordon and others, 'Perceptions of Blue-Collar and White-Collar Crime: The Effect of Defendant Race on Simulated Juror Decisions' (1988) 128(2) Journal of Social Psychology 191.

[31] J-W van Prooijen, 'Retributive Reactions to Suspected Offenders: The Importance of Social Categorizations and Guilt Probability' (2006) 32(6) Personality and Social Psychology Bulletin 715.

a minority ethnic group. The verdicts of the all-white juries showed no evidence of discrimination against defendants from minority ethnic groups.[32] However, it should be noted that a lack of demonstrated bias in one fact pattern cannot be generalized to decisions more broadly due to the range of factors that influence the effect of race in a case (discussed above). In terms of the potential influence of race on the real juries, the study found that jurors at one of the two courts studied (in a predominantly white area but with large minority ethnic populations in some neighbourhoods) seemed to have more difficulty reaching verdicts in cases involving minority ethnic defendants or victims (shown by a higher proportion of hung juries in these cases).[33] This finding, while interesting, is difficult to interpret given the potential for different subject matter in underlying cases and contexts.

Overall, findings in this area can be described as inconsistent.[34] It remains unclear when the characteristics of the defendant and victim are likely to influence jury verdicts. What is clear is that there is potential for those characteristics to influence verdicts, that this potential seems to be case dependent, and that routes of influence should be understood in order to protect against discrimination and bias.

Emotional evidence

Research shows that particularly in cases involving sexual offences (but possibly in broader contexts too), people are more likely to believe a complainant (and, relatedly, convict a defendant) where that complainant demonstrates particular emotions, particularly distress. This effect has been demonstrated in a variety of work and has been termed the 'emotional victim effect'.[35] This effect is problematic since it represents irrelevant context influencing evaluation of evidence. Emotions do not provide reliable and consistent insight into whether witnesses are telling the truth.[36] Also problematically, some work suggests that the effect may differ based on demographic characteristics of the witness, creating a potential source of bias. Specifically, work has found that the effect extends to woman and children,[37] but that it may not extend to adult male complainants (although note that the sample

[32] C Thomas, *Are Juries Fair?* (Ministry of Justice Research Series 1/10, February 2010).

[33] ibid.

[34] In the context of race, see Sommers (n 26).

[35] K Ask and S Landström, 'Why Emotions Matter: Expectancy Violation and Affective Response Mediate the Emotional Victim Effect' (2010) 34(5) Law and Human Behavior 392; FT Nitschke, BM McKimmie, and EJ Vanman, 'A Meta-Analysis of the Emotional Victim Effect for Female Adult Rape Complainants: Does Complainant Distress Influence Credibility?' (2019) 145(10) Psychological Bulletin 953.

[36] B DePaulo and others, 'Cues to Deception' (2003) 129(1) Psychological Bulletin 74; CF Bond Jr and BM DePaulo, 'Accuracy of Deception Judgments' (2006) 10(3) Personality and Social Psychology Review 214.

[37] K Rowsell and MF Colloff, 'Are Sad Children More Believable? A Systematic Review of the Relationship Between Emotional Demeanour of Child Victims and Juror Credibility Judgements' (2022) 28(10) Psychology, Crime & Law 943.

size in this work was relatively small).[38] Thus, the effect may be the result of gendered stereotypes and expectations (of which jurors may or may not be aware).

Emotional content at trial more generally has also been shown to impact the way people evaluate evidence and make verdict decisions. One way that this has been demonstrated is through comparing evaluation of evidence when photographs (a more emotionally evocative form of evidence) are used, as opposed to verbal descriptions conveying the same probative information.[39] Photographs that have been shown to be particularly influential in changing verdicts are 'gruesome' photographs displayed in homicide cases. A recent meta-analysis of mock jury work found that gruesome photographs increased guilty verdicts when compared to neutral photographs, and, to a greater extent, when compared with no photographs.[40]

Pretrial publicity

Publicity surrounding a case itself can have a biasing effect on jurors—changing their perceptions of trial participants prior to trial and, relatedly, their views of evidence in a case. A recent meta-analysis of mock jury work found that pretrial publicity has a modest biasing effect on legal verdicts.[41] Publicity favouring the defendant is associated with the defendant being less likely to be found guilty and publicity that is negative towards the defendant is associated with the defendant being more likely to be found guilty. This work also suggests certain conditions under which the biasing effect of pretrial publicity may be exacerbated, including in cases involving non-violent crimes and longer delays between exposure to pretrial publicity and trial.[42] Pretrial publicity with the potential to bias defendants may not only include explicit judgments about them in the media, but also more general reporting of events with the potential to exacerbate feelings of grief and to increase punitiveness towards a defendant.[43] The impact of pretrial publicity on trial verdicts is particularly important to consider at the current time, where research suggests that increased competition in media reporting is leading to sensationalized reporting and more judgment against defendants in the 'court of public opinion'.[44] Gruesome pictures, associated with effects described above, are now sometimes printed or otherwise displayed in media reports or on media platforms.

[38] S Landström, K Ask, and C Sommar, 'The Emotional Male Victim: Effects of Presentation Mode on Judged Credibility' (2015) 56(1) Scandinavian Journal of Psychology 99.

[39] DA Bright and J Goodman-Delahunty, 'Gruesome Evidence and Emotion: Anger, Blame and Jury Decision-Making' (2006) 30(2) Law and Human Behavior 183.

[40] R Hofstein Grady and others, 'Impact of Gruesome Photographic Evidence on Legal Decisions: A Meta-Analysis' (2018) 25(4) Psychiatry, Psychology and Law 503.

[41] LA Hoetger and others, 'The Impact of Pretrial Publicity on Mock Juror and Jury Verdicts: A Meta-Analysis' (2022) 46(2) Law and Human Behavior 121.

[42] ibid.

[43] R Gimson, 'The Mutable Defendant: From Penitent to Rights-Bearing and Beyond' (2020) 40(1) Legal Studies 113, 126.

[44] ibid.

Section II: Explaining the Relationships Between Case Characteristics and Verdicts

Paths through which case characteristics influence verdicts

According to the model suggested in Chapter 4, there are four primary routes through which case characteristics might result in systematically different verdicts from jurors: through influencing mental representations of pieces of evidence, through influencing mental representations of trial participants, through influencing mental representations of the body of evidence, and through influencing mental representations of legal standards (and, relatedly, the behaviour that falls within or outside those standards). In this section, I will consider existing research that provides insight into how these routes can explain associations between case characteristics and verdicts.

Impacts on representation of evidence

Of course, evidence itself will influence representations of evidence, and, as noted above, research suggests that jurors are sensitive to changes in the probative value of evidence, with predictable exceptions (discussed more below). As in the case of juror characteristics, the room for case characteristics other than evidence to influence representations of evidence is likely to increase as that evidence becomes more ambiguous, leaving more room for subjective interpretation. This reality is demonstrated in some of the research discussed above where, as noted, influence has been found to be most significant in cases involving ambiguous evidence.

There are a number of other ways in which case characteristics can influence representations of evidence, many of which result from those case characteristics influencing representations of trial participants (discussed below) and feeding through into representations of evidence. Most problematically, people may hold explicit discriminatory beliefs that influence how they evaluate trial participants and evidence, such as believing that people from specific ethnic groups are likely to be dishonest or violent. Current legal rules may root out (or at least seek to root out) these types of explicit biases.[45] However, biases against certain trial participants may also be more subtle and operate in more subtle ways. For example, people are more likely to be convinced that evidence given by a witness whom they represent as honest or reliable is accurate and may implicitly associate certain groups with honesty and accuracy as a result of unconscious bias based on skewed experiences or listening to the unfounded opinions of others. These representations of trial participants potentially have a powerful influence not just on the

[45] See eg discussion in Chapter 2 of this book.

testimony of the participant being represented, but on evidence that could favour or disfavour their position more generally. In addition, mechanisms discussed in previous chapters relating to base rates and the simulation heuristic are likely to be important in explaining the influence of case characteristics on verdicts—characteristics of trial participants may make the underlying probability of their account being true appear higher (eg because certain groups are viewed as more likely to make false allegations, or are viewed as being victims of crime more often) or may make their account easier for jurors to imagine.

Emotion can influence how trial participants are seen, which can influence the way evidence given by them is represented (as discussed below), but can also impact the representation of other evidence directly through influencing the meaning attributed to evidence, as discussed in Chapter 4. The specific impact of emotion is likely to depend on the emotion involved.[46] Discrete emotions may all have slightly different impacts, as discussed below, but categorizing emotions can be helpful in identifying commonalities in effects. Dimensional models have suggested that emotion is best understood as being made up of two discrete components—valence and arousal. Valence describes the extent to which an emotion is positive versus negative, and arousal describes the intensity of the emotion.[47] For example, anger or distress would be classified as negative valence and high arousal emotions whereas sadness or boredom would be categorized as negative valence and low arousal emotions. Research in Fuzzy-Trace Theory specifically notes that gist-based representations often incorporate emotion including valence, arousal, and discrete emotions (to put it another way, emotion influences the gist attributed to stimuli).[48] Importantly, legal cases, particularly the more serious cases which are the ones most typically heard by juries, often contain materials that evoke negative valence and high arousal emotions such as anger or disgust. These emotions have been associated with less detailed processing of information and greater reliance on stereotypes.[49] These types of emotions can also be associated with a tendency and motivation to blame.[50] Therefore, case materials with the potential to evoke disgust and anger are likely to lead jurors to be more inclined to interpret evidence

[46] It should also be noted that mood states incidental to a case or evidence rather than caused by the case also have the potential to influence decisions, although this analysis focuses on emotion resulting from exposure to the case and associated evidence.

[47] L Feldman Barrett and JA Russell, 'The Structure of Current Affect: Controversies and Emerging Consensus' (1999) 8(1) Current Directions in Psychological Science 10.

[48] SE Rivers, VF Reyna, and B Mills, 'Risk Taking Under the Influence: A Fuzzy-Trace Theory of Emotion in Adolescence' (2008) 28(1) Developmental Review 107.

[49] GV Bodenhausen, LA Sheppard, and GP Kramer, 'Negative Affect and Social Judgment: The Differential Impact of Anger and Sadness' (1994) 24(1) European Journal of Social Psychology 45.

[50] See eg D Keltner, PC Ellsworth, and K Edwards, 'Beyond Simple Pessimism: Effects of Sadness and Anger on Social Perception' (1993) 64(5) Journal of Personality and Social Psychology 740; JS Lerner, JH Goldberg, and PE Tetlock, 'Sober Second Thought: The Effects of Accountability, Anger, and Authoritarianism on Attributions of Responsibility' (1998) 24(6) Personality and Social Psychology Bulletin 563.

against a defendant. In the legal context, some mock jury work has specifically examined this link between emotional evidence and juror verdicts. For example, one study found that 'emotionally disturbing' case photographs led to greater confidence in the guilt of a defendant through the generation of anger and disgust, which caused moral outrage.[51]

Pretrial publicity clearly has the potential to impact representations of evidence in a trial through confirmatory bias (a cognitive bias introduced in Chapter 4). Confirmatory bias refers to the tendency of individuals to seek out evidence consistent with existing beliefs, expectations, or hypotheses, and to interpret information in line with those beliefs, expectations, or hypotheses.[52] In the legal context, mock juror work has specifically demonstrated the potential for interpretation of specific pieces of evidence to be distorted by a tentatively favoured verdict (such as that which could be introduced prior to trial by pretrial publicity).[53]

Impacts on representation of trial participants

Characteristics of trial participants themselves, and the way that they behave, are likely to feed through into juror judgments in a number of predictable ways. Most obviously, we know that certain characteristics can be linked to stereotypes. These stereotypes represent initial impressions of trial participants that can then colour subsequent interpretations of evidence, as discussed above. For example, a person may find it easier to imagine an assault having occurred with a female complainant or may believe that assaults against women are more common and as a result may be more likely to believe a female who is alleging she has been assaulted than a male alleging he has been assaulted, or a person may find it easier to imagine an attractive person being assaulted or may believe attractive people are assaulted more often and, as a result, may be more likely to believe a complainant who is more attractive.[54] These differences would only be expected in specific and ambiguous fact patterns, which may explain the inconsistencies in research findings, discussed above.

There are also specific mechanisms that have been examined in the literature with the potential to explain the emotional victim effect and the impact of trial participant appearance on the impressions people form of trial participants and their believability. In the case of the emotional victim effect, there is evidence that two

[51] JM Salerno and LC Peter-Hagene, 'The Interactive Effect of Anger and Disgust on Moral Outrage and Judgments' (2013) 24(10) Psychological Science 2069.

[52] See eg A Westerwick, SB Kleinman, and S Knobloch-Westerwick, 'Turn a Blind Eye if You Care: Impacts of Attitude Consistency, Importance, and Credibility on Seeking of Political Information and Implications For Attitudes' (2013) 63(3) Journal of Communication 432; Daniel J Flynn, Brendan Nyhan, and Jason Reifler, 'The Nature and Origins of Misperceptions: Understanding False and Unsupported Beliefs About Politics' (2017) 38 Political Psychology 127.

[53] Carlson and Russo (n 17).

[54] For more information on the simulation heuristic and the impact of base rates, see Chapters 4 and 5.

mechanisms lead female complainants in sexual offence cases to be believed more when they display distress or related emotions.[55] The first mechanism is known as expectancy violation and essentially refers to the extent to which the behaviour displayed by the victim is consistent with what they would expect of that victim. Essentially, when people do what jurors would expect them to do had they been assaulted, people are more likely to believe they are being honest and have been assaulted. A range of research supports the idea that people generally expect female victims to be visibly distressed, and when victims do not appear this way, it is seen as undermining their credibility.[56] This effect may be linked to the simulation heuristic, where people find things that are easier to imagine (eg a real victim being visibly distressed versus a real victim not being visibly distressed) more likely to have really occurred. Importantly, gender stereotyping has the potential to be important in people's expectations of victims,[57] and, in general, high levels of emotionality and sadness (both related to distress) are seen as expected more of women than of men.[58] This stereotyping may explain why a similar effect has, to date, not been observed in men.

The other explanation for the emotional victim effect relates to affective response. Put simply, the emotion of a complainant may trigger an emotional reaction in jurors which leads them to represent a complainant as more reliable. This explanation based on affective response is consistent with work in persuasion more generally which shows that messages that elicit emotions can be more persuasive.[59] An existing study provides support for this proposed mechanism—in that study more emotional complainant accounts did trigger more emotion in mock jurors, and this juror emotion mediated the relationship between complainant emotion and belief in the complainant's account.[60] It is also possible that seeing a complaint emotional increases feelings of anger or disgust, with the predictable effects discussed above, including driving the need to blame someone for what has happened, likely the defendant.

In the case of physical attractiveness, a well-documented cognitive bias can explain why physical attractiveness can influence the way trial participants are represented in a trial. This bias is the halo effect (introduced in Chapter 4), and relatedly, a bias known as the 'What is Beautiful is Good Bias'. In this context, the halo effect refers to people's tendency to attribute socially desirable personality

[55] Ask and Landström (n 35).

[56] L Ellison and V Munro, 'Reacting to Rape: Exploring Mock Jurors' Assessments of Complainant Credibility' (2009) 49(2) The British Journal of Criminology 2021; Ask and Landström (n 35).

[57] J van Doorn and NN Koster, 'Emotional Victims and the Impact on Credibility: A Systematic Review' (2019) 47 Aggression and Violent Behavior 74.

[58] See E Ashby Plant and others, 'The Gender Stereotyping of Emotions' (2006) 24(1) Psychology of Women Quarterly 81.

[59] See eg JP Dillard and E Peck, 'Affect and Persuasion: Emotional Responses to Public Service Announcements' (2000) 27(4) Communication Research 461.

[60] Ask and Landström (n 35).

traits (including trustworthiness) to physically attractive people.[61] This effect has been demonstrated in a range of literature[62] and likely arises as a result of the constructive nature of human judgment, where people may feel positively about another person and treat them positively, without being able to pinpoint the source of those positive feelings.

Impacts on representation of the body of evidence (narratives)

The impact of case characteristics on narrative evaluation is likely to mirror the impacts of juror characteristics on narrative evaluation. The process of evaluating narratives will be influenced by intuitions and beliefs, which may well differ based on irrelevant case characteristics and implicit biases and stereotypes that jurors may hold. Again, as a result of the simulation heuristic, jurors are likely to find narratives (representations of the body of evidence) that they can imagine more easily to be more likely to be true, and therefore will be more confident in them.

Impacts on representation of legal standards

Case characteristics have the potential to impact how legal standards are represented, and, relatedly, judgments of whether what has been shown at trial demonstrates behaviour that breaches legal standards to an appropriate degree of confidence. One case characteristic that is particularly likely to influence the representation of legal standards is emotionality. As noted above, high arousal and negative valence emotions such as anger and distress have the potential to lead to processing based on stereotypes rather than careful consideration, and thus could lead individuals to consider less carefully whether particular behaviour meets the threshold required for a criminal conviction (instead leading people to rely on more of a gut instinct about the case). The motivation to blame when these negative emotions are experienced also has the potential to lead jurors to interpret the standard of proof as a lower threshold (either consciously or unconsciously) or to disregard the standard of proof altogether. There is some support for this idea in existing work suggesting that mock jurors may distinguish less between different standards of proof when they are induced to feel anger.[63]

[61] C Batres and V Shiramizu, 'Examining the "Attractiveness Halo Effect" Across Cultures' [2022] Current Psychology 1.

[62] Although some work also raises questions about the link between attractiveness and perceived integrity (a related characteristic to truthfulness). See AH Eagly and others, 'What is Beautiful is Good, but . . . : A Meta-Analytic Review of Research on the Physical Attractiveness Stereotype' (1991) 110(1) Psychological Bulletin 109.

[63] Y Choi, 'Jurors' Subjective Certainty and Standards of Proof: The Role of Emotion and Severity of Charge in Subjective Probability Emotion and Severity of Charge in Subjective Probability Judgment' (DPhil thesis, University of Nebraska 2013) <https://digitalcommons.unl.edu/cgi/viewcontent.cgi?article=1061&context=psychdiss> accessed 15 June 2023.

Normative acceptability of relationships between case characteristics and verdicts

As with juror characteristics, understanding the causal pathways through which case characteristics are likely to be linked with verdicts is important in assessing the normative desirability of relationships between case characteristics and verdicts, and more broadly in assessing the normative appropriateness of juror function.

The fact-finding role

According to the criteria in Chapter 3, any impact of case characteristics is acceptable only when those characteristics are probative in *arriving at a level of confidence relating to descriptive facts that is appropriately influenced by evidence,* while being *constrained by relevant normative principles including the presumption of innocence and the right to be treated fairly and without discrimination.* An important question in that regard—which may not be as simple as it appears—is precisely which case characteristics are probative and which are not in arriving at an appropriate level of confidence relating to how relevant events occurred. Of course, there are some circumstances in which the characteristics of evidence are clearly probative—probabilities relating to forensic evidence, witness viewing conditions, expert credentials, and corroboration of key points, for example, are all clearly probative. As discussed above, in certain situations additional intervention may be needed to enable jurors to appropriately extract probative value from evidence, but research suggests that generally jurors are quite effective in this regard.

When and if evidence that is not probative in a scientific sense should be considered appropriate in influencing jurors is a more complicated question. One of the key advantages of the early jury system was that juror knowledge of the community and behaviour in that community allowed them to pick up on cues that may have been probative, although not necessarily in a scientific sense (see Chapter 1). Jurors as community members may have known, for example, areas where crimes were most likely to have occurred, the types of people most likely to have committed them, and subtle frictions in the community that may have made offending more likely. This knowledge gave jurors an advantage over experts not just in exercising judgments about standards in a community, but also in making determinations of what happened with appropriate levels of confidence. An important question is the extent to which jurors today still have this advantage, and, if so, whether making decisions in accordance with these types of subtle cues may be normatively problematic for other reasons, for example through introducing discrimination.

Of course, now that the jury is no longer self-informing, jurors no longer have knowledge of particular communities. As noted in Chapter 1, one of the reasons for this change was a recognition that jurors should be judged by people who are not so close to a defendant that they may be biased against them. Now juror judgments are not influenced by personal knowledge of a case or the community it occurred in, but can be influenced the factors discussed above, such as ease of imagination, which are still likely occur as a result of experience of life in society. As noted in Chapter 4, as adaptive creatures in a complex environment, people learn from their experience, for example from connections and frequencies observed in their environment. This learning can allow jurors to pick up on subtle cues in particular cases based on a complex range of context that is too nuanced to be captured by scientific rules. As a result, this learning is a key advantage of the jury.

However, it is important to note that learning from experiences can undermine accurate allocation of probative value in a range of situations, including where experiences in one area are generalized to another and where learning occurs in the absence of representative experience and effective feedback (see Chapter 4). For example, we may find that in everyday life people who have been hurt tend to have an emotional reaction. However, these experiences, while apparently relevant, may not generalize to the much more extreme behaviours involved in criminal contexts. The ability of jurors to learn from experience and thus pick up on probative features of evidence may also be compromised by media reporting of high-profile but rare events. For example, media reporting may make false allegations of sexual assault appear more common than they are and thus lead jurors to unnecessarily discount allegations made by complainants.

In addition, learning from experience can lead jurors to account for factors that undermine the right of trial participants to be treated fairly and without discrimination. Specifically, this type of learning can (even unconsciously) pick up on how people's characteristics tend to, on average, relate to their behaviour. For example, people might experience that, on average, women are more likely to be the victims of violence than men. The learning would be likely to result in (1) base-rate estimates tending to lead jurors to believe female complainants to a greater degree than male complainants, and (2) greater ease of imagining a complainant having been a victim where they are female. As a result, female complainants may be more likely to be believed than male complainants. Similar effects may occur as the result of other characteristics and behaviours of trial participants, including race, attractiveness, and emotion. Importantly, since jurors do not necessarily know the root of their intuitions (eg relating to gender) (as noted in Chapter 4, experience may teach us what is generally connected, but not why) they may not be able to detach proxies from underlying probative information. The criminal law in particular should demand a more individualized approach to the evaluation of evidence. However, this individualized approach is not necessarily intuitive for people. In fact, people get used to relying on proxies and stereotypes in everyday life, rather than consistently engaging with other people and situations in depth. For example, advice suggests that if children get lost, they should look for people such as shop assistants or police officers or parents with children, who are likely to be safe and able to help them.[64] This influence of generalizations is the result of both a lack of more individuating information, and limitations in human understanding and cognitive capacity.[65] Where jurors decide cases without assistance or direction, these types of proxies and stereotypes may feed into decisions, undermining the more individualized approach necessitated by the criminal law and the right to be treated fairly and without discrimination.

Other influences of case characteristics are even more clearly problematic in terms of undermining the right to be treated fairly and without discrimination and in undermining the presumption of innocence—anger or disgust potentially subverting rational processes and leading to a tendency to decide against a defendant, pretrial publicity leading to biased evaluation of trial evidence and case participants, and attractive defendants being viewed as positive in other ways as a result of halo effects. Procedure must guard against these influences to protect the integrity of the juror decision process.

The democratic role

According to the criteria in Chapter 3, any impact of case characteristics is acceptable only when those characteristics are probative in *making decisions that represent values of the community*, while being *constrained by normative principles including the right of innocent persons not to be convicted, the right to be treated fairly and without discrimination and the principle of legality, and by factual accuracy*. The impact of case characteristics on judgments of this type is somewhat unclear due to a lack of relevant research. However, the research discussed above does provide some evidence to suggest that case characteristics that have a problematic influence on fact-finding judgments may have a problematic influence on democratic judgments.

First, research suggests that emotion triggered by case facts has the potential to alter the way that jurors interpret and apply the standard of proof. Any bias leading the standard of proof to be disregarded or downgraded clearly has the potential to undermine the right of innocent persons not to be convicted and should be viewed as normatively problematic. Special care may need to be taken to enforce the standard of proof and to provide necessary safeguards against wrongful conviction in cases in which jurors are likely to experience high levels of anger or related emotions such as disgust.

Secondly, understanding the cognitive biases that can impact assignment of meaning relevant to the fact-finding role shows how those biases also have great

[64] See eg S Gordon, 'How to Teach Your Kids What to Do if They Get Lost' (*Verywell Family*, 27 June 2022) <www.verywellfamily.com/what-to-teach-a-child-to-do-when-lost-620557> accessed 15 June 2023.

[65] These limitations are recognized in the literature on bounded rationality. See eg G Gigerenzer and R Selten (eds), *Bounded Rationality: The Adaptive Toolbox* (MIT Press 2002).

potential to be important in the democratic role. For example, the halo effect has the potential to lead to behaviour being interpreted as honest when performed by an 'attractive' defendant but dishonest when performed by an 'unattractive' defendant. This influence undermines the right to be treated fairly and without discrimination, even if the ultimate judgment ends up being representative of what the judgment of the entire community would be (eg because many people may show susceptibility to halo effects). Other biases such as racism or sexism also have the potential to influence judgments relating to legal standards. Therefore, while research on how case characteristics impact jurors in performing the democratic role is limited, there is clear evidence that juror judgments may be impacted by factors that create a risk of undermining key normative principles relevant to the criminal justice process.

Conclusions

A range of case characteristics have been associated with verdicts, and a number of causal paths can explain these associations. Some of these causal paths are desirable. Most obviously, research confirms that generally jurors are influenced by probative factors in evidence (although they need help responding appropriately to evidence in some predictable ways). However, there is also clear potential for inappropriate generalizations and for proxies that jurors naturally rely on in their environment (eg relating to gender, race, and emotional reactions) to feed through into decision-making in the criminal trial. These generalizations may be incorrect, and even when they are not, they are only probative in a weak sense, and undermine key normative principles in the criminal justice process. Care must be taken to ensure that the influence of these generalizations (even when probative) and cognitive biases triggered by case characteristics, including by emotional content and pretrial publicity, do not feed through into the juror and jury decision process.

7
Legal Standards and Procedure

Introduction

Legal standards and procedure can alter the evidence jurors see, but also what influences them in evaluating evidence and the cognitive processes that they rely on in doing so. For this reason, it is important to understand that legal standards and procedures may not always operate as we would expect from a common-sense or folk psychological perspective. Understanding the ways that legal standards and procedure impact (and do not impact) how jurors work provides important insight into the representations underlying juror decision-making, how those representations can be (and are) shaped, and how legal standards and procedure might be designed to promote optimal juror function.

In this chapter, I identify literature demonstrating associations between legal standards and procedures and verdicts and examine how these associations can be explained by relationships between legal standards and procedures and the meaning assigned to evidence, trial participants, the body of evidence, and legal standards (ie through differences in relevant representations). I consider legal standards and procedure under two headings: (1) legal standards, including *actus reus*, *mens rea*, and defence standards, descriptions of the standard of proof, and alternative verdicts; and (2) rules on evidence including admissibility, judicial warnings/directions, and expert evidence. Note that these procedures have been selected for consideration as they are important illustrations of how legal standards and procedure can influence juror (as opposed to jury) decisions, not as an overview of all legal procedures that can influence juror decisions. Based on this examination, I evaluate the normative acceptability of relationships between legal standards and procedures and verdicts, and discuss how potentially problematic influence (and lack of influence) might be addressed. I conclude by briefly discussing what these relationships can tell us about how jurors work, and how standards and procedure can be used to help jurors work better, without introducing problematic side-effects.

How Juries Work. Rebecca K. Helm, Oxford University Press. © Rebecca K. Helm 2024.
DOI: 10.1093/9780191948107.003.0007

Section I: Associations Between Legal Standards and Procedure and Verdicts

Legal standards

Actus reus, *mens rea*, and defences

First, and most obviously, jurors are likely to be influenced by the law that they are provided with—the *actus reus* (guilty act) and *mens rea* (guilty mind) requirements that must be demonstrated by the prosecution to prove that the relevant crime occurred, and the standards required for any legal defence. Lawmakers spend significant amounts of time developing legal standards to criminalize certain behaviour. However, the way that jurors respond to changing legal standards can, in predictable cases, be complex, and counter to intuitions that lawmakers and commentators may have. This complexity was illustrated in a study examining juror decisions in the context of criminal attempts, when jurors were provided with different standards to determine whether the behaviour engaged in by the defendant was sufficient to impose criminal liability. That work, conducted by Professor Avani Sood, examined mock juror decisions under two different standards for imposing liability for attempts—the 'proximity' test and the 'substantial step' test.[1] The 'proximity' test focuses on how close the defendant came to committing a crime, for example requiring the prosecution to prove that the defendant engaged in conduct that came dangerously close or very near to committing arson. The 'substantial step' test focuses on what steps the defendant has taken towards committing a crime, for example requiring the prosecution to prove that the defendant took a substantial step towards committing the crime. Theoretically, the substantial step test is more prosecution friendly since it allows liability to be imposed at an early stage—when a substantial step has been taken toward committing a crime even where the defendant does not come close to committing the crime.[2] However, Sood's work showed that in ambiguous cases laypeople were actually more likely to impose liability under the proximity test than under the substantial step test, across multiple contexts (despite on average recognizing the substantial step test as a lower bar for criminal liability when shown the tests side by side). Importantly, the work also found that the proximity test seemed to exacerbate bias against a defendant based on religion in a case involving terrorism.[3]

In the context of defences, evidence similarly suggests that jurors do not necessarily respond to changes in legal tests as lawmakers expect. This reality has

[1] AM Sood, 'Attempted Justice: Misunderstanding and Bias in Psychological Constructions of Criminal Attempt' (2019) 71(3) Stanford Law Review 593.

[2] See H Wechsler, WK Jones, and HL Korn, 'The Treatment of Inchoate Crimes in the Model Penal Code of the American Law Institute: Attempt, Solicitation, and Conspiracy' (1961) 61(4) Columbia Law Review 571.

[3] Sood, 'Attempted Justice' (n 1).

been explored in the context of standards for the defence of insanity. Legal debate over the insanity defence has questioned whether the defence should cover only rationality deficits (where defendants cannot tell right from wrong),[4] or whether it should also cover control deficits (where defendants can tell right from wrong but cannot meaningfully control their behaviour).[5] Mock jury work examining decisions in a mock legal case with a defendant with a rationality or control deficit found that regardless of the legal test mock jurors were provided with, they generally excused defendants who clearly lacked meaningful control as well as defendants who lacked rationality.[6]

Descriptions of the standard of proof

The standard of proof required in criminal litigation in order to convict a defendant is typically proof 'beyond a reasonable doubt'.[7] As with *actus reus*, *mens rea*, and defence standards, this standard is not mathematical or scientific, and the important factor for jurors will be their meaningful representations of the standard in a case context. As described in previous chapters, these representations and associated applications of the standard of proof may be influenced by both juror characteristics and case characteristics. Judicial direction relating to the standard of proof also has significant potential to change the meaning that jurors assign to the standard of proof. In England and Wales today, judges no longer explicitly refer to proof beyond a reasonable doubt, and instead describe the standard as 'proof which makes the jury sure'.[8] Regulation also restricts how judges can elaborate on this standard for jurors. A wide range of directions on the beyond reasonable doubt standard are used in other jurisdictions. One study in the 1990s identified a range of different instructions on reasonable doubt used in the United States of America (USA), including some variation in instructions even within the same courts.[9]

These standards are typically designed and evaluated with the aim of enhancing juror understanding.[10] However, the way the standard of proof is described can influence jurors in ways unrelated to their understanding of the standard. One

[4] As in the M'Naghten standard used in England and Wales and in some US jurisdictions, *M'Naghten's Case* [1843] UKHL J16; [1843–60] All ER 229.

[5] As in the US Model Penal Code standard.

[6] RK Helm, SJ Ceci, and KA Burd, 'Unpacking Insanity Defence Standards: An Experimental Study of Rationality and Control Tests in Criminal Law' (2016) 8(2) The European Journal of Psychology Applied to Legal Context 63.

[7] Generally, this standard also applies to defences, so that the prosecution must prove beyond a reasonable doubt that defences do not apply before a defendant is convicted. However, there are exceptions to this rule, including the defence of insanity in England and Wales, which the defence must prove on the balance of probabilities.

[8] See eg *R v Majid* [2009] EWCA Crim 2563.

[9] C Hemmens, KE Scarborough, and RV Del Carmen, 'Grave Doubts About "Reasonable Doubt": Confusion in State and Federal Courts' (1997) 25(3) Journal of Criminal Justice 231.

[10] See eg *R v Majid* (n 8) holding that judges cannot draw distinctions between 'sure' and 'certain' which are thought to be difficult to make clearly, but can direct the jury that they should exclude fanciful possibilities and act only on realistic ones.

variation in instructions that has been examined experimentally is the difference between instructions that ask whether the proof would make someone willing to act ('proof willing instructions') and instructions that ask whether the doubt would make someone hesitate to act ('doubt hesitate instructions'). Results of this work showed that doubt hesitate instructions led to significantly lower interpretations of beyond reasonable doubt (ie requiring less doubt before a not guilty verdict would be delivered), although this difference disappeared when both sets of instructions were phrased in terms of doubt rather than proof.[11]

Alternative verdicts and partial defences

Providing alternative verdicts to jurors (eg verdicts beyond guilty and not guilty) can influence the way that jurors classify defendants, sometimes in irrational ways. Take the not proven verdict in Scotland, for example. This verdict is intended to capture cases in which the jury believe the accused may be guilty, but do not think that this can be proved beyond a reasonable doubt. Logically, it should split what would be the not guilty verdict in other jurisdictions (which should include both cases in which the jury think that the defendant is not guilty, and cases in which they think the defendant may be factually guilty but this cannot be proved beyond a reasonable doubt) but should not influence guilty verdicts (since these verdicts should *only* include cases in which defendant guilt can be proved beyond a reasonable doubt). However, mock jury research in Scotland suggests that the verdict probably not only decreases the number of not guilty verdicts (as it would rationally be expected to do), but also decreases the number of guilty verdicts.[12]

The availability of partial defences may also have an impact that is not necessarily rational on how jurors view and categorize offending. In English law, a partial defence of diminished responsibility is available in cases involving a murder charge—the partial defence recognizes that defendants who fall into its remit are not as culpable as defendants with no defence, but also that some level of liability should be imposed.[13] As with alternative verdicts, some work on partial defences suggests that the presence of a partial defence can change how jurors categorize offending, in irrational (but potentially beneficial) ways. The study considering insanity defence standards, discussed above, found that while jurors irrationally categorized defendants with control deficits as meeting a rationality-based standard for the defence, where a partial defence was included for those with control deficits, those defendants would be categorized using the partial defence and

[11] MK Dhami, S Lundrigan, and K Mueller-Johnson, 'Instructions on Reasonable Doubt: Defining the Standard of Proof and the Juror's Task' (2015) 21(2) Psychology, Public Policy, and Law 169.

[12] J Chalmers, F Leverick, and VE Munro, 'Beyond Doubt: The Case Against "Not Proven"' (2022) 85(4) Modern Law Review 847. Note that the not proven verdict may shortly be abolished as the result of reforms contained in the Victims, Witnesses and Justice (Scotland) Bill.

[13] Homicide Act 1957, s 2, as amended by Coroners and Justice Act 2009, s 52.

would no longer be considered to meet the standard for the full defence (despite that standard not having changed).[14]

Rules of evidence

Admissibility

Admissibility rules govern which evidence can be presented to the jury and through doing so have the potential to significantly impact the representations jurors form and, relatedly, the verdicts that they ultimately reach. Admissibility rules therefore seek to strike a balance between providing jurors with probative information and ensuring that admitted information does not create unfair prejudice against the defendant. Evidential rules on admissibility are often relatively intricate due to difficulties striking this balance fairly and consistently; however, the impacts of rules admitting (or, conversely, excluding) evidence may be more complex than they appear.[15]

One example of a set of admissibility rules often utilized is rules on the admission of bad character evidence against a defendant. Bad character evidence against a defendant is likely to result in jurors representing the defendant in a more negative way and can also influence the way that other trial participants are seen.[16] For this reason, many jurisdictions make bad character evidence inadmissible, subject to exceptions. One such exception, utilized in some jurisdictions, is that bad character evidence can be introduced to refute good character evidence given by the defence.[17] Such rules are intended to create a fair balance between the prosecution and the defence. However, research in social psychology shows that information on bad character of a defendant is likely to be given more weight than information on good character of a defendant.[18] The impact of character evidence may also differ based on existing juror stereotypes. One study examined how admission of character evidence might have a differential impact depending on defendant race and concluded that character evidence had a stronger effect when it was inconsistent with racial stereotypes.[19]

Importantly in regard to admissibility, in some cases jurors may be exposed to evidence that is later ruled to be inadmissible. Jurors may then be asked to

[14] Helm, Ceci, and Burd (n 6).

[15] See eg R Glover, *Murphy on Evidence* (15th edn, OUP 2017) chs 10–17.

[16] See eg BL Bottoms and GS Goodman, 'Perceptions of Children's Credibility in Sexual Assault Cases' (1994) 24(8) Journal of Applied Social Psychology 702; JS Hunt and TL Budesheim, 'How Jurors Use and Misuse Character Evidence' (2004) 89(2) Journal of Applied Psychology 347; EM Maeder and JS Hunt, 'Talking About a Black Man: The Influence of Defendant and Character Witness Race on Jurors' Use of Character Evidence' (2011) 29(4) Behavioural Sciences and the Law 608.

[17] See eg US Federal Rules of Evidence.

[18] Hunt and Budesheim (n 16).

[19] Maeder and Hunt (n 16).

disregard the information that they have heard in making their decisions.[20] However, jurors are unlikely to consistently and effectively disregard information, even when instructed to do so.[21] A meta-analysis of mock jury work examining the impact on juror verdicts of judicial instructions to disregard inadmissible evidence found that inadmissible evidence had a reliable effect on verdicts, consistent with its content, and that judicial instructions to ignore inadmissible evidence did not effectively eliminate its impact.[22] That analysis found that instructions to disregard were more effective when a judicial instruction gave a reason for the inadmissibility (eg explaining that the evidence was not reliable or had no bearing on the case). However, one study found, specifically in the context of prior conviction evidence, that such explanations have the potential to 'backfire', leading mock jurors to pay *more* attention to the evidence they were meant to disregard.[23] Research also suggests that where jurors are aware that evidence has been challenged as inadmissible but has been ruled admissible, the evidence has a greater impact on them than it would have if the evidence had not been challenged.[24]

Judicial warnings

In some cases, evidence that is seen as being potentially unreliable or open to misinterpretation is still shown to jurors but is accompanied by a judicial warning or direction (these will be collectively referred to as warnings). Warnings have been used in a range of areas including cases involving uncorroborated complainant evidence,[25] eyewitness identification evidence,[26] and evidence from disturbing photographs.[27] However, it is unclear that warnings have the impact on juror decisions that they are intended to.

Experimental work in the context of corroboration warnings in sexual offence cases (now widely considered to be inappropriate warnings to provide) suggested that those warnings could lead to a lower percentage of guilty verdicts (as might be expected), although this effect was not statistically significant and so cannot be

[20] See eg in the US context, *Carter v Kentucky* 450 US 288 (1981) 303.

[21] MJ Saks and BA Spellman, 'Instructions to Disregard and to Limit Use' in MJ Saks and BA Spellman, *The Psychological Foundations of Evidence Law* (NYU Press 2016) ch 3, 85.

[22] N Steblay and others, 'The Impact on Juror Verdicts of Judicial Instructions to Disregard Inadmissible Evidence: A Meta-Analysis' (2006) 30(4) Law and Human Behaviour 469.

[23] KL Pickel, 'Inducing Jurors to Disregard Inadmissible Evidence' (1995) 19(4) Law and Human Behavior 407.

[24] Steblay and others (n 22).

[25] eg England and Wales used to require as a matter of practice that the judge direct the jury on the danger of convicting on the basis of certain uncorroborated evidence (including in cases involving evidence of accomplices of the accused, young children, and complainants in sexual cases), see *R v Baskerville* [1916] 2 KB 658; *Davies v DPP* [1954] AC 378.

[26] eg in England and Wales a warning must be given in cases that are reliant on identification evidence, see *R v Turnbull* [1977] QB 224.

[27] See *R v Bowhay* (1998, NSWSC 782); *R v Zammit* [1999] NSWCCA 65 (28 May 1999) in Australia.

treated as reliable, and results also showed that corroboration was not discussed frequently by the jury even following a warning being given.[28]

More extensive research has been carried out on warnings given in the context of cases involving eyewitness identification evidence. This work has examined warnings based on Telfaire and Henderson instructions in the USA and Turnbull directions in England and Wales. All of these directions go beyond just warning jurors about potential unreliability of identification evidence and provide some information on eyewitness identification and factors that may enhance or reduce its accuracy. However, generally mock jury research suggests that these instructions may not lead to effective belief updating,[29] and that where there is an effect of instructions it is often to increase juror scepticism (reducing their belief in any eyewitness identification) rather than to improve juror differentiation of high and low-quality eyewitness evidence.[30] Such an increase in scepticism has also been shown in other contexts, for example work examining warnings relating to complainant emotionality in cases involving sexual offences.[31]

However, research in the eyewitness context has also shown that evidence-based instructions (discussed in more detail below) have the potential to be more effective in improving juror ability to distinguish high-quality from low-quality eyewitness identifications and to allow jurors to effectively account for the likely probative value of evidence in the decision-making process. Specifically, these instructions all provide some level of 'training' to jurors to help them understand the information they have been presented with and apply it to a case context.[32] Research has also shown that warnings targeted specifically at co-witness discussion may be effective in increasing sensitivity in some cases (specifically in cases involving an inconsistent witness).[33]

[28] VR Hans and N Brooks, 'Effects of Corroboration Instructions in a Rape Case of Experimental Juries' (1977) 15(3) Osgoode Hall Law Journal 701.

[29] RK Helm, 'Evaluating Witness Testimony: Juror Knowledge, False Memory, and the Utility of Evidence-Based Directions' (2021) 25(4) The International Journal of Evidence & Proof 264. See also F Leverick, 'Jury Directions' in J Chalmers, F Leverick, and A Shaw (eds), *Post-Corroboration Safeguards Review Report of the Academic Expert Group* (The Scottish Government 2014) 101–17.

[30] AP Papailiou, DV Yokum, and CT Robertson, 'The Novel New Jersey Eyewitness Instruction Induces Skepticism but Not Sensitivity' (2015) 10(12) PloS One e0142695; MK Dillon and others, '*Henderson* Instructions: Do They Enhance Evidence Evaluation?' (2017) 17(1) Journal of Forensic Psychology Research and Practice 1.

[31] FT Nitschke, BM McKimmie, and EJ Vanman, 'The Effect of Trauma Education Judicial Instructions on Decisions About Complainant Credibility in Rape Trials' (2023) 29(1) Psychology, Public Policy, and Law 69.

[32] AM Jones and S Penrod, 'Improving the Effectiveness of the Henderson Instruction Safeguard Against Unreliable Eyewitness Identification' (2018) 24(2) Psychology, Crime & Law 177; AM Jones, AN Bergold, and S Penrod, 'Improving Juror Sensitivity to Specific Eyewitness Factors: Judicial Instructions Fail the Test' (2020) 27(3) Psychiatry, Psychology and Law 366; Helm (n 29).

[33] HM Paterson, DWM Anderson, and RI Kemp, 'Cautioning Jurors Regarding Co-Witness Discussion: The Impact of Judicial Warnings' (2011) 19(3) Psychology, Crime & Law 287.

Expert evidence

Another way to inform jurors in order to assist them in extracting appropriate probative value from evidence is through the use of expert testimony. Typically, both sides (the prosecution and the defence) will have the opportunity to instruct and examine an expert in matters calling for expertise. Precisely when matters are considered to call for expertise varies by jurisdiction. It is also sometimes possible to utilize joint prosecution and defence experts. An important question to consider is whether experts function as intended, to make jurors more informed, or whether experts might actually have unintended effects on the jury, increasing the impact of cognitive biases or misconceptions.

One area in which the impact of expert testimony has been studied is eyewitness identification evidence, particularly in the US context. This research has shown that eyewitness experts (who typically testify on the unreliability of memory) tend to increase mock juror scepticism of eyewitness testimony, rather than increasing their sensitivity to high and low-quality evidence.[34] Research on expert testimony more generally has shown that jurors may struggle to understand and engage with expert testimony. For example, in the field of statistical evidence in forensic science, research has shown that jurors struggle to evaluate and detect errors in evidence given by experts.[35] This issue is often demonstrated in real cases involving miscarriages of justice. For example, this issue was demonstrated in England and Wales in the case of Sally Clark, discussed in Chapter 6.[36]

Research has examined how the way in which expert evidence is presented to jurors can influence their evaluations, despite not changing the evidence itself or its probative value. In the context of DNA evidence, work has shown that jurors can struggle to appropriately interpret quantitative representations given of evidence, such as random match probabilities (RMP). In one study, researchers found that RMPs were misunderstood so badly that a substantial minority of mock jurors interpreted an RMP of 1 in 10 (meaning the chance of a random person matching the DNA sample from a crime scene is 1 in 10) as being stronger evidence against a defendant than an RMP of 1 in 100,000 (meaning the

[34] GL Wells, RCL Lindsay, and JP Tousignant, 'Effects of Expert Psychological Advice on Human Performance in Judging the Validity of Eyewitness Testimony' (1980) 4(4) Law and Human Behavior 275; SG Fox and HA Walters, 'The Impact of General Versus Specific Expert Testimony and Eyewitness Confidence Upon Mock Juror Judgment' (1986) 10(3) Law and Human Behavior 215; BL Cutler, HR Dexter, and SD Penrod, 'Nonadversarial Methods for Sensitizing Jurors to Eyewitness Evidence' (1990) 20(14) Journal of Applied Social Psychology 1197; JL Devenport and BL Cutler, 'Impact of Defense-Only and Opposing Eyewitness Experts on Juror Judgments' (2004) 28(5) Law and Human Behavior 569; MR Leippe and others, 'Timing of Eyewitness Expert Testimony, Jurors' Need for Cognition, and Case Strength as Determinants of Trial Verdicts' (2004) 89(3) Journal of Applied Psychology 524.

[35] See eg JJ Koehler, 'Error and Exaggeration in the Presentation of DNA Evidence at Trial' (1993) 34 Jurimetrics 21; H Eldridge, 'Juror Comprehension of Forensic Expert Testimony: A Literature Review' (2019) 1 Forensic Science International: Synergy 24.

[36] *R v Sally Clark* [2003] EWCA Crim 1020.

chance of a random person matching the DNA sample from a crime scene is 1 in 100,000).[37] This statistic is also often thought to be frequently interpreted by jurors as being the chance that a defendant is innocent—a mistake known as a prosecutor's fallacy.[38] How statistics are framed also has the potential to influence juror interpretation of those statistics. For example, jurors are likely to find DNA evidence stronger when RMPs are presented as probabilities (eg a 0.001 chance of a random match) than when they are presented as frequencies (eg a 1 in 1,000 chance of a random match).[39] Other possibilities of presenting statistical evidence with the potential to prevent misconception have been suggested, including using verbal scales (categorizing the strength of the evidence, for example, as very weak, weak, neutral, strong, very strong) or likelihood ratios (comparing the likelihood of observing matching characteristics if two samples come from the same source to the same likelihood if they came from different sources). However, research has shown risks associated with both of these methods of presentation. Jurors can conflate categories when given verbal scales (eg treating strong, very strong, and extremely strong the same),[40] and the strength of evidence when using those scales can be undervalued.[41] In the case of likelihood ratios, evidence suggests that jurors undervalue these ratios (treating them as less probative than they are).[42]

Finally, there may be issues with the interpretation by mock jurors of expert credentials. Recent research has shown that people may respond appropriately to varying expert credentials, suggesting that providing the jury with information on credentials may be helpful in allowing them to interpret and critique expert evidence.[43] However, this research provided mock jurors with only limited case facts, meaning that the credentials could be evaluated in a relatively neutral context. In a case context with various motivations to believe a particular expert, the way that credentials are weighted may be biased, for example in line with a favoured position (as discussed in Chapter 5).[44]

[37] WC Thompson and others, 'Perceived Strength of Forensic Scientists' Reporting Statements About Source Conclusions' (2018) 17(2) Law, Probability and Risk 133.

[38] S Lindsey, R Hertwig, and G Gigerenzer, 'Communicating Statistical DNA Evidence' (2003) 43(2) Jurimetrics 147.

[39] JJ Koehler, 'When Are People Persuaded by DNA Match Statistics?' (2001) 25 Law and Human Behavior 493.

[40] E Arscott and others, 'Understanding Forensic Expert Evaluative Evidence: A Study of the Perception of Verbal Expressions of the Strength of Evidence' (2017) 57(3) Science and Justice 221.

[41] KA Martire and I Watkins, 'Perception Problems of the Verbal Scale: A Reanalysis and Application of a Membership Function Approach' (2015) 55(4) Science and Justice 264.

[42] KA Martire and others, 'On the Interpretation of Likelihood Ratios in Forensic Science Evidence: Presentation Formats and the Weak Evidence Effect' (2014) 240 Forensic Science International 61.

[43] KA Martire, G Edmond, and D Navarro, 'Exploring Juror Evaluations of Expert Opinions Using the Expert Persuasion Expectancy Framework' (2020) 25(2) Legal and Criminological Psychology 90.

[44] DM Kahan, H Jenkins-Smith, and D Braman, 'Cultural Cognition of Scientific Consensus' (2011) 14(2) Journal of Risk Research 147.

Section II: Explaining the Relationship Between Legal Standards and Procedure and Verdicts

Paths through which legal standards and procedure influence verdicts

According to the model suggested in Chapter 4, there are four primary routes through which legal standards and procedures might result in systematically different verdicts from jurors: through influencing mental representations of pieces of evidence, through influencing mental representations of trial participants, through influencing mental representations of the body of evidence, and through influencing mental representations of legal standards (and, relatedly, the behaviour that falls within or outside those standards). In this section, I will consider existing research that provides insight into how these routes can explain associations between legal standards and procedures and verdicts.

Impacts on representation of evidence

There are a number of ways in which the influence of legal standards and procedures on juror decisions can be explained through those legal standards and procedures influencing juror interpretation and therefore representation of evidence.

First, legal standards and procedures can trigger cognitive biases that will influence how evidence is interpreted and represented. This reality can explain a number of the effects discussed above. One potentially important bias is priming (where exposure to one stimulus influences a reaction to another stimulus), which has the potential to be important in a number of ways. One type of priming that should be considered is anchoring (introduced in Chapter 4). Very broadly, anchoring refers to a bias whereby decisions are influenced by an initial reference point (an 'anchor').[45] In the context of non-numerical decision-making, anchoring language can increase the extent to which people notice features that an anchor and target hold in common.[46] In the context of the work on attempts discussed above, anchoring was used to explain the counterintuitive finding that the proximity test was more prosecution friendly.[47] The proximity test, through focusing on proximity to the offence, mentally anchors decision-makers to a point close to crime commission, which may cause them to be more likely to associate ambiguous behaviour with being close to the commission of an offence. On the other hand, the substantial step test, through its focus on the starting point, anchors decision-makers to a point close to the starting point, which may cause them to be more likely to associate ambiguous behaviour with being close to the

[45] A Tversky and D Kahneman, 'Judgment under Uncertainty: Heuristics and Biases' (1974) 185(4157) Science 1124.
[46] Sood, 'Attempted Justice' (n 1) 643.
[47] ibid 643–44.

starting point. Another potentially important type of priming is the priming of emotions through language. For example, through priming feelings of threat or anger, language has the potential to influence how individual pieces of evidence are interpreted and represented (consistently with work on emotion discussed in Chapters 4 and 6). In the case of the attempts study discussed above, the fact that application of the proximity test was associated with bias based on religion was explained by the author by the fact that use of the words 'dangerously close' may have triggered feelings of threat, which have been shown to increase close-mindedness and bias.[48]

A cognitive bias that can arise as a result of reliance on gist, with the potential to be important, particularly in the context of instructions to disregard inadmissible evidence (or possibly even warnings to not pay too much attention to particular evidence), is known as a 'Streisand effect'. Streisand effects describe a social phenomenon where trying to remove content can draw attention to it and these effects have been shown to be important in the context of censoring information in other contexts.[49]

Reliance on meaningful representations of evidence can also explain how judicial warnings and expert testimony may fail to have the intended effects on evaluation of evidence. Inconsistent effects of these interventions discussed above are predictable based on psychological theory including Fuzzy-Trace Theory (FTT) and a theory of persuasion known as the Elaboration Likelihood Model (ELM). In the case of judicial instructions, information is often conveyed in a simple form, essentially as a series of facts that jurors should be aware of when making decisions.[50] Psychological theory provides good reasons to suggest that providing information in this way may be ineffective or inconsistent in leading to belief updating and may lead people to update beliefs in relation to a heuristic cue such as perceived authority, rather than meaningful engagement with information. ELM distinguishes between two routes to persuasion—the central route (resulting from careful and thoughtful consideration of the merits of information) and the peripheral route (resulting from an association of information with positive or negative cues, such as the status of the person delivering that information). Since jurors are only provided with relatively superficial information when given instructions (eg little or no guidance on scientific support for the statements being presented to them), belief updating can only occur via the peripheral route. This route is inconsistent and subject to bias. A person will only be convinced by the information provided by a judge in this form if they have significant trust in the judge or a tendency to

48 Sood, 'Attempted Justice' (n 1) 645.

49 S Curry Jansen and B Martin, 'The Streisand Effect and Censorship Backfire' (2016) 9 International Journal of Communication 656.

50 See eg Turnbull Guidelines in England and Wales, outlined in Crown Court Compendium Part 1: Jury and Trial Management and Summing Up (2023), Section 15 'Identification' <www.judiciary.uk/guidance-and-resources/crown-court-compendium/> accessed 5 July 2023.

believe the information anyway (eg because it supports a position that they favour for other reasons). In addition, where information such as a warning given by a judge is given as a list of verbatim statements without further context, jurors may struggle to represent this information in a meaningful way (ie as gist) since they are not able to situate it and contextualize it. Thus, statements given by judges may be difficult for jurors to incorporate into decision processes in the gist-based decision-making process that the proposed Representation-Based Model suggests jurors are likely to engage in.

In the case of expert evidence, where jurors are unable to meaningfully engage with information, for example due to its complexity, they are likely to suffer similar problems to those described above—believing information where they are inclined to give credence to the source that the information is coming from or failing to apply information effectively in a gist-based decision process. Where warnings or expert evidence remove the potential for jurors to rely on their existing instincts (eg in the case of witness emotionality), it is also important to consider what will replace reliance on those instincts. Taking away cues which people tend to rely on without replacing those cues with a concrete and meaningful decision strategy has the potential to leave jurors feeling unable to represent evidence at all, potentially contributing to scepticism of that evidence even where this is unwarranted.[51]

Other failures of interventions, specifically expert evidence, to have desired effects can be explained through processing errors, which have been discussed in detail in the FTT framework.[52] These errors are particularly likely to be important in the case of numerical information given in expert evidence. For example, people tend to neglect the denominator when they are interpreting probabilities such as RMPs, which can explain why a 0.001 chance of a random match is interpreted as being smaller than a 1 in a 1,000 chance of a random match (when in fact the two are numerically equivalent). Decision-makers may even know the two numbers are numerically equivalent when they are given them side-by-side but will assign meaning to them differently in the context of a case as the result of denominator neglect.[53]

Impacts on representation of trial participants

Other associations discussed above can be explained as a result of intuitions or beliefs influencing the way that trial participants are represented. Clearly, good or bad character evidence about a trial participant can influence how they are represented in logical and probative ways. However, it is important to note that, as described above, the impact of that information may not always be strictly in line

[51] Nitschke, McKimmie, and Vanman (n 31).

[52] See RK Helm, VP Hans, and VF Reyna, 'Trial by Numbers' (2017) 27(1) Cornell Journal of Law and Public Policy 107.

[53] For more information on processing errors in legal evidence, see ibid.

with its probative value—for example, bad character evidence is likely to have a disproportionate effect on the representation of trial participants compared to good character evidence. This differential impact can be explained, at least partly, as a result of negativity bias (introduced in Chapter 4). Put simply, negativity bias refers to the tendency of humans to give greater weight to negative events, objects, and personal traits than positive ones.[54] There are a range of explanations for this effect in human cognition, many of which are adaptive, resulting from a range of considerations. For example, negative events are more threatening than positive events are beneficial (eg avoiding death, a negative event, is the most important factor from an evolutionary perspective); negative information is more complex (eg while positive things should generally be approached, negative things can warrant a range of different reactions); negative events often develop faster and require a faster response; and negative events are generally more contagious.[55] However none of these rationales suggests that negative information should have a disproportionate impact on the assignment of probative value in the legal decision-making context.

Impacts on representation of the body of evidence (narratives)

The anchoring bias, introduced in Chapter 4 and discussed above in the context of impacts on legal representations, can explain how different descriptions of reasonable doubt can influence juror decisions (eg as requiring more proof or less proof). Specifically, the wording used to describe the legal standard can focus jurors on proof or doubt, and by doing so can influence whether a narrative is represented as one that a juror is highly confident in or less confident in. Authors of the work above examining differences in wording articulating the beyond reasonable doubt standard suggested that the language of the reasonable doubt instructions might inadvertently influence how jurors approach their fact-finding task.[56] Specifically, instructions focusing on proof may lead jurors to focus on proof against a defendant in a narrative, whereas instructions focusing on doubt may lead jurors to focus on doubt surrounding guilt in a narrative. Thus, the switch to directing jurors that they must be 'sure of guilt' as opposed to directing jurors there must be no 'reasonable doubt' may well have unintended consequences on juror decision-making. Representation of the body of evidence also has the potential to be influenced by legal standards and procedures where those standards and procedures change the representation of evidence, trial participants, and legal standards, discussed above and below.

[54] See P Rozin and E Royzman, 'Negativity Bias, Negativity Dominance, and Contagion' (2001) 5(4) Personality and Social Psychology Review 296.

[55] ibid 314–16.

[56] Dhami, Lundrigan, and Mueller-Johnson (n 11) 175.

Impacts on representation of legal standards

Work on the relationship between legal standards and juror intuitions and beliefs illustrates how the way legal standards are represented and applied is coloured by juror intuitions and beliefs and the consistency between those intuitions and beliefs and legal standards. Specifically, the way that legal standards are represented is influenced not only by legal standards themselves, but also by juror intuitions and beliefs (eg about when someone should be excused from criminal liability). Where formal standards clearly conflict with juror intuitions or beliefs, the process of combining intuition and beliefs with standards to form meaningful representations becomes awkward and unpredictable. The work introduced above examining rationality- and control-based defences illustrates this point. The fact that jurors with no intermediate option would excuse defendants with control deficits even when this was not permitted by the legal test was explained by jurors intuitively feeling that the person who lacked meaningful control was not blameworthy and these intuitions overriding the strict legal standard due to incompatibility.[57] This effect may occur consciously, but may also occur as a result of motivated cognition, where people's perceived goals (which could be to treat a defendant fairly or to appropriately recognize moral culpability) shape their thinking, including their interpretation of relevant information such as evidence or standards.[58] Importantly, providing mock jurors with another option for liability in the form of a partial defence based on lack of control demonstrated that jurors could distinguish between rationality and control deficits and would appropriately categorize defendants as having control deficits where they could do so without imposing full legal liability on them (or, in other words, they could do so without significantly departing from underlying intuition).

The work on alternative verdicts also illustrates how juror intuitions and beliefs about defendant responsibility and appropriate characterization creep into their representation and application of legal standards. Again, this effect may occur consciously or as a result of unconscious motivated cognition.[59] As a result, jurors may make decisions that appear inconsistent with black letter law where legal standards are poorly aligned with underlying community standards, particularly where legal standards do not provide clear verbatim standards (such as age in the case of sexual activity with a minor).[60] Research in experimental jurisprudence has highlighted some areas in which lay intuitions and beliefs may be inconsistent with

[57] Helm, Ceci, and Burd (n 6) 67.

[58] AM Sood, 'Motivated Cognition in Legal Judgments—An Analytic Review' (2013) 9 Annual Review of Law and Social Science 307.

[59] ibid.

[60] A Meschkow, 'When Cases Fit the Gist of Rape but Not the Verbatim Definition (and Vice Versa): A Fuzzy-trace Theory of Jurors' Judgments of Guilt' (MA Dissertation, Cornell University 2017) <https://ecommons.cornell.edu/handle/1813/59012> accessed 16 June 2023.

legal standards, creating potential disconnects between legislator intent and juror decision-making.[61]

Normative acceptability of relationships between legal standards and procedure and verdicts

Understanding how legal standards and procedures can influence juror decisions provides important insight into ways in which jurors are unlike machines, and are influenced by intuitions and beliefs, that may lead them to make decisions in ways that depart from legislative expectations. The majority of influences described in this chapter are irrational and have their impact by biasing how jurors assign meaning in unintended ways, with the potential to impact both their fact-finding role and their democratic role.

The fact-finding role

In Chapter 3, success in the fact-finding role is defined as *arriving at a level of confidence relating to descriptive facts that is appropriately influenced by evidence, constrained by relevant normative principles including the presumption of innocence and the right to be treated fairly and without discrimination.* The influences of legal standards on juror determinations of what occurred in the past are obviously problematic. Language in legal standards that biases jurors towards discrimination or interpreting evidence against an accused person, or admissibility rules that create bias against one party are obviously out of line with the goals of the jury set out in Chapter 3. They are non-probative influences and can compromise the presumption of innocence and lead to unfair and discriminatory treatment in legal decision-making. Utilizing balanced legal standards (eg in terms of proximity to a starting point and proximity to an offence) may be helpful in addressing some problems in this area.

In other ways, legal procedures seeking to assist jurors in assigning meaning to evidence may fail to fulfil their role effectively. This reality is particularly true when considering the impacts of expert evidence and judicial instructions. Here, careful design is necessary to ensure interventions have desired effects rather than no effects or even backfire effects. Importantly in this regard, experimental research has confirmed that judicial instructions and expert evidence can influence jurors in desired ways, specifically through allowing them to better discriminate between high-quality and low-quality evidence, but also that instructions must be carefully designed in order to do so.[62]

[61] See eg R Sommers, 'Commonsense Consent' (2020) 129(8) Yale Law Journal 2232.
[62] Jones and Penrod (n 32); Jones, Bergold, and Penrod (n 32); Helm (n 29).

The democratic role

In Chapter 3, success in the democratic role is defined as *making decisions that represent values of the community, constrained by normative principles including the right of innocent persons not to be convicted, the right to be treated fairly and without discrimination and the principle of legality, and by factual accuracy*. As in the fact-finding role, legal standards can have unintended effects that are obviously problematic. Language in legal standards that biases jurors towards conviction is out of line with the right of innocent persons not to be convicted. Again, utilizing balanced legal standards (eg in terms of focus on level of doubt and level of sureness) may be helpful in addressing some problems in this area.

In terms of juror departures from legislative intent in assigning a verdict, it should be noted that some juror interpretation of standards, including departures from legislative intent, for example classifying a condition as constituting legal insanity where is clearly outside the legal definition of insanity, may be considered desirable (provided they lean towards acquittal rather than conviction). As described in Chapters 1 and 3, one of the advantages of the jury is that they can alter the application of legal standards that are out of line with community standards and values; therefore interpreting legal standards in line with intuitions and beliefs as well as based on strict language may be seen as an advantage. However, as judgments become more subjective and less constrained by formal law, they become less predictable, and the chances of different juries reaching different determinations that do not necessarily reflect the judgment of the community and do not respect the principle of legality increase. Legal standards should seek to remain in line with community standards to ensure this consistency and predictability (in keeping with the principle of legality). One way in which legal procedures might compromise between the desire to criminalize behaviour and the desire of the community to excuse that behaviour is in recognizing alternative verdicts. For example, these verdicts might be helpful in pushing jurors to recognize behaviour is unlawful that has been legislated to be unlawful, while also not pushing them to impose full criminal liability where doing so is not consistent with their own intuitions or beliefs (and relatedly, community sentiment). In this way, gradation may be helpful to jurors in scenarios where the imposition of full liability may feel too harsh, resulting in motivation (conscious or unconscious) to avoid a guilty verdict. As noted above, in English law, a type of alternative verdict is recognized in the case of the partial defence of diminished responsibility to a murder charge—the partial defence recognizes that defendants who fall into its remit are not as culpable as defendants with no defence, but also that some level of liability should be imposed. Allowing jurors to categorize offending in a more fine-grained way may even reduce the impact of any irrational influences on decisions, potentially through encouraging specific legally relevant distinctions to be made in ways that do not clearly contradict juror intuitions or beliefs.[63] However, it should be noted that there are downsides of using alternative verdicts too, particularly when considering verdicts that provide jurors with an option indicative of guilt but without guilt having been proved beyond a reasonable doubt. Researchers in Scotland have cautioned of undesirable effects of retaining the not proven verdict, including stigmatizing those who have not actually been convicted of a criminal offence but who receive a not proven verdict.[64]

Conclusions

Research relating to the impacts of legal standards and procedures on juror decisions illustrates how existing associations can be explained through juror attribution of meaning to evidence, trial participants, the body of evidence, and legal standards. These attributions of meaning are influenced by juror intuitions and beliefs as well as information provided at trial. As a result, interventions introduced for one purpose can end up having a counterintuitive effect. The research above shows that the wording of information and the provision of help to jurors can impact (or fail to impact) the representations they encode and rely on. Designing legal standards and procedures specifically to take account of the reality of juror decision-making processes has the potential to enhance the impact of positive influences on juror decisions and to minimize the impact of negative influences on juror decisions. However, it is crucial to consider legal standards and procedures cohesively in terms of their effects on decision-making and how they are likely to interact with underlying decision-making processes. More concrete suggestions on how legal procedure might be designed specifically to *make juries work better* will be developed in Chapters 9 and 10 of this book. However, of course, juror determinations alone do not determine legal outcomes. In order to understand how juries work, it is necessary to understand not only what influences juror determinations, but how these individual determinations are translated into verdicts through deliberation. That process will be considered in the next chapter.

[63] For evidence of such an effect in the context of the insanity defence, see Helm, Ceci, and Burd (n 6).
[64] Chalmers, Leverick, and Munro (n 12).

8
Jury Deliberations

Introduction

In the previous three chapters, I examined a variety of factors that have the potential to influence the meaning that jurors assign to evidence, trial participants, the body of evidence, and legal standards. I highlighted ways in which jurors are well placed to assign meaning to these constructs, but also systematic weaknesses in the process of meaning-assignment that are likely to inhibit the ability of jurors to achieve the goals outlined in Chapter 3. Put simply, the way in which people assign meaning is likely to facilitate the influence of a range of problematic intuitions and beliefs in the decision process. In this chapter, I consider how individual juror verdicts are combined to ultimately result in a jury verdict, and how this process can ameliorate or exacerbate weaknesses of individual juror decisions. While significantly less research has examined jury verdicts compared to individual juror verdicts, research highlights the importance of juror verdicts in predicting jury verdicts. Very broadly speaking, research suggests that the probability of a jury reaching a particular verdict is roughly proportional to the initial number of jurors favouring that verdict.[1]

I begin this chapter by reviewing a range of existing research on factors that affect how individual juror impressions are translated into jury verdicts, complemented by research on group decision-making more generally. This review is intended to highlight important work in this area, not to be a comprehensive summary. It is also important to note that the majority of research considered is in the United States context which requires unanimous decisions (ways in which legal procedure might influence these general processes will be considered in the next chapter). I draw on this research, alongside an existing model of jury decision-making (the DISCUSS Model) and the Representation-Based Model of juror decision-making proposed in Chapter 4, to develop a proposed Representation-Based Model of the translation of individual preferences into jury verdicts. I draw on this model and existing work to assess strengths and weaknesses of the deliberation process and conclude with some notes about how knowledge relating to jury deliberation can be combined with knowledge about how jurors formulate initial impressions (discussed in Chapters 4–7 of this book) to feed into procedures

[1] DJ Devine, *Jury Decision Making: The State of the Science* (New York UP 2012) 31.

How Juries Work. Rebecca K. Helm, Oxford University Press. © Rebecca K. Helm 2024.
DOI: 10.1093/9780191948107.003.0008

designed to improve deliberations and, ultimately, to improve verdicts against the benchmarks laid out in Chapter 3.

Section I: The Majority Rule and Factors Affecting the Translation of Juror Preferences into Jury Verdicts

While significantly less research has examined the deliberation process and jury verdicts compared to individual juror verdicts, this research has still provided important insight that can be drawn on in order to understand how jurors combine individual impressions during the deliberation process. A large amount of relatively early work in the area of jury decision-making sought to predict the probability of a final outcome (eg a guilty verdict) from an initial distribution of member preferences.[2] An important insight of this work was to demonstrate two important effects in the translation of individual to group jury verdicts. The first, termed a majority effect, is that individual verdicts are predictive of ultimate jury verdicts—the probability of a jury reaching a particular verdict is roughly proportional to the initial number of jurors favouring that verdict. This general effect has been observed in both studies of real legal cases and mock jury studies.[3] The effect is relatively unsurprising since more people agreeing with a position is a good sign that the position is ultimately appropriate and supported by evidence and is likely to mean more arguments in favour of that position, such that the majority will have greater informational influence (influence resulting from the communication of information). This reality is enhanced by the fact that generally groups will be more influenced by 'cognitively central' members (members who share information that is known by many in the group) than by 'cognitively peripheral' members (who hold unique information).[4] In addition, the majority also have normative social influence (influence resulting from a desire to be included in a group and to avoid standing out).[5]

The second demonstrated effect is termed an asymmetry effect. Put simply, deliberations tend to produce a leniency shift. Where there is no overall group preference, or only a weak preference, the jury is more likely to move in favour of

[2] I Lorge and H Solomon, 'Two Models of Group Behavior in the Solution of Eureka-Type Problems' (1955) 20(2) Psychometrika 139.

[3] Devine, *Jury Decision Making* (n 1) 31. Note that this is consistent with work on individual versus group decisions more generally, which shows that group discussion tends to move group average preferences towards the side favoured by individual preferences prior to discussion; see DG Myers and H Lamm, 'The Group Polarization Phenomenon' (1976) 83(4) Psychological Bulletin 602.

[4] CR Sunstein and R Hastie, 'Making Dumb Groups Smarter' *Harvard Business Review* (November 2014) 4–5 <https://hbr.org/2014/12/making-dumb-groups-smarter> accessed 19 June 2023. This effect has been explained by the fact that group members generally prefer to hear information that is commonly held and prefer to listen to people delivering such information.

[5] Devine, *Jury Decision Making* (n 1) 152–53.

acquittal.[6] Empirical work collating the results of mock jury studies examining the relationship between juror pre-deliberation verdict preferences (in the context of required unanimous verdicts) and jury verdicts has identified very rough 'critical thresholds' that predict the verdict a jury will reach (provided a verdict is reached, ie excluding hung juries which are more common in experimental work than in practice). Put simply, the authors found that conviction is likely if at least 75 to 83 per cent of jurors favour conviction prior to deliberation, and acquittal is likely if at least 50 to 67 per cent of jurors favour acquittal prior to deliberation.[7] So, the authors state that in a twelve-person jury 'if 7 or fewer jurors favour conviction at the beginning of deliberation the jury will probably acquit, and if 10 or more jurors believe the defendant is guilty, the jury will probably convict. With 8 or 9 jurors initially favouring conviction, the final verdict is essentially a toss-up.'[8] This asymmetry effect can be seen as consistent with the burden of proof, which requires acquittal in the case of uncertainty.

In addition to these two very general effects, work has clearly demonstrated variability in how individual juror verdicts are translated into jury decisions. Importantly, work suggests that the composition of the jury and juror confidence and persuasion resistance can be important in predicting final verdicts.

The composition of the jury

There are a number of ways in which the composition of the jury has been shown to be likely to influence overall jury verdicts. As discussed above, the composition of the jury in terms of the distribution of verdict preferences is likely to influence the overall jury verdict. So, where a particular juror characteristic (eg gender) is associated with a greater likelihood of reaching a particular verdict, generally a jury with more jurors with that characteristic will be more likely to reach the verdict associated with that characteristic. However, it is also important to note that not all jurors are likely to have the same influence on a jury. Existing work suggests that the influence a particular juror has is likely to depend on a number of factors, including their participation (ie how often they speak), their advocacy (ie the extent to which they are seeking to convince other jurors to agree with them), and

[6] See G Stasser, NL Kerr, and R Bray, 'The Social Psychology of Jury Deliberations: Structure, Process, and Product' in NL Kerr and R Bray (eds), *The Psychology of the Courtroom* (Academic Press 1982) 221; RJ MacCoun and NL Kerr, 'Asymmetric Influence in Mock Jury Deliberation: Jurors' Bias for Leniency' (1988) 54(1) Journal of Personality and Social Psychology 21; DJ Devine and others, 'Jury Decision Making: 45 Years of Empirical Research on Deliberating Groups' (2001) 7(3) Psychology, Public Policy, and Law 622; DJ Devine and others, 'Strength of the Evidence, Extraevidentiary Influence, and the Liberation Hypothesis: Data from the Field' (2009) 33(2) Law and Human Behavior 136.

[7] Devine and others, 'Jury Decision Making' (n 6).

[8] ibid 692.

their normative influence (ie the extent to which they as a person are convincing to others).[9]

Importantly, participation, advocacy, and normative influence all have the potential to be influenced by factors that are not probative as to the reliability of the juror in question and thus have the potential to lead to irrational influence on the jury. For example, research conducted in this area with both mock jurors and real jurors (who were surveyed after real trial deliberation and asked for their perspective on their contribution) has found that social class and age predict juror participation and influence on juries, such that jurors with higher social status and middle-aged jurors participate more and are more influential on juries than jurors with lower social status and younger or older jurors.[10] Some work has also suggested that male jurors and white jurors may have greater influence than female jurors and ethnic minority jurors, although other work has questioned this effect.[11]

Work has also shown how normative influence in particular can be impacted by (what are thought to be) irrelevant factors, and how the impact of these factors can have a biasing effect. For example, mock jury work examining the influence of hold-out jurors (dissenters disagreeing with the majority) has found that the expression of emotion can influence persuasiveness, and that this persuasiveness can vary systematically based on juror gender and race. Specifically, this work found that hold-out jurors expressing anger were less influential when they were female (but not male) or Black (but not white)—despite identical arguments and emotion being expressed.[12]

Another way in which jury composition can impact how juror preferences are translated into final verdicts relates specifically to the diversity of juries. In the context of juror race, mock jury research specifically suggests that the quality of deliberations is higher in diverse juries than in all-white juries, and that diversity can have an impact on verdicts. A seminal piece of research in this area examined deliberations in the trial of a Black defendant in racially non-diverse (all-white) and racially diverse mock juries. The work found that the racially

[9] Devine, *Jury Decision Making* (n 1) 166–67.

[10] E York and B Cornwell, 'Status on Trial: Social Characteristics and Influence in the Jury Room' (2006) 85(1) Social Forces 455; E York Cornwell and Valerie P Hans, 'Representation Through Participation: A Multilevel Analysis of Jury Deliberations' (2011) 45(3) Law & Society Review 667; Devine, *Jury Decision Making* (n 1).

[11] DK Marcus, PM Lyons Jr, and MR Guyton, 'Studying Perceptions of Juror Influence *In Vivo*: A Social Relations Analysis' (2000) 24(2) Law and Human Behavior 173; Devine, *Jury Decision Making* (n 1) 166–67.

[12] JM Salerno and L C Peter-Hagene, 'One Angry Woman: Anger Expression Increases Influence for Men, but Decreases Influence for Women, During Group Deliberation' (2015) 39(6) Law and Human Behavior 581; JM Salerno, LC Peter-Hagene, and ACV Jay, 'Women and African Americans Are Less Influential When They Express Anger During Group Decision Making' (2019) 22(1) Group Processes & Intergroup Relations 57.

diverse juries exchanged a wider range of information, and that white jurors made fewer errors when deliberating on these (as opposed to all-white) juries.[13] More recent findings have supported this salutary effect of racial diversity on jury deliberations. For example, recent research found that mock jurors on diverse juries engaged in higher self-monitoring,[14] and that jurors on diverse juries made more 'high-quality' contributions to discussions (specifically in an ambiguous case).[15]

Juror confidence and persuasion resistance

Another factor that is likely to be important in influencing how individual juror preferences are translated into jury verdicts is the confidence that jurors have in their preferred verdicts. Unsurprisingly, research suggests that jurors with lower levels of confidence are more likely to change their verdicts (and, conversely, jurors with higher levels of confidence are less likely to change their verdicts).[16] Thus, juror confidence has been incorporated into models seeking to quantitatively predict final verdicts from juror preference, such as social interaction schemes.[17] This role of juror confidence is consistent with work in social psychology more broadly, which shows that people with greater confidence in their own judgment are less likely to be convinced by advice from others.[18]

The source of juror confidence may be a feeling of competence in relation to particular evidence presented at trial and its correct interpretation; however, some jurors may be predisposed to have greater confidence in their judgments generally, for example as a result of their *power* (their general capacity to influence others).[19] Related to the concepts of confidence and power is persuasion resistance, which essentially refers to a person's stubbornness or willingness to change their mind once they have made a decision. As a result of differences in confidence and, relatedly, persuasion resistance, some jurors are more likely to change their minds than others.

[13] SR Sommers, 'On Racial Diversity and Group Decision Making: Identifying Multiple Effects of Racial Composition on Jury Deliberations' (2006) 90(4) Journal of Personality and Social Psychology 597.

[14] MC Stevenson and others, 'Racially Diverse Juries Promote Self-Monitoring Efforts During Jury Deliberation' (2017) 3(2) Translational Issues in Psychological Science 187.

[15] AN Bergold and M Bull Kovera, 'Diversity's Impact on the Quality of Deliberations' (2022) 48(9) Personality and Social Psychology Bulletin 1406.

[16] G Stasser and JH Davis, 'Group Decision Making and Social Influence: A Social Interaction Sequence Model' (1981) 88(6) Psychological Review 523.

[17] Devine, *Jury Decision Making* (n 1) 33–35.

[18] See eg KE See and others, 'The Detrimental Effects of Power on Confidence, Advice Taking, and Accuracy' (2011) 116(2) Organizational Behavior and Human Decision Processes 272.

[19] ibid.

Section II: Modelling Jury Decisions

The DISCUSS Model

A helpful formal model seeking to represent the group (and jury) decision process is the DISCUSS Model, proposed by Garold Stasser. That model is consistent with Fuzzy-Trace Theory (FTT) in its recognition of the importance of memory in the decision-making process. Specifically, it models how the information in juror memory influences their 'speaking acts' during deliberations, and how those 'speaking acts' shape deliberation and, ultimately, decisions. The model is iterative, capturing multiple steps in the deliberation process. Put simply, each iteration involves the speaking act of a group member. In that act, they draw on information in their own memory to convey information, and the information they convey influences the memories of other group members, who may update their opinions as a result. Importantly, the model also recognizes that some group members are more likely to speak than others, through a 'participation' parameter, and that the impact of a particular speaking act will vary based on an 'advocacy' parameter (recognizing that some jurors disproportionately share information that supports their preferred decision) and a 'normative influence' parameter (recognizing the same information might be given different weight when given by different group members). So, put simply, going into deliberations, group members all have certain information encoded in memory, which will be influenced when other group members speak. The probability of a group member speaking, and their impact on the memories of others when they speak, is determined by the participation parameter, the advocacy parameter, and the normative influence parameter. In this way, group members will update the information that each other has in memory. The model assumes that information in memory has a relatively quantitative weight (the computer simulation implementing the model specifically assigns weight to each item of information), and that jurors reach verdicts based on a weighted sum of the information in memory.[20] The model therefore assumes relatively rational and quantitative processing. As Dr Dennis Devine has noted, the model (along with other earlier models of jury decisions) retains 'a level of dependence on rational modes of calculation that assume the evidence is presented in a spreadsheet fashion'.[21] While the model can account for many of the effects discussed above, as well as replicating the majority effect,[22] its assumptions about how group members store information in memory and combine information to

[20] Devine, *Jury Decision Making* (n 1) 36–38.

[21] ibid 40.

[22] G Stasser, NL Kerr, and GH Davis, 'Influence Processes and Consensus Models in Decision-Making Groups' in PB Paulus (ed), *Psychology of Group Influence* (Lawrence Erlbaum Associates 1989) 279–326.

reach decisions are inconsistent with FTT and associated evidence, discussed in Chapter 4.

Updating DISCUSS—a representation-based model

As noted above, the DISCUSS Model is consistent with FTT in its recognition of the importance of information represented in memory in the decision-making process. The importance of deliberation in updating memory is also recognized in legal decisions.[23] However, the way that FTT conceptualizes both memory and its updating differs from the predictions of the DISCUSS Model.

According to FTT (discussed more fully in Chapter 4), the representations in memory that adults are likely to rely on in legal decision-making are gist-based representations. These are representations of the underlying meaning of information in context, do not have a quantitative weight, and cannot be combined in a calculation-type process. Because the representations in memory that are most likely to be important in decision-making are gist-based representations, updates to verbatim representations that do not correspond to updated gist-based representations are unlikely to influence the decision-making process. To put it another way, if jurors share verbatim information with each other, this verbatim information is unlikely to feed through into the decision process of other jurors unless the information leads other jurors to encode new gist-based representations or to update existing gist-based representations (of evidence, trial participants, the body of evidence, or legal standards). The deliberation process will therefore influence decision-making through jurors leading others to encode new gist-based representations or to update existing gist-based representations. This change could occur through a juror providing others with information that those others may not have remembered, or through a juror changing the way others think about or perceive information that they had already remembered. The extent to which information conveyed will lead others to update how they perceive meaning (ie the meaning they ascribe to evidence, trial participants, the body of evidence, and legal standards) will likely depend on the information itself, and other factors—which have been introduced in the discussion of existing work above—including how information is conveyed, who is conveying the information, and characteristics of those receiving information, as well as likely interactions between these variables.

Information itself

Clearly certain information has the potential to be more meaningful to jurors than other information, based on, for example, its strength and relevance to the case.

[23] See eg *Apodaca et al v Oregon* 406 US 404 (1972) 389.

Some information will clearly be stronger and more relevant than other information. For example, in a case that is heavily reliant on digital evidence, information on weaknesses in digital evidence backed up by evidence given by a reliable expert is likely to be viewed as more persuasive than information on a particular juror's general suspicion of forensic evidence or the criminal justice system.[24]

The way information is conveyed

Existing models and empirical work, discussed above, highlight ways in which how information is conveyed can influence how it is interpreted by jurors. For example, as noted earlier, existing work has shown that the influence particular information has can depend on the extent to which jurors are seeking to convince others to agree with them, and by the emotion of the person conveying the information.

FTT also provides additional insight into how the way information is conveyed may be important in determining whether it leads jurors to encode new gist-based representations or to update existing gist-based representations. Specifically, research drawing on FTT suggests that the most effective way to convey meaning (and thus lead others to update their conceptions of meaning) is to provide a clear causal structure for information presented.[25] So, juror statements are likely to be most effective in updating the beliefs of others where they do not just convey verbatim information, but present information in a narrative form (either incorporating it into the wider picture of what happened, or presenting an independent narrative relating to the individual piece of evidence). A similar sentiment is captured by Devine's 'Story Sampling' Model, which suggests that the most persuasive information shared by jurors will be information shared in narrative form.[26]

Who is conveying the information

The persuasiveness of information in altering conceptions of meaning can also be changed by who is presenting the information. In simple terms, information will have the most weight when provided by someone whom a person trusts and respects. A wide variety of factors may influence whether a person conveying information is trusted and respected, including the person's standing in a group (eg whether they are in a minority or majority),[27] a person's social status,[28] and whether the message being conveyed fits with existing viewpoints.[29] This

[24] For a review of work relating to the impact of information itself on deliberations, see Devine, *Jury Decision Making* (n 1) 163–65.

[25] DA Broniatowski and VF Reyna, 'To Illuminate and Motivate: A Fuzzy-Trace Model of the Spread of Information Online' (2020) 26 Computational and Mathematical Organization Theory 431.

[26] Devine, *Jury Decision Making* (n 1) 201–04.

[27] ibid 153.

[28] York and Cornwell (n 10); Cornwell and Hans (n 10); Devine, *Jury Decision Making* (n 1) 166–67.

[29] KA Carlson and JE Russo, 'Biased Interpretation of Evidence by Mock Jurors' (2001) 7(2) Journal of Experimental Psychology: Applied 91.

differential trust and respect can explain why some jurors are more influential than others, including in the ways discussed above. In addition, some jurors may have a tendency towards better advocacy in general and can be more persuasive in that way. Considering the differential effects of jurors of different genders and ethnicities expressing anger, effects that have been observed may have occurred as the result of emotions leading other jurors to infer different things about an emotional speaker based on their gender, and these inferences influencing the trust that jurors have in the information being expressed.[30] The way that people make inferences about those from whom they are getting information is likely largely a result of the learning described in Chapter 4 of this book.

Characteristics of those receiving information

Finally, the characteristics of those receiving information have the potential to make them more or less receptive to changing their attributions of meaning and can also change the particular information that may be persuasive for them. As noted above, some jurors may be resistant to persuasion, and thus will be less likely to update meaningful representations than those more open to persuasion. For example, some jurors may adhere to belief in discredited information, or may be particularly committed to initial preferences as a result of confirmatory bias.[31]

Summary

The Representation-Based Model of juror decisions presented in Chapter 4 of this book suggests that jurors will come into deliberations with their own meaningful representations of evidence, trial participants, the body of evidence (narrative), and legal standards. During the deliberation process, jurors are expected to share their own representations in addition to their own outstanding questions in an attempt to reach a consensus. Existing work illustrates that the extent to which jurors participate in discussions will vary and may differ systematically in line with juror characteristics such as social status and age. Jurors will influence others in discussions when they successfully lead others to encode new gist-based representations or to update existing gist-based representations. Ultimately, jurors' impressions on verdict will be shifted where representations of the body of evidence or legal standards are changed (including as a result of representations of evidence or trial participants changing) or, relatedly, when perceptions of the overlap between these two representations change. The extent to which jurors will change representations will depend on a number of factors, including the information being conveyed, the way information is conveyed, characteristics of the person conveying

[30] Salerno and Peter-Hagene (n 12).

[31] D Tait and J Goodman-Delahunty, 'The Effect of Deliberation on Jury Verdicts' in D Tait and J Goodman-Delahunty (eds), *Juries, Science and Popular Culture in the Age of Terror: The Case of the Sydney Bomber* (Palgrave Macmillan 2017) 235, 236–37.

the information, and characteristics of those receiving the information (as well as interactions between these factors).

As a result of discussions, jurors will either come to update their representations (or at least their confidence in them) or to maintain existing representations. If they update representations (or confidence in them), updated representations will be what is drawn on in discussions going forward. This process will continue until jurors update their representations so that the required number are in agreement as to the presence or absence of the necessary degree of overlap between their representation of the body of evidence (narrative) and legal standards, or until jurors fail to reach such an agreement, resulting in a hung jury. A rough depiction of this process and how it might work for an individual juror is outlined in Figure 8.1.

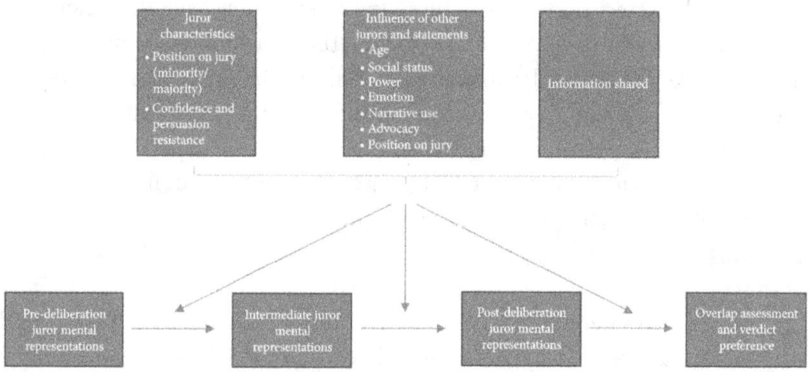

Figure 8.1 Impact of deliberations on juror representations and verdict preference

Thus, a Representation-Based Model accounts for many effects demonstrated in the literature and also incorporates many of the factors recognized as important by the DISCUSS Model, but in a slightly different framework, linking to the Representation-Based Model of juror decision-making discussed in Chapter 4 of this book.

Section III: Strengths and Weaknesses of the Deliberation Process

As noted in previous chapters of this book, one of the key advantages of the jury is the pooling of knowledge and insight gained by citizens as members of the community. As members of the community, we gain subtle insight through our experiences and interactions, some of which cannot be articulated in clear rules or calculations. Jurors have an educated intuition both on how events occur in society and the standards that we have as community members, and this allows them to insightfully assign meaning to evidence, trial participants, the body of evidence, and legal standards. However, as described in Chapters 4–7, there are predictable weaknesses in the way humans assign meaning to information. Ultimately, a range of intuitions and beliefs have the potential to feed through into the decision-making of jurors, some of which are non-probative and/or can undermine the presumption of innocence, the right to be treated fairly and without discrimination, the right of innocent persons not to be convicted, and/or the principle of legality.

Deliberations have the potential to improve the quality of decision-making through increasing insight (which is generally more likely to be representative of community insight and less likely to be influenced by an individual's problematic intuitions or beliefs where more viewpoints are represented), but also through allowing jurors to collectively correct errors and reduce memory deficiencies that might be experienced by individual jurors.[32] However, understanding how people deliberate as groups and what influences them when doing so highlights key ways in which the deliberation process may not achieve these aims and could in predictable cases even lead to a decline in quality when compared to individual decisions.

Ultimately, the effect that deliberation has will not be consistent, and will vary depending on a range of factors including strength of the evidence and the number of jurors influenced by particular intuitions or beliefs. Where the evidence is objectively very strong or very weak, it is much less likely that there will be significant variation in opinions among jurors as long as clear errors are corrected (and note there may be cases in which they are not, for example cases in which expert evidence is not properly critiqued). In this context, if any jurors are initially voting against the clear weight of the evidence, they are likely both to be in the minority and to have weaker arguments. In the absence of a complicating factor, such as a juror with a desire to nullify the law or a juror with very high persuasion resistance in the minority who is not persuaded by the majority viewpoint, deliberations are likely to be helpful in these cases through facilitating unanimous verdicts in line with the weight of evidence. However, the situation in more ambiguous cases is likely to be far more complex. In these cases, there are greater risks that deliberations could fail to address problematic influences on individual juror impressions or could even spread them. In this context, the precise distribution of initial preferences among individual jurors is likely to be important.

First, in more ambiguous cases, there is a far greater risk that the majority could favour a verdict that results from problematic intuitions or beliefs. Where the majority are influenced by problematic intuitions or beliefs, these undesirable influences are susceptible to spread, per the majority effect. In this way, deliberation may reinforce or even spread problematic opinions. An important question in this context is therefore how likely a jury is to contain a majority of members whose relevant mental representations are influenced by problematic intuitions or beliefs.

[32] See eg J Surowiecki, *The Wisdom of Crowds: Why the Many Are Smarter Than the Few and How Collective Wisdom Shapes Business, Economies, Societies, and Nations* (Doubleday 2004).

In relation to problematic intuitions and beliefs learned through experience, it is helpful to look back at the discussion in Chapter 4 relating to how intuitions and beliefs develop. Unfortunately, some problematic intuitions and beliefs that develop through experience are likely to be held by a significant proportion of the population, and, in particular, a significant proportion of the majority population. There are at least two clear reasons for the pervasiveness of these potentially problematic intuitions and beliefs. First, majority groups often share common experiences that can be insightful when applied in contexts with which they are familiar, but misleading when applied to minority groups. Secondly, many people in the population rely on similar media sources to get information, and, as noted in Chapter 4, media coverage is often skewed towards particular events and thus may be misleading. Problematic influences resulting from cognitive bias also have the potential to influence the majority of jurors. Biasing influences such as emotion or anchoring that can influence a verdict are generally predictable in human cognition and are likely to influence multiple jurors in similar ways (although the extent of the influence will depend on the particular cognitive bias, and some biases, such as confirmatory bias, may lead to divergences rather than convergences of opinion).

Unfortunately, where most members of a group share problematic intuitions and beliefs, group agreement may be seen as proof that reasoning is correct.[33] Importantly, existing research in the context of cognitive biases has confirmed the potential for the influence of biases to be exacerbated rather than attenuated in group decision-making (although note that where biases affect different individuals differently, for example where different things are easier/harder to imagine for different individuals in the case of the simulation heuristic, the impact of biases may be attenuated by group discussion).[34]

Secondly, in more ambiguous cases there is a greater probability that minority jurors could form persuasive arguments and thus have informational influence. This influence could be present even where those arguments are based on problematic intuitions and beliefs, rather than representation of community views. This risk is particularly apparent where minority jurors in question are people who are particularly likely to (a) speak and (b) be persuasive. The research discussed above suggests that people who are most likely to speak and be persuasive are generally middle-aged and of relatively high social status. Importantly, these groups may be particularly susceptible to inappropriate generalization from experience since their experiences (and the learning from those experiences) may not match the reality of life in the contexts they are making legal judgments about, which disproportionately involve young people from groups perceived as having lower

[33] Sunstein and Hastie (n 4).
[34] ibid 2.

social status.[35] The potential for jurors to be persuasive despite being inaccurate is supported by some existing mock jury work. One experimental study specifically found that the mock jurors who control deliberation are not always the most accurate, and, relatedly, those likely to change their verdict through deliberation are not those with the least accurate memories, but those with the least confidence in their memories.[36]

The multiple factors that are likely to influence how deliberation impacts the quality of legal decision-making can explain conflicting findings in previous work.[37] As the discussion above demonstrates, deliberation can be beneficial, but may also fail to correct or even amplify problematic influences on jurors. Legal procedure can seek to improve the impact of deliberations either through changing the initial distribution of juror preferences, or through changing how those initial preferences are combined to reach a group verdict.

Conclusions

Ultimately, deliberations are necessary in order for legal verdicts to reflect community judgment rather than the judgment of an individual citizen. However, the extent to which jury deliberations lead to verdicts that are appropriate in line with the goals laid out in Chapter 3 of this book (both in terms of the fact-finding function and the democratic function) is likely to be case dependent.

Problematic intuitions and beliefs that feed into juror representations of evidence, trial participants, the body of evidence, and legal standards through the attribution of meaning, discussed in Chapters 4–7 of this book, clearly have strong potential to feed through into the final jury verdict. This is particularly likely to be true in ambiguous cases where those factors have impacted the majority of jurors or have impacted a persuasive minority of jurors. Importantly, the nature of these factors means that there is a real possibility that they could be impactful for either the majority or an influential minority. The disproportionate influence of certain individuals may also compromise the ability of the jury to reach a determination that the community as a whole would have made.

In this context, understanding the composition of the jury and viewpoints on a jury is important. Existing work, discussed above, has demonstrated the benefits of diverse jury composition. However, work in group decision-making more broadly suggests that potential benefits of diversity could extend beyond those resulting

[35] See T Newburn, 'Who Commits Crime?' in T Newburn, *Criminology: A Very Short Introduction* (OUP 2018).

[36] ME Pritchard and JM Keenan, 'Does Jury Deliberation Really Improve Jurors' Memories?' (2002) 16(5) Applied Cognitive Psychology: The Official Journal of the Society for Applied Research in Memory and Cognition 589.

[37] See Devine, *Jury Decision Making* (n 1) 177–79.

from diverse jury composition alone. Juries often have a significant amount of information (incorporating both information from trial and learning from experience) that they can utilize. However, key probative information is lost where some juror views are neglected. A key puzzle piece in improving the function of the jury may therefore be not only to ensure diversity in composition of the jury, but also to ensure that all viewpoints feed appropriately into the deliberation process, particularly in cases where jurors in a minority or other low-influence group actually have the most relevant experience relating to a particular case. How that might be achieved will be considered in the next part of this book, where I examine how we can tailor legal procedure to make juries work better.

9

Improving Juror Decisions

Introduction

In Chapter 4, I introduced a new model of how jurors work, the Representation-Based Model. I then developed this model in Chapters 5–7 by identifying a range of factors that have been associated with differences in juror decisions, and explaining these associations through the impact that relevant factors have on juror attribution of meaning to evidence, trial participants, the body of evidence, and legal standards (in line with the Representation-Based Model). This analysis makes clear that there are both normatively desirable and undesirable influences on jurors, based on the criteria outlined in Chapter 3. Broadly, the experience that jurors have in society gives them adaptive insight that can promote good decision-making in both the fact-finding and democratic roles; however, they are also susceptible to the influence of predictable misconceptions and biases that can be non-probative and also undermine key normative principles. As discussed in Chapter 8, juror decisions are highly predictive of jury decisions. Therefore, in seeking to improve jury decisions, a good place to start is to assess and improve the decisions of individual jurors.

In this chapter, I draw on the Representation-Based Model of juror decision-making and accompanying research discussed in this book to evaluate the consistency between theory relating to the jury and juror decision-making in practice. I then consider how interventions might improve juror decisions. Recommendations include changes to directions and guidance, changes to the way expert evidence is introduced, the utilization of targeted decision aids, the utilization of agreed questions for cross-examination, evidence-based rules on admissibility, and more careful design of legal standards. In some areas, discussions focus primarily on England and Wales, although some references are made to other jurisdictions, and many recommendations apply more broadly. An important preliminary note is that this chapter covers a lot of territory, and so does not comprehensively cover the body of existing research in each sub-area. These suggestions should therefore be considered alongside existing research on the jury in considering jury reform in a complete and cohesive way.

How Juries Work. Rebecca K. Helm, Oxford University Press. © Rebecca K. Helm 2024.
DOI: 10.1093/9780191948107.003.0009

Section I: Juror Decisions: Consistency Between Theory and Practice

In Chapter 4, I proposed the Representation-Based Model of how jurors evaluate evidence and compare that evidence to legal standards in order to reach legal verdicts. Central to that model is the fact that jurors (as human decision-makers) are unlikely to rely on verbatim information itself but rather will rely on gist-based representations of that information in memory. As a result, the central information on which jurors rely, likely relating to evidence, trial participants, the body of evidence, and legal standards, will be influenced not only by information itself (ie evidence itself, trial participants themselves, a list of pieces of evidence, and legal standards themselves) but also by intuitions and beliefs of jurors that will interact with context to influence the meaning ascribed to that information. Through an examination of existing jury research and causal paths explaining associations between juror decisions and other factors, I identified a number of influences on jurors. Table 9.1 provides a summary of those influences (which are intended to be representative and important, rather than comprehensive) and a note on the normative desirability of each influence, based on my evaluations in each chapter. Ideally, desirable influences would be reflected in juror (and relatedly overall jury) decisions, but problematic influences would not be.

Table 9.1 Summary of influences on juror decision-making

Influence	Primary representation(s) influenced	General desirability	Chapter(s) discussed
Beliefs or intuitions about evidence (eg reliability of testimony)	Evidence	Desirable only when probative and consistent with normative principles	5, 6
Beliefs or intuitions about relative prevalence of events	Evidence	Desirable only when probative and consistent with normative principles	5, 6
Beliefs or intuitions about particular classes of people	Trial participants	Problematic	6
Ethical standards	Legal standards	Desirable only when consistent with normative principles	5
Perceived risk of wrongful conviction and future offending	Legal standards	Problematic when undermining the right of innocent persons not to be convicted	5

Table 9.1 Continued

Influence	Primary representation(s) influenced	General desirability	Chapter(s) discussed
Motivated cognitions (eg identity-protective cognition, culpable control theory of blame attribution)	Evidence, trial participants, legal standards	Problematic	5, 6
Halo effects	Trial participants	Problematic	5, 6
Empathy	Trial participants	Generally problematic	5
The simulation heuristic	The body of evidence, trial participants	Desirable only when ease of imagination not influenced by incorrect information or normatively undesirable factors	5, 6
Emotion	Evidence, trial participants, body of evidence, legal standards	Problematic (particularly since relevant emotion likely to be negative valence and high arousal)	6
Confirmatory bias	Evidence, trial participants	Problematic	6
Expectancy violation	Trial participants	Problematic	6
Priming effects (including anchoring)	Evidence, the body of evidence	Problematic	7
Streisand effects	Evidence	Problematic	7
Peripheral persuasion	Evidence	Problematic	7
Negativity bias	Evidence	Problematic	7
Processing errors	Evidence	Problematic	7

The extent to which each of these influences is important in a case will depend on the extent to which the influence changes the meaning ascribed to evidence by jurors. Notably, problematic influences are likely to play a much smaller role in cases involving clearly strong or weak evidence where the way evidence should be interpreted is clearer. However, in relatively ambiguous cases (or strong or weak cases where limited juror understanding prevents appropriate assessment of evidence) problematic influences are likely to feed into juror decisions and therefore jury decisions. There is therefore clear evidence that jurors can malfunction in important and predictable ways. In both their fact-finding and democratic roles jurors are likely to be influenced by misconceptions and cognitive biases that compromise both their ability to appropriately arrive at levels of confidence relating to descriptive facts and their adherence to relevant normative principles (including the presumption of innocence, the right of an innocent person not to be convicted, the right to be treated fairly and without discrimination, and the principle of legality). A range of approaches informed by the Representation-Based Model may be used in order to improve juror decision-making through maintaining desirable influences on decisions while reducing problematic influences on decisions.

An important preliminary note in this regard is that while many of the problematic influences identified above result from reliance on meaningful interpretations of information rather than verbatim information itself, pushing jurors to rely on verbatim representations of information will not have a beneficial impact on decision-making. Because verbatim representations are superficial, reliance on such representations will not be conducive to assigning weight to evidence, something that it is necessary for jurors to do. Where verbatim representations have the potential to lead to more accurate decision-making is in simple mathematical tasks, where information can be combined based on set rules in a quantitative way. Juror decision-making is not a quantitative task and requires evaluation of meaning and weighting of evidence. It is this very nature of juror decision-making that means that the task is well suited to lay human decision-makers rather than machines or experts with advanced knowledge of precise quantitative rules. As noted in Chapter 4, reliance on gist-based representations is developmentally advanced and has a beneficial impact on decisions requiring qualitative insight, such as juror decisions. So, what we are looking to do in improving juror decisions is essentially to educate intuition in order to improve the process of assigning meaning—to enhance the impact of desirable influences on jurors and to reduce the impact of problematic ones. Such a goal is in line with recent research finding that, in reasoning tasks, cognitive capacity predicts performance not because people high in cognitive capacity are better at correcting intuitions through deliberation but because people high in cognitive capacity have more accurate intuitions.[1] In this context, an important question is whether, how, and when we can educate and guide juror intuition. A number of interventions, both already utilized and proposed, have the potential to effectively provide this education and guidance.

[1] M Raoelison, VA Thompson, and W De Neys, 'The Smart Intuitor: Cognitive Capacity Predicts Intuitive Rather Than Deliberate Thinking' (2020) 204 Cognition 104381.

Section II: Improving Juror Decisions (Educating Intuition)

Directions/guidance to provide information

Existing intervention

As noted in Chapter 7, many jurisdictions already utilize directions or warnings (which I will refer to collectively as warnings) delivered by a judge in attempts to prevent the impact of problematic influences, most often incorrect beliefs, on jurors. These warnings are designed to improve the ability of jurors to arrive at a level of confidence relating to descriptive facts that is appropriately influenced by evidence.

Warnings seeking to dispel incorrect beliefs are generally utilized where legal systems identify a systemic risk that jurors may have misconceptions that could influence their legal decision-making. One area where this is done, as discussed in Chapter 7, is in cases involving eyewitness identifications. In England and Wales, warnings given in this context are known as Turnbull directions.[2] These warnings were introduced following a number of significant miscarriages of justice that were attributed to mistaken identifications by eyewitnesses and a subsequent report on identification evidence. That report concluded that there was a 'special risk' of wrongful conviction in cases dependent on eyewitness identification evidence.[3] Following the publication of this report, a specially constituted Court of Appeal in the case of *Turnbull*[4] issued guidelines designed to reduce the risk of miscarriages of justice resulting from eyewitness misidentification. As well as requiring the court to prevent prosecutions based entirely or almost entirely on weak identification evidence, these guidelines require courts to deliver a Turnbull direction, which underlines the dangers inherent in eyewitness identification evidence, where the prosecution case depends 'wholly or substantially on the correctness of one or more identifications of the accused which the defence alleges to be mistaken'.[5] Essentially, the direction provides information to jurors intended to make them aware of the limitations of identification evidence and to improve their evaluations of it. The direction must be tailored to a particular case but includes warning jurors of the need for caution in interpreting identification evidence, explaining that witness who is convinced in his or her own mind (ie a confident witness) may be wrong, explaining that a convincing witness may be

[2] For examples in the US context, see *United States v Telfaire* 469 F 2d 552 (DC Cir 1972); *New Jersey v Henderson* (2011) 27 A 3d 872.

[3] Lord Devlin, *Report to the Secretary of State for the Home Department of the Departmental Committee on Evidence of Identification in Criminal Cases* (HC 338 HMSO 1976).

[4] *R v Turnbull* [1977] QB 224.

[5] ibid 228.

wrong, and commenting on factors relevant to the quality of the evidence in the particular case.[6]

Another area in which warnings are commonly used is in targeting misconceptions relating to rape ('rape myths' or 'false assumptions'). In England and Wales, for example, evidence relating to belief in rape myths among potential jurors led the Court of Appeal to accept judges giving warnings to counter the potential impact of stereotypes and assumptions about sexual offending and the behaviour of victims.[7] The Crown Court Compendium now provides guidance to judges on warnings that can be given, at their discretion, in this area. These warnings should be tailored to a particular case and can relate to (amongst other things) the delay in making a complaint, inconsistency in accounts, emotion displayed when giving evidence, and clothing worn by the complainant. An example of a warning that might be given includes the following wording:

> [A]s a juror you have taken a legal oath or affirmation to try D based only on the evidence you hear in court. This means that none of you should let any false assumptions or misleading stereotypes about rape affect your decision in this case. To help you with this I will explain what we know about rape/sexual offences from experience that has been gained in the criminal justice system. We know that there is no typical rape, typical rapist, or typical person that is raped. Rape can take place in almost any circumstances. It can happen between all different kinds of people, quite often when the people involved are known to each other or may be related. We also know that there is no typical response to rape. People can react in many different ways to being raped. These reactions may not be what you would expect or what you think you would do in the same situation.[8]

Similar warnings are utilized in other jury systems.[9] Although these types of warning are quite widely used, the extent to which they actually facilitate better evaluation of case evidence is probably limited, and empirical research has generally shown that many jury directions are likely to be ineffective.[10] This

[6] Crown Court Compendium Part 1: Jury and Trial Management and Summing Up (2023), Section 15 'Identification' < https://www.judiciary.uk/wp-content/uploads/2023/06/Crown-Court-Compendium-Part-I-June-2023-updated-Feb-2024.pdf >accessed 25 April 2024. See also R Munday, *Evidence* (10th edn, OUP 2019) 504–05.

[7] See *R v D* [2008] EWCA Crim 2557; *R v Breeze* [2009] EWCA Crim 255; *R v Miller* [2010] EWCA Crim 1578.

[8] Crown Court Compendium Part 1: Jury and Trial Management and Summing Up (2023) Section 20 'Sexual Offences' 20-5–20-6 < https://www.judiciary.uk/wp-content/uploads/2023/06/Crown-Court-Compendium-Part-I-June-2023-updated-Feb-2024.pdf> accessed 25 April 2024.

[9] See eg J Quilter, L McNamara, and M Porter, 'New Jury Directions for Sexual Offence Trials in New South Wales: The Importance of Timing' (2022) 46(3) Criminal Law Journal 138.

[10] See eg J Goodman-Delahunty, A Cossins, and N Martschuk, *Jury Reasoning in Joint and Separate Trials of Institutional Child Sexual Abuse: An Empirical Study*. Sydney: Royal Commission into Institutional Responses to Child Sexual Abuse (2016); F Leverick, 'Jury Directions' in J Chalmers, F Leverick, and A Shaw (eds), *Post-Corroboration Safeguards Review Report of the Academic Expert Group* (The Scottish Government 2014) 101–17.

ineffectiveness can be explained for a number of reasons, some of which were explored briefly in Chapter 7. At the outset, it should be noted that commentators have raised concerns about the ability of the jury to understand instructions.[11] Even where jurors do understand instructions, there are likely to be limitations to their effectiveness.

First, warnings typically provide jurors with verbatim information, but do not provide context to facilitate the encoding of appropriate gist-based representations. They provide conclusions, sometimes from substantial bodies of research, in a simplistic way. For example, as noted above, Turnbull directions note that there is not necessarily a correlation between confidence and identification accuracy. This statement sums up decades of research examining the relationship between confidence and accuracy in a very simplistic way. However, without being told about the factors that are thought to undermine (or not undermine) the relationship between confidence and accuracy, jurors are left unable to learn about the relationship, and to encode information in a meaningful way that they can then apply to assess the probative value of confidence in a particular case. Instead, they will encode the verbatim representation that confidence does not necessarily equate to accuracy. This representation may not be encoded in gist-based form at all and may have no impact, or may increase scepticism of all identifications.[12] This potential for warnings to merely increase scepticism rather than facilitating better evaluations (ie evaluations that appropriately distinguish between high- and low-quality identifications) is exacerbated by the fact that some warnings tell people what they should not rely on or how they should not make decisions, rather than helping them understand what they should be influenced by. Removing the cues people typically rely on without replacing those cues may lead them to be uncertain of what to rely on and may generate scepticism as a result.[13] Warnings simply telling jurors that a witness who is convinced in his or her own mind may be wrong are interesting in this regard. While it is certainly true that predictable factors can disrupt the typical relationship between confidence and accuracy[14] and that highly confident false memories are possible,[15] confidence generally remains predictive

[11] See eg J Temkin, '"And Always Keep a-Hold of Nurse, for Fear of Finding Something Worse": Challenging Rape Myths in the Courtroom' (2010) 13 New Criminal Law Review 710, 722.

[12] For experimental work demonstrating increased scepticism, see AP Papailiou, DV Yokum, and CT Robertson, 'The Novel New Jersey Eyewitness Instruction Induces Skepticism but Not Sensitivity' (2015) 10(12) PloS one e0142695; MK Dillon and others, '*Henderson* Instructions: Do They Enhance Evidence Evaluation?' (2017) 17(1) Journal of Forensic Psychology Research and Practice 1.

[13] For experimental work and discussion relating to this possibility, see FT Nitschke, BM McKimmie, and EJ Vanman, 'The Effect of Trauma Education Judicial Instructions on Decisions About Complainant Credibility in Rape Trials' (2022) 29(1) Psychology, Public Policy, and Law 69.

[14] See eg ER Spearing and KA Wade, 'Long Retention Intervals Impair the Confidence–Accuracy Relationship for Eyewitness Recall' (2022) 11(3) Journal of Applied Research in Memory and Cognition 384.

[15] See eg EF Loftus, 'Memories of Things Unseen' (2004) 13(4) Current Directions in Psychological Science 145.

of identification accuracy in identifications of suspects and so may be a useful cue in at least some cases.[16]

Secondly, the fact that warnings provide verbatim information rather than targeting underlying gist-based representations means that even where jurors are persuaded by the information given at a superficial level it is unlikely to change underlying schemas that are relevant to evidence evaluation and may influence jurors, including unconsciously. As Julia Cooper has stated in the context of warnings used in rape trials, guidance relies on the 'rationalist assumption' that if jurors are told about the reality of rape and are aware of misconceptions then they will arrive at more just outcomes.[17] However, jurors are not 'rationalist' in a strict sense; they are intuitive decision-makers focused on meaning. Merely providing information is unlikely to be sufficient to counter engrained intuitions and beliefs that influence attribution of meaning, although it may lead to updating of surface-level beliefs. For example, in the context of rape myths, warnings may convince jurors that sexual offences do not always involve force. However, that information is unlikely to go against years of juror experience that may make it easier for them to picture a sexual offence occurring when it involves force than when it does not (and which therefore have the potential to feed into decisions via the simulation heuristic). Thus, though warnings can change explicit beliefs, they cannot necessarily undo schemas related to those beliefs that can influence decisions, sometimes outside of conscious awareness. As a result, although warnings may alter explicit beliefs, and may even alter what jurors discuss during deliberation, those alterations may not translate into differences in decision-making in a concrete task.[18]

Finally, the information provided in warnings is provided in a very direct way, intended to be authoritative rather than persuasive as a result of information contained. As a result, warnings may actually be ineffective at influencing even verbatim beliefs. Jurors are expected to believe the information and integrate it into their assignment of meaning purely because it is provided by a judge in court. As noted in Chapter 7, an empirically grounded psychological theory relating to persuasion (the Elaboration Likelihood Model) suggests that persuading people to accept new information can be done via two routes—the Central Route or the Peripheral Route.[19] The Central Route involves attitude change based on

[16] See SL Sporer and others, 'Choosing, Confidence, and Accuracy: A Meta-Analysis of the Confidence-Accuracy Relation in Eyewitness Identification Studies' (1995) 118(3) Psychological Bulletin 315.

[17] J Cooper, 'Judges as Myth-Busters: A Re-Examination of Jury Directions in Rape Trials' (2022) 31(4) Griffith Law Review 485, 486.

[18] See discussion on abstract versus applied myths in E Daly and others, 'Myths About Myths? A Commentary on Thomas (2020) and the Question of Jury Rape Myth Acceptance' (2022) 7(1) Journal of Gender Based Violence 189. Relatedly, see O Smith and others, 'State Compensation as Rape Justice: Are Public Attitudes a Legitimate Foundation for Reform of the UK's Criminal Injuries Compensation Scheme?' (2022) 6(1) Journal of Gender-Based Violence 79.

[19] RE Petty and JT Cacioppo, 'The Effects of Involvement on Responses to Argument Quantity and Quality: Central and Peripheral Routes to Persuasion' (1984) 46(1) Journal of Personality and Social Psychology 69.

thoughtful consideration of the merits of information and is associated with more consistent attitude change. The Peripheral Route involves attitude change resulting from the information being associated with positive or negative heuristic cues (eg the perceived authority of the person providing the information) and is associated with less consistent attitude change, which can be influenced by bias. In the context of jury trials, because jurors are not provided with sufficient detail to engage with, critique, and appreciate evidence underlying warnings, they can only be persuaded by its content when this persuasion occurs via the Peripheral Route. Therefore, persuasion will be inconsistent and most likely in people who are predisposed to believe the information they are being given anyway, for example due to trust in the legal system or existing beliefs that align with the information.

Improving intervention

In order to address the problems noted above, general warnings should be avoided and instead guidance should be used to provide information in a way that allows jurors to extract gist as well as verbatim representations from it. Where jurors can encode meaningful rather than superficial information this has the potential to translate more easily into the gist-based decision-making process. Meaningful information has the potential to educate underlying intuition (rather than just surface-level representation) and, as a result, to facilitate appropriate application of new information to a particular case and potentially to facilitate the updating of schemas that may influence decisions unconsciously (eg through cognitive biases). Experimental research designing and testing guidance that essentially educates jurors through giving meaningful insight has shown promise in this regard in the area of eyewitness identifications. This research has used guidance to educate jurors rather than passively providing them with information. Specifically, the following techniques have been used successfully:

(1) *Providing specific detail on appropriate methods for assessing the probative value of evidence, where possible.* For example, the interview-identification-eyewitness factor (I-I-Eye) method is designed to help jurors identify and organize different types of eyewitness factors that affect accuracy and provides a framework for applying those in a case setting.[20]

(2) *Providing detail on why and how jurors should consider particular details.* For example, instead of stating 'You must ask yourselves . . . how long was it between the time of the incident and the time when the witness identified the defendant to the police', proposed instructions might state 'Memories

[20] NB Pawlenko and others, 'The Interview-Identification-Eyewitness Factor (I-I-Eye) Method for Analyzing Eyewitness Testimony' (2013) 25(3) The Jury Expert: The Art and Science of Litigation Advocacy 1 <www.thejuryexpert.com/wp-content/uploads/1305/JuryExpert_1305_IIEye.pdf> accessed 19 June 2023.

fade with time. As a result, delays between the commission of a crime and the time an identification is made can affect the reliability of the identification. The more time that passes, the greater the possibility that a witness's memory of a perpetrator will weaken.'[21]

(3) *Providing detail on evidence underlying statements that will allow jurors to understand and scrutinize their source, and examples to help jurors contextualize findings.* For example, 'Research in this area has shown that . . .' or 'For example, in one illustrative case . . .'[22] Providing jurors with examples of real cases that have the potential to really change the way that jurors picture and think about evidence may be promising in this regard, although note that this approach must be balanced against the need to avoid judges being seen to give expert evidence.

Designing guidance in line with these principles has the potential to facilitate updates to juror understanding based on the Central rather than the Peripheral Route, and to result in the encoding of meaningful gist-based representations that can be appropriately applied in context. This guidance should be given consistently and using clear language. It should also be delivered prior to evidence being presented rather than afterwards so that it can influence the gist-based representations that are encoded from evidence (rather than trying to retrospectively alter already engrained representations) and to avoid inappropriate gist-based representations influencing the interpretation of other information at trial, for example through their role in narratives or through creating an initial impression that then generates confirmatory bias. Empirical research supports this suggestion that guidance will be most effective when provided prior to evidence being presented rather than afterwards.[23]

There is therefore potential for evidence-based guidance to be effective in improving juror, and therefore jury, decision-making. An effective way to identify misconceptions that might be targeted in this way may be to consider predictable limitations in intuitions and beliefs, discussed in Chapter 4. However, such guidance is clearly not a panacea for a number of reasons. First, guidance cannot be so strong as to compromise juror autonomy or the benefits of utilizing lay decision-makers will be compromised. Secondly, guidance can only be used where there is objective information to provide which is clearly reliable and applicable in a

[21] AM Jones and S Penrod, 'Improving the Effectiveness of the *Henderson* Instruction Safeguard Against Unreliable Eyewitness Identification' (2018) 24(2) Psychology, Crime & Law 177.

[22] RK Helm, 'Evaluating Witness Testimony: Juror Knowledge, False Memory, and the Utility of Evidence-Based Directions' (2021) 25(4) The International Journal of Evidence & Proof 264.

[23] See J Chalmers and F Leverick, 'Methods of Conveying Information to Jurors: An Evidence Review' Research Findings 66/2018 (Scottish Government Justice Directorate 2018) 27–31. See also A Elwork, BD Sales, and JJ Alfini, 'Juridic Decisions: In Ignorance of the Law or in Light of It?' (1977) 1(2) Law & Human Behavior 163, 177.

particular case. Finally, even well-designed guidance is unlikely to be convincing to all jurors, particularly where it needs to override strong existing intuitions or beliefs.

Directions/guidance to reduce bias and other problematic influence

Another type of guidance that might be provided to jurors in order to reduce the impact of problematic factors on the assignment of meaning is guidance aimed directly at reducing potential unfair and discriminatory treatment. For example, guidance may seek to make jurors aware of implicit biases they might have and how to counter them in decision-making or may seek to assist jurors in identifying sources of intuitions or beliefs that they may have that should be tempered in the legal decision-making process. This intervention is important as it has the potential to help the jury avoid unfair and discriminatory influence.

Some research suggests that giving people information relating to discrimination against particular trial participants can trigger values that can be used to suppress any bias against those participants. One area in which this idea has been tested is discrimination based on race, through a theory called Aversive Racism Theory (ART). ART highlights the role of implicit biases (associations outside conscious awareness) relating to race which can impact decisions.[24] Where people hold egalitarian values, triggering awareness of implicit biases can potentially trigger those egalitarian values that can be used to recognize and suppress bias. The theory can therefore explain the findings discussed in Chapter 5, where racial bias appears to be reduced when the issue of race is made salient (ie where the presence of racially charged issues is clear). In the legal context, race may be made salient in case facts, may be made salient by racial tension in society that is brought into the courtroom, or may be made salient by awareness of the race of other jurors.[25]

If this theory is correct, then making race (or other potentially biasing factors) salient through guidance should trigger egalitarian values and thus lead jurors with implicit (but not explicit) bias to counter that bias. Instructions based on this theory have been examined in experimental work testing guidance designed to trigger egalitarian values. Specifically, experimental work tested the impact of the following guidance on people's evaluations of case evidence: 'Whatever your verdict may be, it must not rest upon baseless speculations, nor may it be influenced in any way by bias, prejudice, or sympathy. Research has shown that some individuals have unconscious biases that affect their judgments, so please monitor any

[24] SL Gaertner and JF Dovidio, 'The Aversive Form of Racism' in C Stangor (ed), *Stereotypes and Prejudice: Essential Readings* (Psychology Press 2000) 289.

[25] See discussion of implicit race salience in E Ingriselli, 'Mitigating Jurors' Racial Biases: The Effects of Content and Timing of Jury Instructions' (2014) 124(5) The Yale Law Journal 1346, 1690.

such biases you may have and do not let them affect your judgments.'[26] The study found some evidence that these instructions could be important in reducing biases (particularly when combined with race salience in a case), although this effect was only demonstrated in sentencing judgments, and not in guilt judgments. Results therefore provide some evidence that guidance may be helpful in reducing implicit biases, but are mixed, and highlight the need for further development and testing of potential guidance in this area.

Work on intuitions and beliefs more generally (discussed in Chapter 4) may also be drawn on to develop guidance with the potential to reduce other problematic influences related to juror intuitions and beliefs. These problematic influences include where intuitions and beliefs are influenced by heuristics and cognitive biases, where we inappropriately generalize (eg due to limited experience and learning what is connected but not why), where we do not have representative experience and effective feedback, and where we accept what we are told by others without scrutiny. Work on intuition has suggested that potentially triggering people to consider where their intuitions arise from and how appropriate they are to apply may be helpful in improving the quality of intuitive decision-making.[27] For example, it might be helpful, when jurors have a particular intuition, for them to ask themselves what kind of feedback they have received relating to this kind of intuition in the past, and how clear and immediate that feedback was. Triggering jurors to critique their own intuitions and beliefs in this way may improve the quality of those intuitions and beliefs where jurors can recognize and account for relevant limitations (although note a significant amount of introspection is needed to know where intuitions and beliefs come from).

Expert evidence

Existing intervention

Introducing expert evidence has the potential to enhance the extent to which jurors arrive at a level of confidence relating to descriptive facts that is appropriately influenced by evidence. Typically, jurisdictions will allow expert evidence to be introduced to assist the jury, particularly where expertise is required that is likely to be outside the knowledge of the jury.[28] As noted in Chapter 7, typically both sides (the prosecution and the defence) will have the opportunity to instruct and examine an expert in matters calling for expertise. Precisely when matters are considered to call for expertise varies by jurisdiction. In England and Wales, a relatively restrictive approach has been adopted towards the admission of expert

[26] ibid 1690.
[27] Robin M Hogarth, *Educating Intuition* (University of Chicago Press 2010) 219.
[28] In England and Wales see Turner [1975] QB 834.

evidence, particularly evidence from experts specializing in psychiatry and psychology.[29] Put simply, court decisions imply that generally matters relating to the human mind are within the normal range of knowledge of the jury, and therefore expert evidence is not necessary. Where expert evidence is given, it is typically given by opposing experts, although it is sometimes also possible to utilize joint prosecution and defence experts.

Improving intervention

First, rules on the situations in which expert evidence can be admitted should be closely considered based not on assumptions of subject matter within the experience of the jury but rather on examination of where juror knowledge, intuitions, and beliefs are likely to diverge from established evidence. This examination should consider not only where jurors have experience, but also where such experience is likely to lead to intuitions and beliefs that are accurate (eg where sufficient feedback has been received alongside appropriate existing experience, see Chapter 4). An important note in this regard is that, as discussed in Chapter 5, many people hold erroneous beliefs about memory and mental states. A relatively permissive approach to the admission of expert evidence in these areas may therefore be helpfully considered.

Secondly, the utility of expert evidence may be improved through greater utilization of agreed evidence, signed off by a prosecution and defence expert, rather than by opposing experts in court. Such an approach would enhance the potential for evidence presented to jurors to appropriately highlight strengths and weaknesses in evidence that jurors could then engage with, rather than being led by cognitive biases such as favouring the side they are drawn towards due to existing biases or prior evidence. Where evidence is presented by opposing experts (who have a strong tendency to favour the side that they are instructed by, even where they have appropriate training and expertise),[30] the way that jurors interpret the scientific evidence will be coloured by a range of cognitive biases given that jurors lack their own expert knowledge with which to scrutinize accounts.[31] As a result, they may fail to identify which position accurately reflects general scientific consensus (where there is one) or to recognize which limitations are most important in expert accounts. Importantly, adversarial experts may lead jurors to unnecessarily discredit evidence where the risks of such evidence being unreliable are very low. For example, introducing expert evidence on false memory in a case where the probability of false memory is very low (eg due to a large amount of independent corroboration) may provide an unnecessary opportunity for jurors with a tendency to

[29] Munday, *Evidence* (n 6) 327–31.

[30] See DC Murrie and MT Boccaccini, 'Adversarial Allegiance Among Expert Witnesses' (2015) 11 Annual Review of Law and Social Science 37.

[31] For related discussion, see E Giffin, 'Experts for Hire: A Dangerous Practice Which Increases the Risk of Bias and Disadvantages the Accused' (2018) 26 Dalhousie Journal of Legal Studies 1.

discredit victims to selectively interpret scientific evidence to support their viewpoint.[32] Utilizing agreed expert evidence has the potential to avoid this risk, and ensure that the weight of scientific opinion, as well as competing interpretations, are appropriately presented. Utilizing agreed experts also avoids the risks that jurors may assign meaning to expert evidence based on the personality and persuasiveness of the person delivering the evidence, rather than scientific value. As a review in England and Wales prepared by the United Kingdom Register of Expert Witnesses and published in 2005 stated, the approach can 'deal with the "cult of personality" that can develop at trial'.[33] Approaches such as 'hot-tubbing', where experts appear concurrently and are able to interact with one another, might also help bring out strengths and weaknesses of expert evidence more clearly, although the evidence available in this area suggests that this approach would be limited in its utility since it does not appear to reduce adversarial biases, at least in experts.[34]

Providing other aids to assist with understanding and decision-making

Existing intervention

The quality of the gist-based representations that jurors encode and apply (most obviously the extent to which they are appropriately influenced by evidence) may also be improved by providing aids to assist with understanding and decision-making. These aids have the potential to help jurors to arrive at a level of confidence relating to descriptive facts that is appropriately influenced by evidence, and also to avoid inaccuracy in assigning meaning to legal standards.

However, as with guidance, existing aids have not focused specifically on gist and the importance of meaning, and their utility may be limited. Two such aids that may have relatively limited utility are note taking and allowing jurors to ask questions. Generally, research on some such procedures has found positive effects on recollection and comprehension; however, little or no research suggests that these improvements translate into differences in verdict.[35]

In terms of note taking, the purpose of allowing jurors to take notes or see trial transcripts is primarily to avoid issues with recollection—where jurors are unable to remember evidence, they may unduly disregard important evidence during

[32] For discussion in the context of a real case, see J Fanelli and C Ramey, 'Ghislaine Maxwell Trial Will Put Memories of Jeffrey Epstein Accusers on Trial' *The Wall Street Journal* (26 November 2021) <https://www.wsj.com/articles/ghislaine-maxwell-trial-will-put-memories-of-jeffrey-epstein-accusers-on-trial-11637938801> accessed 19 June 2023.

[33] The UK Register of Expert Witnesses, 'Submission to Lord Carter's Review of Legal Aid Procurement: The Expert Witness Dimension' (2005) 16 <www.jspubs.com/downloads/PDFs/UKREW_Carter_Review_(Public).pdf> accessed 19 June 2023.

[34] JT Perillo and others, 'Testing the Waters: An Investigation of the Impact of Hot Tubbing on Experts from Referral Through Testimony' (2021) 45(3) Law and Human Behavior 229.

[35] For a more in-depth summary of these and other procedures, see Chalmers and Leverick (n 23) ch 2.

deliberations. In England and Wales, courts are required to permit note taking, but some other jurisdictions have more restrictive rules.[36] Australia and New Zealand permit note taking, which may be encouraged or discouraged at the discretion of the judge,[37] and some United States (US) jurisdictions only permit note taking if it is agreed to by the prosecution and the defence.[38] Note taking does have the potential to improve recollection of information, but the impact of the note taking is likely to depend on the notes that jurors take. Where jurors take note of verbatim information this information may ultimately be neglected in the gist-based decision-making process. Importantly, the gist-based representations that jurors are most likely to rely on and be influenced by are likely to be information that they would remember anyway. As discussed in Chapter 4, research informed by the Story Model suggests that people interpret evidence as a whole, with evidence being viewed as more persuasive where it fits in with an overarching narrative (in the Representation-Based Model, the representation of the body of evidence). Unless jurors check their notebooks for information throughout trial, this means that the information that is most influential to them (and which influences how other information is interpreted) will be information that fits in with their overall representation of the body of evidence. This information is also more likely to be recalled and may well be remembered even without notes. Thus, while note taking may trigger specific verbatim memory it may not alter the overall gist relied on by jurors. Questions about the efficacy of note taking are supported by experimental work in this area. Mock jury work in the criminal law context has confirmed that generally note taking helps jurors remember evidence more effectively but has not yet shown that note taking has an influence on verdicts.[39]

In terms of asking questions, in England and Wales, jurors can submit questions via notes to a judge.[40] While there is clear potential for questions to enhance the ability of jurors to encode gist appropriately, this potential is limited by juror understanding of what they need more information on. In many cases, intuitions and beliefs will guide the questions that they ask. Therefore, where these factors are

[36] C Thorley, 'Note Taking and Note Reviewing Enhance Jurors' Recall of Trial Information' (2016) 30(5) Applied Cognitive Psychology 655, 655.

[37] J Clough and others, 'The Jury Project 10 Years On—Practices of Australian and New Zealand Judges' (The Australasian Institute of Judicial Administration 2019) <https://aija.org.au/wp-content/uploads/2019/04/AIJA-The-Jury-Project-A-Survey-final-18-April-2019.pdf> accessed 19 June 2023.

[38] Thorley (n 36) 655.

[39] See eg D Rosenhan, S Eisner, and R Robinson, 'Notetaking Can Aid Juror Recall' (1994) 18 Law and Human Behavior 53; Thorley (n 36); C Thorley, R Baxter, and J Lorek, 'The Impact of Note Taking Style and Note Availability at Retrieval on Mock Jurors' Recall and Recognition of Trial Information' (2016) 24(4) Memory 560. Although see BM Dann, VP Hans, and DH Kaye, 'Can Jury Trial Innovations Improve Juror Understanding of DNA Evidence?' (2006–07) 90 Judicature 152 (where note taking was not even found to increase understanding) and IA Horowitz and L ForsterLee, 'The Effects of Note-Taking and Trial Transcript Access on Mock Jury Decisions in a Complex Civil Trial' (2001) 25(4) Law and Human Behavior 373 (a study in the civil context where jurors did perform better—in terms of effectively distinguishing among worthy plaintiffs—when they were allowed to take notes).

[40] See eg *R v Gynane* [2020] EWCA Crim 1348.

misleading, the ability to ask questions may not be as helpful as it first appears. In addition, while relevant research is quite limited, it suggests that generally people may not have many questions to ask during trial. One mock jury study examined the impact of juror questions on juror understanding and decisions in the context of a trial involving mitochondrial DNA evidence. Overall, the study found that jurors did not ask many questions despite being permitted to do so (only 22 per cent of jurors allowed to ask questions actually did so), and the ability to ask questions was not found to enhance juror understanding.[41]

Improving intervention

Other aids may have greater potential to enhance juror performance, by guiding jurors through the process of allocating meaning to information they are given. One aid with the potential to improve decision-making in this way targets juror understanding of the law and is called a 'route to verdict'. Routes to verdict involve a series of written questions that are given to jurors, designed to lead them to an appropriate verdict. They are now used frequently in courts in England and Wales.[42] While empirical evidence has highlighted the potential for written directions more generally to assist with juror comprehension,[43] there is currently limited evidence relating to how routes to verdict are likely to influence jurors. Broadly speaking, there is clear potential for the route to verdict to help jurors effectively extract meaning from what can sometimes be complex law.[44] However, drafters of routes to verdict (judges) must be careful to ensure that these directions, while encouraging jurors to encode meaning based on accurate understanding, are not so prescriptive as to undermine the ability of the jury to infuse meaning into relevant legal standards in a way that is consistent with viewpoints in the community, rather than viewpoints of the judge. To put it another way, they should avoid turning the task of applying legal standards into a checklist exercise that orients jurors towards more superficial application of facts to the law and that may influence their impressions in undesirable ways.[45]

[41] Dann, Hans, and Kaye (n 39). The fact that jurors ask relatively few questions has also been supported by research with real jurors, see L Heuer and S Penrod, 'Increasing Jurors' Participation in Trials' (1988) 12(3) Law and Human Behavior 231; L Heuer and S Penrod, 'Juror Notetaking and Question Asking During Trials: A National Field Experiment' (1994) 18(2) Law and Human Behavior 121.

[42] See eg *R v Atta-Dankwa* [2018] EWCA Crim 320 [31]; *R v Toure* [2019] EWCA Crim 1961; [2020] 4 WLR 17 [32].

[43] See eg for England and Wales, C Thomas, *Are Juries Fair?* (Ministry of Justice Research Series 1/10, February 2010) 35–40; C Thomas, 'Avoiding the Perfect Storm of Juror Contempt' (2013) 6 Criminal Law Review 483; C Thomas, 'The 21st Century Jury: Contempt, Bias and the Impact of Jury Service' (2020) Criminal Law Review 987, 992–97.

[44] For a discussion of this and other benefits of routes to verdict, see D Ormerod and C Thomas, 'Routes to Verdict—What We Know and What We Need to Know' (2021) 8 Criminal Law Review 615, 617.

[45] For a discussion of concerns in the US context, see M Comiskey, 'Tempest in a Teapot—The Role of the Decision Tree in Enhancing Juror Comprehension and Whether It Interferes with the Jury's Right to Deliberate Freely?' (2016) 6(2) Oñati Socio-legal Series 255.

Another type of aid that may have the potential to help jurors appropriately extract meaning from evidence is jury checklists or visual guides.[46] Research has suggested that these tools may improve understanding, at least once jurors have deliberated as a group.[47] However, their likely impact on verdict will depend on (1) the relevance of the particular evidence for verdict decisions, and (2) the extent to which they are designed to effectively facilitate the extraction of meaning. Work grounded in Fuzzy-Trace Theory has discussed visual decision aids that could be given to jurors to assist them in extracting appropriate gist from numbers and, specifically, to help them avoid processing errors (discussed in Chapter 6). Essentially, people can extract meaning from visualizations more easily than they can extract meaning from numbers themselves, avoiding processing errors associated with dealing with numbers. Put simply, these processing errors are 'bookkeeping' errors that can be cured by presenting numerical information in a clear visual way. This might be done through using tables, graphs, or simple graphics that aid the extraction of appropriate gist.[48] For example, where random match probabilities are provided in a graph, jurors can clearly extract meaning from numerical estimates while avoiding biases—there is no risk that 1/10 and 10/100 would be interpreted differently (see Figure 9.1).[49]

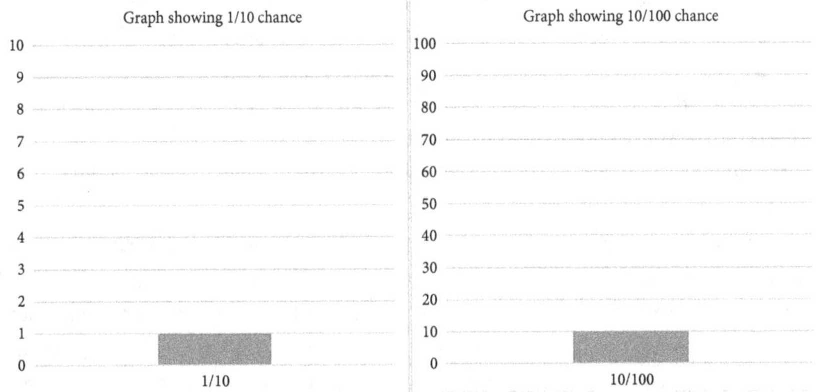

Figure 9.1 Illustrative graphical depiction of information to convey gist and to avoid processing errors

[46] Dann, Hans, and Kaye (n 39).

[47] ibid.

[48] R Helm, VP Hans, and VF Reyna, 'Trial by Numbers' (2017) 27(1) Cornell Journal of Law and Public Policy 107.

[49] ibid 128 and 135 for further examples.

Agreed questions for cross-examination

A relatively novel approach that may allow jurors to arrive at a level of confidence relating to descriptive facts that is appropriately influenced by evidence, and to avoid influences that undermine the right to be treated fairly and without discrimination, the presumption of innocence, and the right of an innocent person not to be convicted is for cross-examination questions to be reviewed by judges before they are shown to the jury in cases in which there are particular facts that may be prone to misinterpretation. This review could be conducted at a ground rules hearing—a hearing at which judges can set the parameters for fair treatment of defendants and witnesses.[50]

Currently, ground rules hearings are commonly used in England and Wales to ensure proper care of vulnerable defendants and witnesses; however, they might helpfully be used more extensively in order to ensure that the questions that are put to defendants and witnesses are not likely to mislead, or to lead to responses that will mislead, the jury. For example, in cases involving sexual offences, judges might be asked to screen cross-examination questions in advance to ensure that advocates questioning witnesses do not draw attention to factors known to be misleading or discriminatory, for example questions relating to clothing, past sexual history, or minor inconsistencies in testimony. In Scotland, ground rules hearings have been conducted for this purpose since 2017. At these hearings, parties to a trial agree key aspects of how evidence will be taken, including agreeing, among other things, the scope of questions asked in cross-examination.[51] During such hearings, non-probative questions likely to draw attention to misleading factors can be screened out, reducing the risk of an influence of problematic intuitions and beliefs on juror representation of evidence and associated decision-making.

Ground rules hearings could be utilized in a similar way to improve the quality of juror decision-making in other cases where existing juror intuitions or beliefs create a risk of inappropriate interpretation of, and assignment of meaning to, evidence. To give one example, such hearings may be used in cases heavily reliant on witness memory. In these cases, questions could be screened to ensure, for example, that they do not focus on minor inconsistencies that evidence suggests are not probative in assessing the quality of memory but which may be convincing to jurors, particularly when significantly disrupting the overall flow of testimony.[52]

[50] P Cooper, P Backen, and R Marchant, 'Getting to Grips with Ground Rules Hearings: A Checklist for Judges, Advocates, and Intermediaries to Promote the Fair Treatment of Vulnerable People in Court' (2015) 6 Criminal Law Review 420.

[51] Scottish Government, 'Improving Victims' Experience of the Justice System: Consultation' (May 2022) ch 2 <www.gov.scot/publications/improving-victims-experiences-justice-system/pages/5/> accessed 19 June 2023.

[52] See RP Fisher, A Vrij, and DA Leins, 'Does Testimonial Inconsistency Indicate Memory Inaccuracy and Deception? Beliefs, Empirical Research, and Theory' in BS Cooper, D Griesel, and M Ternes (eds), *Applied Issues in Investigative Interviewing, Eyewitness Memory, and Credibility Assessment* (Springer 2013).

Restrictions on admissibility

In some cases, the potential for evidence to hamper rather than enhance the ability of the jury to reach decisions in accordance with goals may necessitate restrictions on the admissibility of evidence. This reality is recognized by existing exclusionary rules which prevent some relevant evidence from being put before the jury (at least as long as an exception to the rule does not apply). It is beyond the scope of this book to engage in detailed discussion of exclusionary rules of evidence. However, it is worth noting that understanding how jurors assign meaning to evidence, and, relatedly where problematic influences are likely to influence this assignment, can inform an evidence-based approach to admissibility.

In some cases, the current law employs exclusionary rules based on assumptions about the operation of the jury that are not consistent with how jurors assign meaning to evidence. A clear example here is the hearsay rule, which essentially prevents a witness from giving evidence that they have heard from another witness who is not in court. Broadly, this rule is intended to safeguard the quality of verdicts by keeping unreliable evidence (evidence that is likely to be assigned value inappropriately) from 'inherently poor consumers' of that evidence: the jury.[53] The rule is thus grounded in the idea that the jury will struggle to assign appropriate evidential value (meaning) to hearsay. As Lord Bridge stated in the case of *R v Blastland*:

> Hearsay evidence is not excluded because it has no logical probative value . . . The rationale of excluding it as inadmissible, rooted as it is in the system of trial by jury, is recognition of the great difficulty . . . of assessing what, if any, weight, can properly be given to a statement by a person whom the jury have not seen or heard and who has not been subject to any test of reliability by cross-examination.[54]

However, this rationale is based on reasoning about the ability of the jury that is grounded in common sense rather than in evidence. Consider the problematic influences on juror reasoning outlined in Table 9.1. None of these weaknesses clearly applies to hearsay evidence to a greater extent than it applies to other types of evidence of relatively ambiguous strength. As Professor Justin Sevier noted in a recent article on hearsay evidence, 'hearsay evidence is indeed imperfect, but imperfect evidence is routinely admitted in the adversary system insofar as juries hear from duelling experts, biased character witnesses, and potentially faulty eyewitnesses, among others.'[55] In fact, intuitions and beliefs that feed into the assignment of

[53] J Sevier, 'Evidence-Based Hearsay' (2023) 76(6) Vanderbilt Law Review 1799, 1803. Although note that the reasons for considering this evidence unreliable have evolved over time. As noted in Chapter 1, the exclusion was initially introduced since statements were considered unreliable when not made under oath.

[54] [1986] AC 41.

[55] Sevier (n 53) 1804.

meaning by jurors in these areas (including in the consideration of hearsay) may actually represent a key strength of jurors in evaluating evidence. Although the evidence cannot easily be assigned weight scientifically, the reliability of rumours and reported statements made by others is likely to be something well within the experience of jurors—jurors may well have experienced such statements and also have had feedback on their reliability. Thus, the intuitions that jurors have from experience in society makes them well placed to pick up on considerations that influence likely reliability (including relatively nuanced considerations). Empirical research supports this contention by suggesting that jurors do appropriately discount the value of hearsay statements compared to statements made in court and that jurors are generally responsive to factors influencing the likely reliability of hearsay evidence.[56] Therefore, while jurors may not be able to assess hearsay evidence perfectly, no clear limitations in juror decision-making apply particularly to hearsay evidence, and actually strengths of jurors are likely to facilitate relatively effective evaluation in this area.[57]

To some extent the ability of jurors to appropriately assess hearsay evidence is reflected by provisions of the Criminal Justice Act 2003, which created exceptions to the exclusion of hearsay, including a broad exception allowing hearsay evidence to be introduced where 'the court is satisfied that it is in the interests of justice for it to be admissible'.[58] However, maintaining an exclusion that has to be overturned is unjustified by robust theory or empirical evidence—as Sevier stated in the US context, 'it is unclear that the hearsay rule should categorically exclude *any* of the evidence that it currently excludes'.[59]

In other areas, knowledge of how jurors assign meaning to evidence can justify the exclusion of evidence from the jury. One clear example is in the case of highly emotional evidence. Such evidence can typically be excluded from consideration by the jury by broad rules that require judges to balance the probative value of evidence with the potential for it to introduce prejudice. For example, in England and Wales, trial judges have general discretion to exclude technically admissible evidence where they feel its prejudicial effect exceeds its probative value.[60] There is a clear basis on which to exclude highly emotional evidence from the jury, particularly when it is likely to invoke anger—as discussed in Chapter 6, such emotion has been shown to affect the way that jurors assign meaning to evidence and thus could impede their decision-making (both in terms of leading to inappropriate

[56] See eg S Landsman and RF Rakos, 'Research Essay: A Preliminary Empirical Enquiry Concerning the Prohibition of Hearsay Evidence in American Courts' (1991) 15 Law and Psychology Review 65; MK Pathak and WC Thompson, 'From Child to Witness to Jury: Effects of Suggestion on the Transmission and Evaluation of Hearsay' (1999) 5 Psychology Public Policy and Law 372.

[57] For detailed discussion of flaws in the evidence-base underlying the hearsay rule, see Sevier (n 53).

[58] Criminal Justice Act 2003, s 114(1)(d).

[59] Sevier (n 53) 1807.

[60] *DPP v Christie* [1914] UKHL 641; [1914] AC 545. In the US context, see Federal Rules of Evidence, r 403.

allocation of probative value to evidence, and undermining normative principles such as the presumption of innocence). Even in cases where there is clearly an enhanced risk of weaknesses in juror decision-making, knowledge of how jurors assign meaning combined with empirical evidence has the potential to inform procedure to ameliorate weaknesses without excluding evidence from the jury. Consider, for example, where evidence is likely to influence the way jurors assign meaning to evidence through raising emotion such as anger (and thus might be excluded in the interests of justice). Interventions have been developed that might assist in reducing prejudice in these cases. For example, some research suggests that while gruesome crime scene photographs may be prejudicial when presented to jurors in colour (as the result of emotionality), this effect may be attenuated or even eliminated when the same photographs are presented in black and white.[61] Such interventions may help to ameliorate weaknesses in juror decision-making without relying heavily on exclusionary rules.[62]

Where such amelioration is not possible, it may be necessary to withhold evidence from the jury, or, if highly prejudicial evidence is essential to a case, to utilize other decision-makers (see Chapter 10 for examples). However, such cases are likely to be relatively rare. Such cases are best identified through individualized assessment based on tailored and relevant evidence rather than broad exclusionary rules, due to the nuance involved in assessments of potential weaknesses in decision-making and methods through which they might be ameliorated. For example, while in some cases a negative impact of high emotion might be ameliorated by showing a photograph in black and white, in other cases the nature of the photograph might mean that it may evoke strong emotion even in black and white, or the nature of the information conveyed may make display in colour necessary. It is important to note in this regard that decisions on admissibility often require judges to engage in evaluation of metacognition—assessing how certain information is likely to influence jurors.[63] Such judgments are complex, and intervention should assist judges in making assessments in a way that appropriately reflects knowledge relating to how jurors make decisions and what influences them.

Careful design of legal standards

As discussed in Chapter 7, the way in which legal standards are designed and phrased can have unintended consequences for the meaning jurors ascribe to

[61] JM Salerno, 'Seeing Red: Disgust Reactions to Gruesome Photographs in Color (But Not in Black and White) Increase Convictions' (2017) 23(3) Psychology, Public Policy, and Law 336.

[62] See also discussion of 'forensic reasoning rules' in P Roberts and A Zuckerman, *Roberts & Zuckerman's Criminal Evidence* (3rd edn, OUP 2022).

[63] For discussion, see MJ Saks and BA Spellman, *The Psychological Foundations of Evidence Law* (New York University Press 2016).

information and juror (and consequently jury) decision-making. These unintended consequences must be borne in mind when designing legal standards. Two identified consequences were priming effects caused by the language used in legal standards, and deviation from legal standards and unpredictability where legal standards do not sufficiently accord with juror intuitions or beliefs. These effects will be focused on to illustrate how legal standards can be designed to take into account relevant research and, relatedly, to reduce problematic influences on juror decisions.

Broadly, priming effects can be reduced by careful and balanced crafting of legal standards where effects could predictably arise. Legal standards should avoid anchoring decision-makers to a particular starting point, for example a time (in attempts liability) or doubt or sureness (in standards of proof). Balanced legal instructions can include language relating to both closeness and distance, or both sureness and doubt, for example. This may also be done through judicial directions relating to legal standards that might detach jurors from a particular anchor point (eg the commission of a crime or the beginning of actions leading towards a crime) and move them towards a more neutral starting point. For example, standards of proof might be discussed both in terms of level of doubt and level of sureness—'you must be sure of guilt, meaning that you have very little or no doubt.' Importantly, wherever possible, legal standards should also avoid the inclusion of threatening language which may trigger emotional reaction, punitiveness, or outgroup bias. Phrases such as 'dangerously close' should be avoided for that reason, and might be replaced with phrases such as 'sufficiently close to create a real risk of harm.'

As discussed in Chapter 7, where legal standards detach significantly from juror intuitions or beliefs relating to offending, this can lead to awkward application of legal standards and sometimes decision-making that is detached from legal standards, and a lack of predictability in the application of law (thus undermining the principle of legality). Jurors are less likely to be able to engage with legislation and imbue it with meaning where the distinctions contained in it are not distinctions that are meaningful for them, and combining intuitions and beliefs with legal terms that do not accord with those intuitions and beliefs results in clear complexity. Care should therefore be taken to ensure that legal standards are roughly in line with lay intuitions and beliefs relating to offending. Including offences providing for partial liability may help here, for example, in recognizing a lay intuition to excuse behaviour combined with strong policy reasons to criminalize. In some areas, keeping legal standards in line with lay intuitions and beliefs will involve creating new categories of offending where laypeople generally agree that behaviour should be criminalized, but where that behaviour does not sit easily (for them) within traditional legal standards. For example, current law in England and Wales classifies defendants as being liable for rape and related offences where they deceive a sexual partner, for example as to use of contraception[64] or biological gender,[65] since this deception can legally vitiate consent (under specific conditions). However, research (at least in the US context) suggests that while laypeople 'largely agree that coercion and incapacitation invalidate consent, they believe that deception does not'.[66] In ensuring such cases are dealt with appropriately, it may therefore be helpful to categorize such offending in its own way—not centred on the vitiating of consent (although the underlying rationale for policymakers may still relate to consent and, relatedly, autonomy) but on the wrongfulness and harm of the deception itself, that is, someone consented to sexual activity but only because they were deceived. This might be achieved through a specific offence of sexual assault or rape by fraud (which is already utilized in some jurisdictions).[67]

It should be noted that designing laws that appropriately reflect legislator intent and are also in line with lay intuitions and beliefs may result in increasing complexity in legislation, since, intuitions in particular can be complex and account for a wide variety of factors that are sometimes difficult to articulate. Some might argue that such added complexity makes the law less clear and therefore undermines the principle of legality both in terms of the ability of citizens to abide by the law and the ability of jurors and other legal decision-makers to uphold it. However, it is important to note that, in terms of citizens, the majority do not read legislation and, if they did, they would often not truly be able to engage with or understand it, and such understanding may be impossible anyway without knowing how flexible terms might be interpreted in court. In terms of jurors, it is important to note that, while complexity in legislation could undermine the ability to apply the law, so might oversimplification that does not appropriately take into account relevant intuitive distinctions (as discussed above). Jurors are much more likely to be able to appropriately interpret and apply legal constructs where they fit with their existing intuitions and beliefs. Thus, oversimplification of law that overlooks concepts and distinctions important to jurors introduces its own type of undesirable complexity. Professor John Gardner drew a helpful distinction in this regard (in the context of a discussion relating to the 1861 Offences Against the Person Act in England and Wales) between *textual clarity* in law (meaning language being straightforward, unornamented, avoiding great technicality or complexity of drafting, and minimizing the scope for conflicting interpretations)[68] and *moral clarity* in law (meaning adequate replication in the law of clear distinctions and significances which apply

[64] *Assange v Swedish Prosecution Authority* [2011] EWHC 2849 (Admin).

[65] *R v McNally* [2013] EWCA Crim 1051.

[66] R Sommers, 'Commonsense Consent' (2020) 129(8) The Yale Law Journal 2232, 2236.

[67] For broader discussion relating to such an offence and where it is used, see J Syrnick, 'Challenging the Use of Fraud to Get into Bed After *Suliveres v Commonwealth*—A Call for Legislative Reform' (2009) 43 New England Law Review 321, 335–36; M Mullen, 'Rape by Fraud: Eluding Washington Rape Statutes' (2017) 41 Seattle University Law Review 1035.

[68] J Gardner, 'Rationality and the Rule of Law in Offences Against the Person' (1994) 53(3) The Cambridge Law Journal 502, 512.

outside the law, together with reasonably clear indication of which cluster of distinctions and significances people can expect to find replicated in which legal contexts).[69] Replicating distinctions that laypeople find significant outside of law in the law (ie ensuring moral clarity) can help citizens conform their conduct to the law and also help with clear and predictable application of the law by juries. Research in psychology and law and in the emerging field of experimental jurisprudence[70] can help to identify accord between lay intuitions and beliefs and the law, and where detachment between these two factors may be compromising the application of law. As noted above and in Chapter 7, the use of more fine-grained verdicts which strike a compromise between juror intuitions and beliefs and legislative intent may be helpful in this regard.

Conclusions

Ultimately, we cannot entirely eliminate the influence of problematic factors on juror decisions, particularly since we cannot (and even jurors themselves cannot) know what underlies each decision. We can enhance understanding where objective understanding is possible (ie where there is clear objective truth), but enhancing decision-making is much harder in situations where more scientific rules will not provide a 'right' answer. We can enhance conformity with normative principles such as the presumption of innocence but cannot guarantee that such principles will always be respected. Although the suggestions made above are likely to help, they are by no means a panacea and further evaluation and monitoring is necessary to optimize juror performance. One other way that weaknesses in juror decisions might be addressed is through the deliberation process. If the deliberation process is to address such weaknesses, it is important that the strengths and weaknesses of each juror's viewpoint is appropriately accounted for, in order to maximize the potential for collective wisdom to enhance jury decisions and to minimize the possibility of the group setting exacerbating problematic influences, and jurors 'cascading' to a 'wrong' answer.[71] In the next chapter, I consider how to improve the translation of juror decisions into jury verdicts. I also briefly identify situations in which unavoidable weaknesses mean that the jury may helpfully be replaced or supplemented by other decision-makers.

[69] ibid 513.

[70] R Summers, 'Experimental Jurisprudence' (2021) 373(6553) Science 394 <www.science.org/doi/10.1126/science.abf0711> accessed 19 June 2023.

[71] CR Sunstein and R Hastie, 'Making Dumb Groups Smarter' *Harvard Business Review* (November 2014) <https://hbr.org/2014/12/making-dumb-groups-smarter> accessed 19 June 2023.

10

Improving Deliberations and Utilizing Other Decision-Makers

Introduction

In the previous chapter, I introduced a range of suggestions as to how interventions might improve the quality of juror decisions against normative goals. However, as noted in that chapter, no interventions can entirely eliminate the impact of problematic influences on juror decisions. An effective way to reduce the impact of problematic influences on jury decisions is to improve the way that individual preferences are translated into group verdicts. However, although deliberations have the potential to reduce any impacts of problematic influences, as well as to bring democratic voice to the jury process, they also have the potential to amplify the impact of problematic influences and can lead to decisions that do not truly represent the views of the community as a whole. Importantly, as discussed in Chapter 8, deliberations tend to favour majority opinions and the people who are most influential on the jury are not necessarily those who are most likely to hold opinions that are most valid from either a fact-finding or democratic perspective.

In this chapter, I discuss a range of interventions that have the potential to alter the way that individual preferences are translated into group verdicts and, as a result, to potentially change the impact of minority voices, and to promote the influence of those with the most appropriate contributions (rather than those with high social status or power). These interventions focus on increasing the diversity and representativeness of the jury, as well as ensuring that the most valuable contributions effectively feed through into ultimate decisions. As in the previous chapter, an important preliminary note is that this chapter covers a lot of territory and so does not comprehensively cover the body of existing research in each sub-area. These suggestions should therefore be considered alongside existing research on the jury in considering jury reform in a complete and cohesive way. I also briefly outline some examples where limitations of juror and jury decision-making mean that other decision-makers may helpfully be used to supplement the jury. I conclude with four final take-home messages relating to the recommendations in this chapter and the previous chapter, and highlight the fact that although juries can work, they have important weaknesses that should be addressed through evidence-based intervention.

How Juries Work. Rebecca K. Helm, Oxford University Press.
DOI: 10.1093/9780191948107.003.0010

Section I: Improving Deliberations

Broadly, in the fact-finding role juror intuitions and beliefs with the greatest potential to have high probative value should be represented and prioritized in the decision-making process (subject to relevant normative principles including the presumption of innocence and the right to be treated fairly and without discrimination). Where jurors with different experiences converge on one intuition or belief it is most likely to be accurate (although note that factors which systematically mislead, for example intuitions gained from the media or from experience without feedback, may be misleading for many jurors even when those jurors have diverse experience). Where intuitions and beliefs in the population differ, including a diverse range of jurors has the potential to improve the decision-making of the jury through causing the jury to scrutinize more deeply their own intuitions and beliefs and even through triggering recognition that the minority intuitions and beliefs may be more informative than those of the majority due to more closely matched experience (particularly when the value of those experiences is appropriately recognized during deliberation, see discussion of deliberation dynamics below).[1] Note that this may be particularly important in areas such as ethnic minority representation where minority groups are over-represented in many criminal justice systems and therefore minority juror intuitions and beliefs, which are likely to be more in tune with the people being judged, are particularly important to account for.[2] To give one example, a recent study found that Black jurors were more effective than white jurors at assessing the likely accuracy of eyewitness identifications of Black defendants. This result may have been due to Black jurors having more experience with when members of their own ethnicity (such as themselves) tend to be remembered.[3] In order to capture the benefits of a range of experience (both in terms of convergence of intuitions and beliefs and the representation of

[1] On the importance of heterogeneity in juries to challenge biases, see also LJ Curley, J Munro, and IE Dror, 'Cognitive and Human Factors in Legal Layperson Decision Making: Sources of Bias in Juror Decision Making' (2022) 62(3) Medicine, Science and the Law 206.

[2] See eg B Yasin and G Sturge, 'Ethnicity and the Criminal Justice System: What Does Recent Data Say on Over-Representation?' (*House of Commons Library, UK Parliament*, October 2020) <https://commonslibrary.parliament.uk/ethnicity-and-the-criminal-justice-system-what-does-recent-data-say/> accessed 19 June 2023 (England and Wales); AJ Beck, 'Race and Ethnicity of Violent Crime Offenders and Arrestees, 2018' Statistical Brief NCJ255969 (*US Department of Justice*, January 2021) <https://bjs.ojp.gov/content/pub/pdf/revcoa18.pdf> accessed 19 June 2023 (USA); Government of Canada, 'Overrepresentation of Black People in the Canadian Criminal Justice System' (15 December 2022) <www.justice.gc.ca/eng/rp-pr/jr/obpccjs-spnsjpc/index.html> accessed 19 June 2023 (Canada); Australian Law Reform Commission, 'Pathways to Justice—Inquiry into the Incarceration Rate of Aboriginal and Torres Strait Islander Peoples' (ALRC Report 133 2018) paras 3.13–29 <www.alrc.gov.au/publication/pathways-to-justice-inquiry-into-the-incarceration-rate-of-aboriginal-and-torres-strait-islander-peoples-alrc-report-133/3-incidence/over-representation/> accessed 19 June 2023 (Australia).

[3] RK Helm and ER Spearing, 'The Role of Race in Evaluations of Memory: Insensitivity to the Cross-Race Effect and Inaccuracy in Cross-Race Identification Evaluation' (forthcoming).

minority intuitions and beliefs that may be probative), it is important both that juries are diverse and that diverse viewpoints are appropriately accounted for.

In the context of the democratic role, juries should make decisions that represent values of the community, constrained by normative principles including the right of innocent persons not to be convicted, the right to be treated fairly and without discrimination, and the principle of legality, and also by factual accuracy. This task is most easily achieved where diverse viewpoints in the population are represented on the jury proportionately to their representation in society. This diversity maximizes the extent to which views that would feed through into overall community judgment feed through into the judgment of the jury roughly in representative proportions. In this judgment it is important that all views are allowed to feed equally into decisions, in a democratic way. Although it is not possible to monitor the extent to which specific viewpoints are represented, it is possible to make the jury representative in terms of key demographics that are likely to be associated with systematic differences in relevant viewpoints. For example, where jurors of different genders are likely to differ systematically in opinions relevant to a case, it is important that the jury is representative in terms of gender.

One consequence of the above arguments is that there are benefits to jury diversity (in terms of the fact-finding role) and representativeness (in terms of the democratic role) even where jurors do not show evidence of out-group bias. In this regard, it is important to note research in England and Wales, specifically in the context of ethnicity, which concluded that all-white juries are not prejudiced against minority defendants.[4] While this work is valuable, it does not undermine arguments relating to the importance of diversity and representativeness, since the benefits of diversity and representativeness extend beyond preventing discrimination to maximizing the accurate allocation of probative value and ensuring subjective judgments are made in a way that represents the judgments of the community as a whole rather than just majority opinion or the idiosyncrasies of a particular jury. For example, an all-white jury may not discriminate against a minority defendant compared to a white defendant but may have weaknesses in appropriately allocating probative value to evidence, particularly in cases involving minority defendants (where they may have less experience). In addition, all-white juries may reach conclusions as to responsibility that do not represent those of the population as a whole (eg the views of the population as a whole as to whether a defendant has been dishonest). These arguments are supported by findings of existing experimental work, discussed in Chapter 8, that suggest that diverse juries can perform better than non-diverse juries in a range of ways (including exchanging a wider range of information, engaging in more self-monitoring, and having higher-quality discussions).[5]

[4] C Thomas, *Are Juries Fair?* (Ministry of Justice Research Series 1/10, February 2010).

[5] SR Sommers, 'On Racial Diversity and Group Decision Making: Identifying Multiple Effects of Racial Composition on Jury Deliberations' (2006) 90(4) Journal of Personality and Social Psychology

Therefore, the work in this book contributes to existing work highlighting the benefits of both diversity and representativeness on the jury. An ideal jury should be both diverse and representative, and this diversity and representativeness should feed through appropriately into legal decisions. Rules and practice relating to jury composition and deliberations have the potential to improve the function of the jury in this regard.

Jury size

Developing formal mathematical models of ideal jury size and voting requirements is beyond the scope of this book, as is making very specific recommendations about ideal size. However, clear evidence-based arguments relating to size can be made based on the need to maximize diversity and representativeness on the jury. Clearly, in seeking to achieve a diverse jury that also represents the underlying population jury size is key. Some differing approaches that have been utilized in determining jury size are discussed in detail in Chapter 2. Broadly, the research developed in this book suggests that the jury must be big enough that sufficiently diverse opinions are represented in a way that is roughly proportionate to their occurrence in the general population.

Existing models in economics and law have attempted to model the optimal jury size (and voting requirements) given specific needs of the justice system, for example to reduce the risk of wrongful conviction, to maximize 'accuracy', and to promote efficiency. However, these models, necessarily, are based on assumptions that may not be justified, for example that an 'accurate' verdict (even in the fact-finding judgment) is one that the community as a whole would reach,[6] or that all jurors reach decisions based on a simultaneous vote rather than as part of a group decision-making process.[7] In fact, developing an ideal jury size to fit all cases may not be possible based on the criteria outlined above, since the 'ideal' sample size may be dependent on the heterogeneity of a population in terms of demographics and in terms of opinions and experiences relevant to a particular case. In a completely homogeneous society, a very small jury might be representative and match diversity in the underlying population. As populations become more heterogeneous a greater jury size will be needed to match diversity in the population and

597; MC Stevenson and others, 'Racially Diverse Juries Promote Self-Monitoring Efforts During Jury Deliberation' (2017) 3(2) Translational Issues in Psychological Science 187; A Nicholson Bergold and M Bull Kovera, 'Diversity's Impact on the Quality of Deliberations' (2022) 48(9) Personality and Social Psychology Bulletin 1406. See also Curley, Munro, and Dror (n 1).

[6] T Watanabe, 'A Numerical Study on Efficient Jury Size' (2020) 7(1) Humanities and Social Sciences Communications 1.

[7] A Guerra, B Luppi, and F Parisi, 'Jury Size and Voting Requirements for Criminal Convictions: Assessing the Tradeoffs' (2020) 28 Supreme Court Economic Review 221.

remain representative. Evidence-based research in specific populations of interest is needed to pinpoint precise jury sizes at which judgments of a subset of the population are broadly consistent with what judgments of the population as a whole would likely have been (and note that the precise number required may vary based on case facts).

The research discussed in Chapter 5 provides insight into the characteristics of jurors that might be associated with differences in intuitions and beliefs relevant to legal decision-making, and thus which should be considered in setting jury size to maximize diversity and representativeness. Specifically, that chapter highlights how intuitions and beliefs tend to vary based on political opinions, legal attitudes, case-specific beliefs, experiences, need for cognition, gender, and race. Many of these factors are likely to vary sufficiently in the population that diverse viewpoints will be reflected even in relatively small jury sizes. However, one way in which small juries may not contain sufficient representation is in the area of juror race, where majority racial groups are often highly dominant numerically in society (and note, as described in Chapter 8, that they are also often more likely to speak and more influential overall on juries). As mentioned above, ideally juries should be both diverse and representative. We want sufficient minority representation that minority voices are heard (and ideally diverse minority voices are heard since opinions may systematically vary amongst different minority groups) and can make a difference in deliberations but for this representation to be roughly numerically proportionate to representation in the population. In terms of race this means consistently having at least one, and probably ideally two, minority jurors, and for their representation on the jury to be roughly proportionate to their representation overall in society.[8]

In terms of diversity, clearly numerical representation of any group is likely to be larger in a larger sample, and so as jury size increases the representation of minority jurors is likely to increase. Unsurprisingly, a 1997 meta-analysis examining differences in representation based on jury size (including experimental work and one field study) found that twelve-person juries were more likely than smaller juries to contain at least one minority member.[9] A more recent field examination in the United States (US) civil jury context (which is complicated by procedures

[8] Note that, in this regard, minority jurors are grouped together despite important differences based on specific race/ethnicity. However, this grouping is necessary to capture differential experience but to maintain the size of the jury within realistic limits.

[9] MJ Saks and M Weighner Marti, 'A Meta-Analysis of the Effects of Jury Size' (1997) 21(5) Law and Human Behavior 451. See also S Landsman and D McCord, '12-Member Juries and Unanimous Verdicts: A Debate' (2005) 88(6) Judicature 300:

> The smaller the jury, the less representative it becomes . . . For example, in a community with a 10 percent minority population, a 12-person jury is 25 percentage points more likely to contain a member of that group than is a 6-person jury (72 percent of 12-person juries versus 47 percent of 6-person juries) . . . A jury of one's peers in a heterogeneous community can hardly be expected to remain representative if it is progressively downsized.

for selection) found that 28.1 per cent of the eighty-nine six-member juries studied ended up with no Black jurors serving on them, compared to 2.1 per cent of the 188 twelve-member juries studied, and that 41.7 per cent of the six-person juries ended up with two or more Black jurors serving on them, compared to 82.2 per cent of twelve-member juries.[10] In terms of representativeness, mathematically, sampling theory demonstrates that a randomly selected smaller sample will be less representative than a randomly selected larger sample.

The appropriate jury size to ensure minority representation and also to maintain numerical representativeness is clearly highly dependent on the underlying population that a jury is drawn from. For example, in a society in which 10 per cent of the population are members of a particular minority, juries would have to have at least ten members to allow the inclusion of a minority member proportionate to minority representation in society (for discussion on ensuring such proportionate representation, see discussion of selection procedures below). Distributions may differ significantly by jurisdiction. In England and Wales, the 2021 census found that 81.7 per cent of residents identified their ethnic group as 'white' (with 74.4 per cent identifying as 'English, Welsh, Scottish, Northern Irish, or British'); 9.3 per cent identified their ethnic group as 'Asian, Asian British, or Asian Welsh'; and 2.5 per cent identified their ethnic group as 'Black, Black British, Black Welsh, Caribbean, or African'.[11] Thus, a twelve-person jury drawn completely at random from the entire population would be expected to contain ten white members, one Asian member, and one member of another ethnicity. However, research has shown that in England and Wales a relatively significant number of juries end up being all-white, at least partly as a result of the distribution of minority citizens geographically.[12] Research examining racial composition in juries in this context has found that racially mixed twelve-person juries are only likely in courts where minority ethnic groups make up at least 10 per cent of citizens in the relevant area, and note that only twenty (out of a total of ninety-one) Crown Court areas in England and Wales have a minority ethnic population of 10 per cent or more.[13] In this context, juries, as a general rule, require more than twelve members to consistently achieve diversity while remaining representative of the underlying population, and calls to reduce jury size[14] should be resisted. Using fifteen jurors, as is done in Scotland, may be helpful. In a jury of fifteen members, at least one

[10] S Seidman Diamond and others, 'Achieving Diversity on the Jury: Jury Size and the Peremptory Challenge' (2009) 6(3) Journal of Empirical Legal Studies 425.

[11] Saks and Weighner Marti (n 9).

[12] C Thomas, 'Diversity and Fairness in the Jury System' (Ministry of Justice Research Series 2/07 June 2007).

[13] A Lever, 'Democracy, Epistemology and the Problem of All-White Juries' (2017) 34(4) Journal of Applied Philosophy 541.

[14] See eg PA News Agency, 'Reduced-Sized Juries Could Help Clear Court Backlog' *Telegraph & Argus* (21 June 2021) <www.thetelegraphandargus.co.uk/news/national/19388778.reduced-sized-juries-help-clear-court-backlog---lord-chief-justice/?ref=rl&lp=1> accessed 19 June 2023.

minority member could be included on the jury while maintaining representativeness as long as at least 7 per cent of members of the population were from minority groups (on using selection procedures to ensure representativeness, see discussion of jury selection below).

Potential difficulties with increasing the size of juries are clear from a practical perspective. In England and Wales, the courts are currently facing significant backlogs, predating but also exacerbated by the Covid-19 pandemic.[15] Increasing the number of jurors has the potential to be expensive (juror expenses are paid for the duration of trial). It also has the potential to increase hung juries and therefore cost the system time which it cannot afford. However, it should be noted that hung juries are generally rare in England and Wales. For example, in 2006–08 only 0.6 per cent of juries failed to reach a verdict.[16] In addition, research in the US context has suggested that adoption of smaller juries may actually have little to no impact on hung jury rates.[17] For these reasons, a slight increase in jury size may not be a significant risk in this regard, particularly if combined with appropriate voting rules. It is also possible that larger juries may be utilized only in cases identified as involving a particular risk of bias or partisan issues, to reduce pressure on the system.

Voting requirements

Turning to voting requirements (introduced and discussed in Chapter 2), the potential for minority impact is clearly greatest where a verdict cannot be issued against the wishes of minority jurors (eg where a minority of two jurors can block a majority verdict). In addition, guilty verdicts are likely to be more reliable where they have been agreed by all jurors—consistent with the presumption of innocence.[18] However, particularly as juries become larger, unanimity may be a difficult threshold to reach, and requiring unanimous verdicts could lead to a significant increase in the number of hung trials. In this context, previous work has described a trade-off between jury size and voting requirements, with decisions being most reliable when either juries are larger *or* verdicts must be unanimous.[19] Therefore, in increasing jury size, concessions may need to be made in terms of unanimity. Crucially, these concessions may actually be beneficial in other ways. Perhaps most

[15] See G Davies, 'Reducing the Backlog in Criminal Courts' (Ministry of Justice and HM Courts & Tribunals Service 2021) 732; M Millar and others, 'Covid-19 and the Jury Trial' in E Johnson (ed), *Covid 19 and Criminal Justice: Impact and Legacy in England and Wales* (Routledge 2023).

[16] Thomas, *Are Juries Fair?* (n 4) 27.

[17] See PL Hannaford-Agor and others, 'Are Hung Juries a Problem?' (National Center for State Courts 2002).

[18] See eg PJ Coughlan, 'In Defense of Unanimous Jury Verdicts: Mistrials, Communication, and Strategic Voting' (2000) 94(2) The American Political Science Review 375.

[19] Guerra, Luppi, and Parisi (n 7). See also *Burch v Louisiana* 441 US 130 (1979).

importantly, where minority jurors can block a verdict, only one juror with problematic attitudes (eg racist or sexist attitudes) can prevent a conviction.

It is important to note in this regard that, as discussed in Chapter 8, diversity can be beneficial even where minority jurors do not have the power to block verdicts. Merely hearing the voices of the minority, particularly in a process involving appropriate deliberation dynamics (discussed below) has the potential to have a positive impact on majority jurors and ultimately group verdicts. Thus, in terms of the positive impacts of a range of viewpoints being represented in the fact-finding judgment of the jury, prioritizing greater jury size over unanimity requirements appears beneficial.[20] It is better to have a larger jury with more minority voices deciding by a majority verdict than a smaller jury without minority voices deciding unanimously. However, allowing simple majority verdicts creates a situation in which the minority need to affect a significant number of the majority to have an impact on verdict, and the majority are aware that there is not a real need to engage heavily with the minority.

Larger juries with supermajority requirements (eg twelve/fifteen) have the benefit of, ideally, leaving minority jurors with numerical influence (since not many jurors need to agree with even a small minority to block a verdict) but also allowing the jury to triage the views of the minority (at least given appropriate deliberation dynamics), and to be influenced by appropriate views (where the experience of minority jurors gives their opinions particularly important probative value) but not by inappropriate views (eg racist or sexist attitudes). Utilizing 'supermajority verdicts' may therefore be a promising way of allowing an increase in jury size to ensure sufficient diversity and representativeness while maintaining the efficiency of the jury and limiting minority voices that may feed into deliberations in problematic ways.

Jury selection and representation on juries

I have argued that juries will function best when they are diverse and representative. The extent to which they are diverse and representative, and along which lines, is likely to be at least partially dependent on methods of jury selection. While random selection and a large jury size may create good chances of representativeness, there is still a reasonable chance that random selection could result in an imbalanced jury (eg a jury without proportionate minority representation or a jury with disproportionate representation of one gender).

As discussed in Chapter 2, jurisdictions have reached different conclusions as to which method of jury selection will best achieve representativeness and, relatedly,

[20] For analysis of the trade-off between jury size and voting requirements, see Guerra, Luppi, and Parisi (n 7).

neutrality. The *voir dire* system utilized in the United States of America (USA) is intended to ensure a representative and unbiased jury; however, commentators have raised concerns about the process actually increasing bias as a result of bias and stereotypes of lawyers feeding into the selection process and thus the composition of the jury.[21] On the other hand, as discussed above, random selection, as utilized in England and Wales, has the potential to result in some juries in which particular populations are over or under-represented.[22] Since initial majorities are so predictive of final verdicts, even a slight imbalance, particularly in favour of a group with less relevant experience, may impair the performance of the jury. For example, in the context of sexual offences, research suggests that men may be particularly susceptible to endorsing rape myths.[23] Juries may therefore be particularly susceptible to the influence of rape myths in their decision-making where they are majority male, and the risk of rape myth influence could be reduced through appropriate gender balance.[24]

As noted above, increasing jury size has the potential to increase representativeness but still does not guarantee it. A relatively simple solution to this problem may be to identify key lines along which the jury should be representative, and to provide a right for a party to argue that the jury should be reconstituted where it is significantly imbalanced along these lines (particularly where a clear case can be made that representation along specific lines is important). The research presented in this book has the potential to inform ways in which the jury should be both diverse and representative, specifically where intuitions and beliefs of different groups are likely to differ and particularly where one group may hold intuitions and beliefs that are susceptible to error and bias (for examples see Chapters 4 and 5). Simple procedures may also help facilitate proportionate participation of minority groups, including providing funding to help those with

[21] A full analysis of the *voir dire* process is beyond the scope of this book, but for relevant discussion, see AL Tayman, 'Looking Beyond Batson: A Different Method of Combating Bias Against Queer Jurors' (2019) 61(6) William & Mary Law Review 1759; A Sloan, '"What to Do About Batson?": Using a Court Rule to Address Implicit Bias in Jury Selection' (2020) 108(1) California Law Review 233; A Lowe, 'The Call for an Adequate Remedy: The Lack of Deterrence and Judicial Consequences for Prosecutors Who Habitually Violate Batson' (2020) 43 University of Arkansas at Little Rock Law Review 261; TJ Conklin, 'The End of Purposeful Discrimination: The Shift to an Objective Batson Standard' (2022) 63(3) Boston College Law Review 1037.

[22] See eg C Gallagher, 'Women Under-Represented on Juries in Serious Criminal Trials' *The Irish Times* (17 July 2017) <www.irishtimes.com/news/crime-and-law/women-under-represented-on-juries-in-serious-criminal-trials-1.3156886> accessed 19 June 2023.

[23] See M Davies and S McCartney, 'Effects of Gender and Sexuality on Judgements of Victim Blame and Rape Myth Acceptance in a Depicted Male Rape' (2003) 13(5) Journal of Community & Applied Social Psychology 391; DJ Angelone and others, 'Does Sexism Mediate the Gender and Rape Myth Acceptance Relationship?' (2021) 27(6–7) Violence Against Women 748; AM Zidenberg and others, 'Tipping the Scales: Effects of Gender, Rape Myth Acceptance, and Anti-Fat Attitudes on Judgments of Sexual Coercion Scenarios' (2021) 36(19–20) Journal of Interpersonal Violence NP101784.

[24] Note that it is not the case that all men will endorse rape myths and all women will not, but just that the risk of rape myth influence is heightened as male representation on the jury increases, based on average levels of acceptance.

dependent relatives to act as jurors, and reconsidering how districts are drawn for jury selection.[25]

Jury deliberation dynamics

Another way to influence how individual preferences feed into the jury decision process (provided sufficiently diverse views are represented on the jury) is by seeking to alter the dynamics of jury deliberation. In fact, the dynamics of deliberation are key to ensuring any benefits of minority representation on juries and interact closely with the discussion above. In this regard, it should first be noted that any interference with jury deliberation might be seen as compromising the decision-making freedom of the jury. Potential intervention to alter the influences on jury decisions should be weighed up against this concern.

One factor with the potential to influence the dynamics of deliberation is the use and selection of a jury foreperson, who acts as a spokesperson for the jury and chairs jury deliberations. In many jurisdictions the jury select their foreperson themselves, although other jurisdictions may have rules in place for foreperson selection, such as selecting the first person chosen to sit as a juror.[26] Research in the US context suggests that where jurors do select their foreperson, the process may be fairly brief and 'even perfunctory, seemingly driven more by a desire to pick someone and get on with things rather than identify the best person for the role'.[27] On the whole, research has shown that forepersons are more likely to be male, well educated, and extraverted (although note that much of this research was conducted a relatively long time ago, and more recent research is needed to confirm this finding today).[28] Note that these characteristics broadly mirror the characteristics of those thought to have the most influence on the jury anyway (see Chapter 8). Importantly, evidence suggests that the foreperson role may also provide increased influence on the jury. For example, field research in the USA suggests that pro-acquittal advocacy by the foreperson can change the relationship between evidence strength and the probability of conviction.[29] Allowing jurors themselves to select a foreperson may represent a missed opportunity to guide the translation of individual preferences into jury verdicts in a positive way. Research conducted by Professors Reid Hastie and Cass Sunstein suggests that in improving the decision-making of groups, it is helpful to 'quieten high status members'.[30]

[25] See Lever (n 13).

[26] See eg New York State Unified Court System, 'Foreperson's Role' (*nycourts.gov*) <www.nycourts.gov/judges/cji/1-General/CJI2d.Foreperson.pdf> accessed 19 June 2023.

[27] DJ Devine, *Jury Decision-Making: The State of the Science* (NYU Press 2012) 154.

[28] ibid 155.

[29] DJ Devine and others, 'Evidentiary, Extraevidentiary, and Deliberation Process Predictors of Real Jury Verdicts' (2016) 40(6) Law and Human Behavior 670.

[30] CR Sunstein and R Hastie, 'Making Dumb Groups Smarter' *Harvard Business Review* (November 2014) <https://hbr.org/2014/12/making-dumb-groups-smarter> accessed 19 June 2023.

Quietening high-status members can be beneficial in allowing more diverse voices to feed into jury discussions, and the benefits of diversity to be realized. Appointing a member of a lower-status group as foreperson may be a promising way to balance out the voices that are heard and thus the contributions that feed into the jury process (something which may be especially beneficial given the discussed benefits of jury diversity).

Another way to balance out the voices heard during deliberation would be to provide some kind of structure to jury decisions that encourages all jurors to speak and to share insight that has the potential to be valuable, thus reducing the current imbalance where jurors from certain demographics speak more than others (see Chapter 8). Jurors might be encouraged to consider as a group the unique and distinctive contributions that each member may be able to make, and be given guidance on the importance of engaging with minority opinion (and the potential insights of minority opinion), potentially in conjunction with debiasing instructions discussed in the previous chapter. Time should then be given to each juror to contribute to discussions accordingly—with the foreperson encouraging information to be shared from group members, even where their viewpoints go against majority beliefs. It may also be helpful to encourage jurors to enter deliberations as open-mindedly as possible—once jurors have split into 'factions' the impact of social pressures and related biases has far greater potential to influence decision-making. Initial votes are likely to be unproductive in this regard. One way to promote open-mindedness may be to encourage jurors to engage in critical thinking, and to raise possibilities that run counter to what may appear to be the preference of the majority. Where no jurors are clearly advocating for a position, it may even be helpful to appoint 'devil's advocates' to attempt to think about the facts from a different point of view and to advocate from that point of view.[31]

Giving reasons

As a final note, one intervention that is sometimes discussed as having the potential to increase the quality of jury deliberations and verdicts is requiring juries to provide reasons for their verdicts, as is done, for example, in Spain.[32] As noted in Chapter 2, requiring juries to give reasons is seen as a way of enhancing jury accountability and correcting errors or contradictions in jury reasoning. There has been some impetus for such a requirement recently. In the 2010 case of *Taxquet v Belgium*, the Grand Chamber of the European Court of Human Rights confirmed that juries must give sufficient reasons for their verdicts in order to comply with Article 6 of the European Convention on Human Rights (although note that

[31] ibid.

[32] M Jimeno-Bulnes, 'Jury Selection and Jury Trial in Spain: Between Theory and Practice' (2011) 86(2) Chicago-Kent Law Review 585, 585–96.

this requirement does not necessitate provision of sufficient reasons to identify or correct errors).[33] In 2021, in England and Wales, the Criminal Cases Review Commission argued for the introduction of reasoned verdicts, which they say would help to identify miscarriages of justice.[34] However, from the perspective of jury accountability and enhancing the impact of desirable influences (and minimizing the influence of problematic ones) the duty to give reasons may be limited in terms of any beneficial effect. As described in Chapters 4–7, jurors may be unaware of many potentially problematic influences feeding into their decisions. Presumably, juries generally, as a group, make their decisions in a way that appears rational and based on the evidence. However, rationalization may be post hoc and cover more subtle influences on decisions. Thus, requiring jurors to give reasons is likely to be limited in its ability to truly shed light on the intuitions and beliefs feeding into jury decisions.[35]

Section II: Utilizing Other Decision-Makers

Finally, it should be noted that there may be some areas where jurors and juries may fundamentally struggle to make appropriate decisions, even given the interventions discussed in this chapter and the previous chapter. It is therefore helpful to consider how other decision-makers might be utilized effectively in order to supplement and support the jury. Two clear situations in which jurors may struggle to make appropriate decisions are (1) when there is a very high risk of bias in a case and that risk cannot be ameliorated, combined with relatively limited benefits of lay judgment, and (2) when jurors are engaging with highly complex evidence that they do not understand and which cannot be sufficiently simplified. Here, there is a heightened risk that jurors and juries may be influenced by problematic intuitions and beliefs or misconceptions that will jeopardize their ability to achieve the goals outlined in Chapter 3 of this book.

First, there may be situations in which there is such a risk of bias (despite evidence being reliable) combined with limited utility of lay decision-making, that the jury may not be appropriate decision-makers at all. This may, for example, be the case where it is known that defendants have committed serious and distressing crimes and jurors are asked to make a neutral decision as to, for example, the applicability of a defence based on mental health (essentially a clinical judgment). Such cases involve the fact-finding role of the jury, where relevant facts can be

[33] *Taxquet v Belgium* App no 926/05 (ECtHR, 16 November 2010).

[34] See J Robins and N Robinson, 'Miscarriage of Justice Watchdog Calls for a Review of Juries' (*The Justice Gap*, 5 January 2021) <www.thejusticegap.com/miscarriage-of-justice-watchdog-calls-for-a-review-of-juries/> accessed 19 June 2023.

[35] For further discussion of the requirement to give reasons, see KA Burd and VP Hans, 'Reasoned Verdicts: Oversold?' (2018) 51(2) Cornell International Law Journal 319.

determined in a robust way based on scientific analysis (and thus advantages of lay insight are limited), and where the ability of the jury to reach a determination consistent with scientific analysis is likely to be compromised.

Existing research in the USA, specifically in the context of determinations of intellectual disability, provides some support for the suggestion that juries may struggle to make unbiased decisions in such contexts. In the USA, it is unconstitutional for the death penalty to be imposed on the intellectually disabled.[36] In this context, there is a risk that crimes found to have been committed by defendants (which are without exception very grave since they have been found to warrant the imposition of the death penalty) will bias the jury against finding in their favour on intellectual disability (see discussion of motivated cognition and the culpable control theory of blame attribution in Chapters 4, 5, and 6). In line with this suggestion, research examining outcomes in real cases has found that juries are significantly less likely than judges to find a defendant to be intellectually disabled and thus ineligible for the death penalty (despite the fact that research more generally suggests juries are more lenient than judges).[37] The authors of this work concluded that:

> perhaps juries are more lenient than judges in ordinary guilt and sentencing determinations but harsher in determinations of intellectual disability because—in the context of a horrible crime—judges are more able to set aside their feelings and correctly apply a legal standard than jurors.[38]

They also stated that since judges generally make pretrial rulings while jurors make rulings after hearing evidence, judges have the advantage of having been exposed to 'fewer emotional, retributive triggers'.[39] In these specific situations, decisions may be better made by professional judges (although, as noted below, professional judges are also not immune from bias).

In other cases, for example those involving complex corporate crimes, jurors may be unable to effectively engage with evidence without significant assistance. Here, there are predictable weaknesses of the jury which have the potential to be addressed by other decision-makers, but also strengths of the jury that should be retained where possible. These cases could potentially be handled in a novel way (at least for common law systems)—by allowing professional judges to sit alongside jurors. It should be noted that this option would require a significant departure from precedent in existing traditional jury systems, however it may be preferable

[36] *Atkins v Virginia* 536 US 304 (2002).

[37] JH Blume and others, 'A Tale of Two (and Possibly Three) Atkins: Intellectual Disability and Capital Punishment Twelve Years After the Supreme Court's Creation of a Categorical Bar' (2014) 23(2) William & Mary Bill of Rights Journal 393.

[38] ibid 411.

[39] ibid 412.

to taking cases away from the jury entirely where there are aspects of a case that jurors clearly cannot engage with, but where there is still a clear benefit of community judgment. In fact, 'mixed tribunals' containing judges and jurors are already utilized in some jurisdictions, which provide useful examples to learn from. For example, Germany, Italy, and Japan all utilize lay judges (jurors) alongside professional judges to reach collective verdicts in criminal cases.[40] In theory, these systems provide both the benefits of lay decision-making and also a safeguard against mistakes and misunderstandings. However, questions have been raised about the voice of lay members in these courts, where the expert judges are expected to exert a strong influence. In some jurisdictions this reality is exacerbated by other aspects of procedure. For example, in Germany lay tribunal members cannot view the case dossier, but judges can,[41] and in some Swedish cases professional judges have the majority of votes.[42] These limitations on lay members arise as a result of legal systems that do not prioritize lay voices in legal decision-making. It may be possible to design a system where expert judges sit alongside jurors in order to provide information and to correct clear misunderstanding, while lay decision-makers still guide the deliberation process and ultimately have power to assign a verdict.

One area where 'juryless trials' have recently been considered is in trials involving sexual offences. In England and Wales, this possibility was raised in a 2023 Law Commission consultation.[43] However, these cases do not easily fall into a category of case in which the jury can helpfully be replaced or supplemented by another legal decision-maker. Although there is a risk of problematic influence, particularly resulting from endorsement of rape myths (discussed in Chapter 5), there are clear advantages to utilizing insight from the jury rather than judges in such cases. First, the fact-finding judgments involved in such cases are often challenging, involving competing accounts that cannot be resolved scientifically—cases have been described as involving 'inexact science'.[44] This challenge makes cases particularly appropriate for resolution by citizens rather than experts. It is in cases involving scientific ambiguity that the adaptive insight of citizens, incorporating the subtleties of everyday life in society, can be most advantageous. Experience of situations akin to those described in legal proceedings and diverse experience of life in society more generally have the potential to facilitate collective judgment that more accurately captures what is likely to have taken place than the experience

[40] RK Helm and VP Hans, 'Procedural Roles: Professional Judges, Lay Judges, and Lay Jurors' in DK Brown, J Iontcheva Turner, and Bettina Weisser (eds), *The Oxford Handbook of Criminal Process* (OUP 2019).

[41] VP Hans and CM Germain, 'The French Jury at a Crossroads' (2011) 86 Chicago-Kent Law Review 737.

[42] C Diesen, 'Lay Judges in Sweden: A Short Introduction' (2001) 72(1–2) International Review of Penal Law 313.

[43] Law Commission, *Evidence in Sexual Offences Prosecutions: A Consultation Paper* (Law Com No 259, 2023).

[44] A Cossins, *Closing the Justice Gap for Adult and Child Sexual Assault* (Springer 2020) 96.

and even training of judges or experts. It is cases involving 'inexact science' that jurors rather than experts may have the best judgment, given their adaptive insight (although note that there will also be aspects of cases where jurors are unlikely to have relevant experience and thus may need to be provided with additional support or guidance). Secondly, such cases involve democratic judgments that cannot appropriately be made by judges or experts, who cannot accurately capture community sentiment relating to legal concepts (ie the judgment that would have been reached by the community as a whole) such as what constitutes a reasonable belief—how are judges as lone individuals expected to effectively consider an issue and reach the same judgment on it as the community as a whole would have reached? What a judge or expert might consider to be (un)reasonable may well not appropriately reflect what the majority of people in society would deem (un)reasonable, and therefore is an inappropriate standard against which to assess behaviour, at least without far clearer guidance. This challenge is particularly important given the evolution of ethical standards and behaviours. It is also necessary to note in this regard, and when considering the utilization of judges more generally, that judges themselves are not immune from bias.[45] Ultimately, although the potential influence of rape myths on the jury represents a significant problem, this is likely to be best addressed through interventions to improve juror and jury decisions discussed in this chapter and the previous chapter, rather than through replacing the jury with a judge or several judges.

Conclusions: Making Juries Work Better

Overall, at least some jury research paints a relatively encouraging picture in terms of the ability of the jury to account for evidence strength. However, understanding the nature of people generally (and jurors specifically) as intuitive decision-makers provides insight into ways in which jurors may be susceptible to influences that are problematic, as well as into their key strengths in making both factual and democratic judgments. When we think about improving juror and jury decision-making, we need to think not just about providing verbatim information to jurors or about correcting explicitly biased or incorrect beliefs that jurors may hold, but also about how procedure and other infrastructure surrounding the jury can improve the ability of the jury to allocate meaning to information appropriately (eg through educating juror intuition). Traditionally, legal systems have had a tendency to presume that jurors are able to make sound decisions primarily as a result of experience and to encourage jurors to rely on their own intuitions and good sense. However, the research discussed in this book highlights some systematic

[45] See eg C Guthrie, JJ Rachlinski, and AJ Wistrich, 'Inside the Judicial Mind' (2000) 86(4) Cornell Law Review 777.

weaknesses in juror decisions and finds that the deliberation process can fail to address such weaknesses. We must acknowledge that lay decision-makers have inherent strengths and weaknesses as finders of fact. In some respects, the way that humans make decisions is actually in direct conflict with the way that we want the jury to operate. Through targeted use of procedure, we can capitalize on strengths and reduce weaknesses, for example through correcting problematic intuitions and beliefs (at the juror level) and altering how individual impressions are translated into verdicts (at the jury level). Four central take-home messages capture much of the discussion in this chapter and the previous chapter about how procedure may be utilized.

First, to impact juror decisions, we must make the information given to jurors meaningful. Verbatim information is unlikely to feed through into decision processes where jurors cannot meaningfully engage with that information in context. New information can be made meaningful through education and/or contextualization, or targeted guidance can trigger relevant existing intuitions or beliefs to inform appropriate assignment of meaning. Secondly, legal standards must take into account existing intuitions and beliefs and how they will interact with legal standards to inform meaningful representations. Where laws are inconsistent with existing intuitions or beliefs, application of law becomes unpredictable, undermining the principle of legality. Thirdly, jury deliberation is not inherently beneficial in translating individual preferences into verdicts. Deliberation must be engaged in by suitably diverse and representative groups and guided to bring out the strengths of intuitions and beliefs in different jury members. Finally, jurors and juries will not always behave in strictly rational ways. We need to be careful what jurors see and how factors that would not be expected to be influential from a rational perspective may impact jurors. In this regard, any innovation that could impact the jury should be carefully examined in terms of its potential influence.

Luckily, there are ways to predict where we will see normatively desirable and normatively problematic influences on the jury, which provide avenues through which interventions should be targeted. Ultimately, juries can work, and often do work, but they do have weaknesses that should not be overlooked or glossed over. Evidence-based procedural intervention can help juries work better.

Index

For the benefit of digital users, indexed terms that span two pages (e.g., 52–53) may, on occasion, appear on only one of those pages.

Tables are indicated by an italic *t* following the page number

The manufacturer's authorised representative in the EU for product safety is Oxford University Press España S.A. of el Parque Empresarial San Fernando de Henares, Avenida de Castilla, 2 – 28830 Madrid (www.oup.es/en or product.safety@oup.com). OUP España S.A. also acts as importer into Spain of products made by the manufacturer.

www.ingramcontent.com/pod-product-compliance
Lightning Source LLC
LaVergne TN
LVHW011819200926
848484LV00005B/1240
* 9 7 8 0 1 9 2 8 5 7 2 9 3 *